Donald Barton, born in industrial Lancashire in 1927, was educated at Chepstow Secondary School, and after two and a half years in the army, at Oxford. Drawn to Africa in his mid-teens, he entered the Colonial Administrative Service and served in Tanganyika from 1952-1961. Accompanied by his wife, both their children were born there. He later joined the British Council, where his concern for the less developed world was reflected in postings to Nigeria, Malaysia, and Afghanistan, mainly administering a wide range of educational aid and technical assistance. He lives with his wife in Hampshire

To my best friends, my family

AN AFFAIR WITH AFRICA

Tanganyika remembered

Donald Barton

With best wishes to Jill

Don Barton 2005

Authors On Line

Visit us online at www.authorsonline.co.uk

ISBN 0 7552 0122 1

Authors OnLine Ltd
40 Castle Street
Hertford SG14 1HR
England

This book is also available in e-book format, details of which are available at
www.authorsonline.co.uk

ii

CONTENTS

AUTHOR'S PREFACE AND ACKNOWLEDGEMENTS

This account of the work of a latter-day District Officer in the long defunct Colonial Administrative Service had its genesis in the question posed by parents and relatives: 'I know *what* you were and *where* you were – but what did you *do* exactly?' Weekly air-letters home tended to record mundane domestic matters, and there was little time – or indeed inclination – to describe in any detail the manifold local matters which preoccupied me; what follows is only a partial answer to the question. There is little or no mention of the long hours spent poring over files, and compiling papers and memoranda on local concerns such as education, forestry, agriculture, the changing rôle of chiefs, or game control. Nor is there much reference to the time spent supervising the local treasury accounts, mulling over district development plans, or composing representations to distant seniors. Every job has its routine tasks which, though essential and perhaps absorbing to the practitioner, are less than enthralling to the outsider; but the work of a District Officer in Africa offered a range of interest which was probably unique. This book describes events which did not occur on a daily basis, but which were nevertheless typical, and indicative of the issues and problems which engaged us. It will, I hope, show something of the nature of district administration in Africa, and perhaps give some idea of why we found it so engrossing and satisfying.

Before plunging into the narrative I would like to thank my wife Sylvia for her patience, forbearance, and support during our years in Tanganyika,[1] and for processing this text. I am also grateful to Tony Kirk-Greene, Colin Baker, John Iliffe, and John Cooke for their various advice, encouragement, and comment; and to the friends who have cajoled and bullied me into getting on with it.

I would also like to acknowledge the part played in our expatriate lives by our African domestic staff. After a few hiccups during our early months, we retained the services of two trusted and valued friends, Mzee Hamsini and

---

[1] Now the mainland part of Tanzania.

Issa Saidi. With their families they accompanied us on our several postings until our departure. Thereafter we corresponded with them over the years until their deaths in the late 1980's.

Similarly the work of our African colleagues in both the civil service and local government merits recognition. Like employees everywhere – including ourselves – they were variously good, average, and indifferent. The poor were criticised, the good often taken for granted; but in general, with little or no training, they served their country well. In retrospect, we relied on them more than we acknowledged, and perhaps appreciated their contribution too little. Finally, a few words of tribute to that great survivor, the African peasant farmer, whose advancement was one of our primary concerns. He survived our good intentions, and will survive whatever his own governments may throw at him.

2004

The verse quoted on page 231 is reproduced with permission of Curtis Brown Ltd., London on behalf of the estate of Christopher Isherwood.

INTRODUCTION

No-one with an interest in British colonial history will need to be told what a District Officer was, but others may appreciate a brief description. All members of the Colonial Administrative Service were generically described as Administrative Officers, and collectively they directed and managed the main business of government, supported by specialist, technical, and professional officers in various functional departments. Those working in the Secretariat, the colonial equivalent of Whitehall, had designations related to the job they were doing. In the Provincial Administration, responsible for the provinces and districts, all Administrative Officers were known as District Officers (DOs); and in Tanganyika the senior DO in charge of each of the 56 districts had the courtesy title of District Commissioner or DC. In the mid to late 1950's, Africans were increasingly recruited as Assistant District Officers, essentially a training grade but with every prospect of rapid promotion. During this period Dunstan Omari became the first Tanganyikan DC.

The administrative cadre in Tanganyika probably numbered something in the order of 250, of whom perhaps 40 were out of the country on leave at any given time. The manner in which work was allocated between DOs was a matter for the DC, but between them they were responsible for the good government and administration of the district. As the senior official, the DC was the informal leader of the district team, which comprised local representatives of specialist departments as well as his DOs. His key personal responsibilities were to implement government policies, manage government expenditure, ensure the collection of revenue, and maintain law and order. He also had the important task of promoting and developing local government institutions and supervising associated staff. All DOs were magistrates, and in all but the largest districts the DC was also officer in charge of police and, if there was one, the prison. The DC was also, by default, the local representative of all departments which did not have a presence in the district. In short he was actively and intimately concerned with pretty well everything for which Government had a responsibility or interest. By European standards all this was very basic and unsophisticated and the resources available derisory, although even in an average district in a relatively backward territory such as Tanganyika, the DC and his colleagues managed several million pounds worth of expenditure annually.[2] It was this lack of sophistication plus the variety of experience offered which seduced us; only the brain-dead could fail to respond.

The DO was very much a colonial creation, and there had been no comparable rôle in Britain since late medieval times. He was an expedient rather than a model, but – important in a poor country – cheap in relation to his wide range of duties. Where did a DO's loyalty lie, and to whom was he accountable? In denigrating colonialism the critics usually fail to distinguish between the acquisition and retention of colonies on one hand and the process of disengagement foreshadowed for Africa in the early 1920's, albeit not perceptibly begun until after the 1939-45 war, when it accelerated. They also tend to assume unanimity and complicity between Westminster, Whitehall, territorial governments, and the administrator in the field; this was by no means the case. We were not employed by the Colonial Office in London but by the government of the country in which we served, a government which had considerable discretion to act and legislate on its own account. It was answerable to both the British Government and, increasingly, its own people.[3] Similarly the DO was accountable to his territorial government, but also in varying degrees, albeit informally, to the people of his own district; the welfare of *his* people in *his* district was usually a major preoccupation. To this extent most of us went native, with a strong inclination to respond to or advance local needs and priorities. This is not of course entirely true, but it is a fair generalisation; we were not merely agents of a distant government in Europe.

The events described in this narrative are a record of one DO's experiences in Tanganyika; they will not have been precisely replicated elsewhere, but were of a kind familiar to any former DO who served anywhere in British colonial Africa. Most of the incidents were directly related to work, but I have

---

[2] 2004 values.

[3] And in the case of Tanganyika, a United Nations Trust Territory, to the UN.

also tried to convey something of the flavour of domestic and social life in a rural district. In this I may have sold our womenfolk short, and my wife Sylvia would say that her recollections have a different emphasis from my own. Although aware of my official activities and preoccupations and unfailingly supportive, her main concerns were with running the household, raising the children, and latterly teaching the older of them the three Rs. Like many others she gritted her teeth at the oft-repeated observation that 'of course, this is a man's country', with its implied acknowledgement of the lack of amenities and opportunities taken for granted by women in England. Absorbed by my work, I was largely oblivious to the deprivations and occasional hazards of domestic life; probably a majority of expatriate wives in remote districts enjoyed the life more in retrospect than in the event.

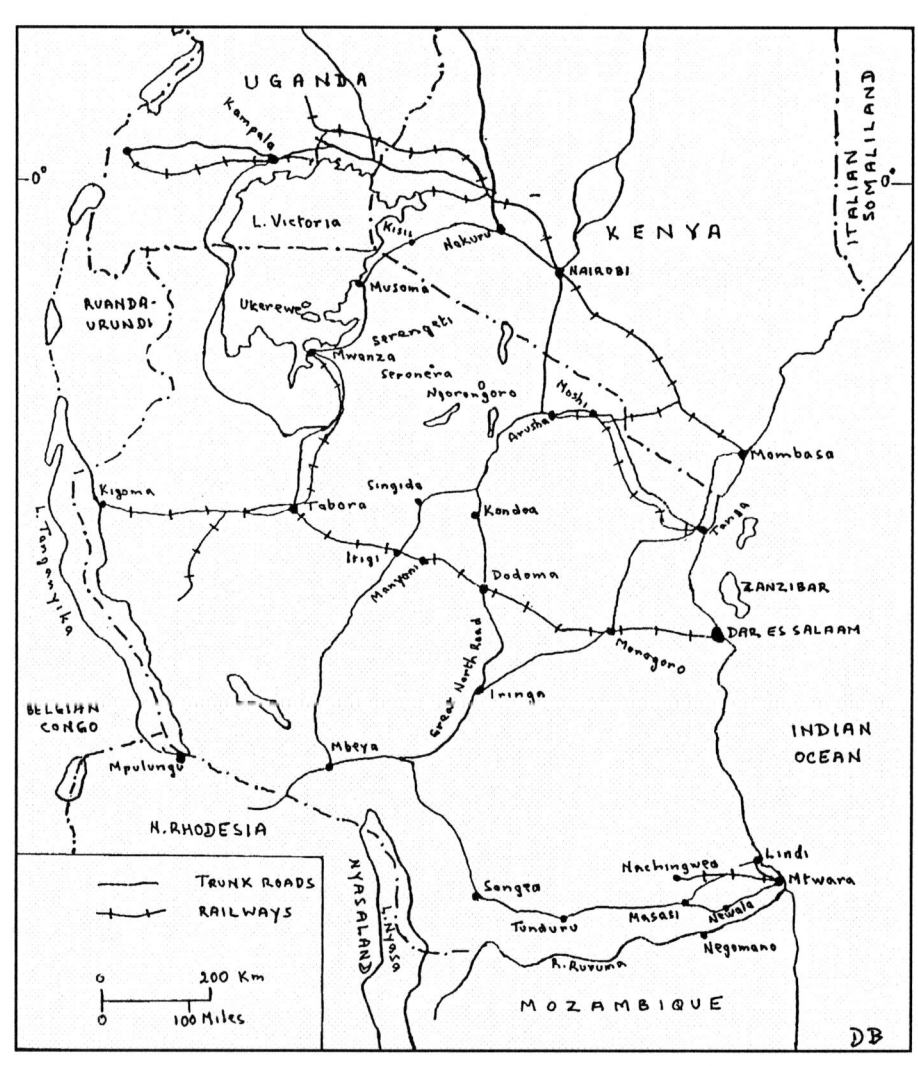

Tanganyika and neighbours, 1955

CHAPTER ONE

How It Began

Stirrings

In the years leading up to the outbreak of war in 1939 I attended a number of elementary schools in different parts of the country. North or south, metropolitan or provincial, they all had at least one thing in common – the celebration of Empire Day. The general holiday atmosphere, sports, and handouts of a cardboard box containing sandwich, bun, banana and orange made the twenty-fourth of May a day to be looked forward to. The years 1936 and 1937 were particularly heavy with imperial pomp and circumstance; King George V died in January 1936, not long after his Silver Jubilee; Edward VIII dashed quickly across the scene, leaving in his wake mementoes in the form of mugs, beakers, and aluminium medals distributed to the school population; and the next year there was the Coronation of George VI. To this came contingents of exotically-garbed Dominion and Colonial troops, and there were constant reminders that a disproportionately large part of the world's map was coloured deep pink.

During this period I discovered in the public library of my grandparents' home town in Lancashire, a series of books recounting the adventures of one Trooper Ouless – nicknamed Useless – of the British South Africa Police[4]. Trooper Useless was an engaging hero, never likely to be promoted, a victim at every turn of Murphy's law, and regularly falling foul of his Sergeant, Inspector, and officialdom in general. But like the Mounties, he always got his man – murderer, diamond thief, or the brutal farmer who was too free with his fists or whip. Indeed, to all intents and purposes he *was* a Mountie; same horse and bedding roll, same breeches, same revolver and holster; and the high-necked tunic was of the same cut, but a sober green instead of scarlet. Only the headgear

---

[4] The police force of Southern Rhodesia, now Zimbabwe.

1

was completely different, and Trooper Useless wore a khaki solar topee to prevent his brains from boiling in the tropical sun. Whilst – for all I knew – the background was as fictitious as the ripping yarns themselves, this boyhood reading sparked off an interest in Africa which was to propel me into the Colonial Service[5] a decade and a half later.

Halfway through the Second World War, aged fifteen or sixteen, I was captivated by Kenneth Bradley's 'Diary of a District Officer' – so much so that I promptly wrote off to the Colonial Office, a little prematurely it might be thought, for whatever recruitment literature they had. The booklet 'Appointments in the Colonial Service' was distinguished by the Royal Coat of Arms, but otherwise resembled a school examination paper in layout and visual appeal. The prose style was correspondingly prosaic and understated, a colony dealt with briskly in a short paragraph. It was commonly reported that 'good rough shooting is to be had in up-country districts' or – less appealingly – of some low-lying coastal territory or island, that 'Europeans may find the humidity trying (or enervating) in the hot season', and that 'children over the age of five are generally sent home to England'.

The pay looked reasonably good, as I suppose any adult salary does to a schoolboy. Starting at about £400 (£10,000)[6] a year and without promotion to dizzier heights, a District Officer could expect to get £1,000(£25,000) after nearly twenty years service – a princely income beyond my imagining. Another publication asserted that 'only in the Colonial Service is it possible to live the life of an English country gentleman on a civil servant's salary'. Not numbering the offspring of any country gentlemen amongst my acquaintances, I had only the dimmest conception of what this might mean; but it sounded all right – as if the prospect unfolded by Kenneth Bradley was not enough, with his description of life on safari in Northern Rhodesia (Zambia), elephant in the Luangwa Valley, the District Office at Fort Jameson, and his hilarious encounter with buffalo bean, besides which, I was later to discover, itching powder was a very inferior product.

Five years later, after a couple of years in the army, I was reading geography at Oxford, with Africa as my chosen region for detailed study, and as a special

---

[5] From 1954 Her Majesty's Overseas Civil Service (HMOCS).

[6] 2004 equivalents.

subject 'the social and political geography of the British Colonial Empire'. In my final year I applied for appointment to the Colonial Administrative Service, putting Tanganyika as my first choice if selected. Climatic consideration played a greater part than perhaps they should have done, for I found an averagely hot summer day in England uncomfortable. West Africa would be too hot; Basutoland and Bechuanaland (Lesotho and Botswana) were tempting – but the level of recruitment derisory. Attention focused on the high plateau of East Africa. Kenya was better publicised and more developed; but here, I thought, Government's freedom of action would be constrained by the white settler community. Tanganyika next door looked more promising ground; more 'backward', there would be more to do, and as a UN Trust Territory under international scrutiny, economic and political advance might be swifter than elsewhere.

The first interview took the form of a very friendly chat with a District Officer from Northern Rhodesia on secondment to the Colonial Office. The board was a more formidable affair, officials ranged along the other side of a heavy polished table, faces dim against the bright summer sunlight. I have no detailed recollection of the interview, and of course on these occasions it is the questioning which largely determines which of one's thoughts and motives are revealed for scrutiny and judgment. Certainly my own motives were mixed, but they were consistent. The idea of the wide open spaces and work which was not tied to an office desk had great appeal, and all my reading suggested that the work would be varied and interesting. By now I also had some knowledge of the problems of colonial development, and it seemed to me that there was a worthwhile job to be done; and whilst I did not at this stage envisage the early prospect of working myself out of a job, to play a part in preparing a dependency for eventual independence struck me as being a better way of spending my time than any of the alternatives on offer. And there was the further thought, essentially egotistical, that with so much to be done in the field, the opportunity to make a personal and visible contribution would be greater than in some highly structured monolithic organisation at home. My own country already had an abundance of what I assumed, not entirely correctly, Tanganyika wanted and needed; and perhaps I needed Tanganyika more than I needed Britain. I did not leave the interview light footed and confident, but felt that I'd had a fair crack of the whip and that if I failed I had only myself to blame.

Preparations and departure

Some weeks later a telegram announced 'Subject to medical fitness and satisfactory degree result you have been selected for appointment to Colonial Administrative Service. Formal offer and allocation follows'. Both requirements were met, and I was appointed to Tanganyika. In the autumn of 1951 I returned to Oxford for another year to join twenty or so others on the First Devonshire Course. This was based in the Colonial Service Club under the direction of Jerry Cornes, a pre-war Olympic hurdler and former District Officer. We attended lectures on native administration, accounting, tropical agriculture, forestry, East African history, economics and development, Islamic history and theology, and anthropology. We did a rapid theoretical course on the construction of buildings, roads, and bridges; and on several warm summer afternoons we might have been seen under the guidance of Mr.Longland in the University Parks, making a simple compass traverse, marking in prominent buildings on a plane table, or laying out imaginary building plots with line and tape. They were simple techniques, later to be recollected with relief when surveying the line of a new road or putting up my first bridge – which in the event looked like a heap of debris thrown together by the river; but it worked! Most important, in an absolute sense, were language and law; failure to pass future examinations would result in a personal pay freeze. For the eight of us who were bound for Tanganyika[7], and the one for Kenya, the language was Swahili; another group destined for Northern Nigeria, learned Hausa; and a very aloof young man who thought himself a cut above the rest of us was alone in grappling with Arabic, his posting the Aden Protectorate. He was welcome to it.

In charge of our Swahili tuition was Robbie Maguire, a retired Provincial Commissioner from Tanganyika, silver haired and silver tongued; he was a spellbinder, each lesson carried along on a tide of anecdote, usually relevant and invariably entertaining. Explaining a particular construction he would

---

[7] The others were Tom Moon, Tony Moore, Ashley Dixon, Eric Lawson, John Boxall, Jerry Nettleton (South African), and Peter McLaughlin (Canadian).

relate how once, on *safari,* he was out shooting for the pot. As he walked up to the carcass of a shot antelope a figure appeared from nowhere, and reaching the dead beast a few yards ahead, observed with approval ' *Itanitoshea'* - it will suffice me. Abdullah, his Zanzibari assistant, thought the Maguire technique rather frivolous, and favoured the more traditional method of learning by rote and repetition.

Not a natural linguist, my own progress was further retarded by a preoccupation with persuading Sylvia Perry – partner at a summer ball the previous term, and secretary to the Professor of Zoology – to abandon all prospects of a safe, secure and comfortable life in England, marry me, and come to Tanganyika. Towards the end of our year's training Robbie Maguire invited his class to tea on the lawn of his country home near Abingdon. In an informal valedictory speech he offered a final bit of advice; 'Do not for Heaven's sake think about marriage until you have done two or three years in the country'. It was good advice, and well meant. Afterwards, a little sheepishly, I confessed that a wedding was planned for the following month.

Seventy years or so earlier, in more pressing circumstances, General Gordon was summoned by the Prime Minister and asked to undertake an ambiguous errand in the Sudan. The very same evening he caught the boat train at Charing Cross to connect with an eastbound steamer at Brindisi; those Victorians were no slouches. *We* still had five or six weeks to prepare for departure, and it seemed little enough. We started with an expedition to London to order essential purchases from a firm of tropical outfitters, Baker's of Golden Square. It was perhaps as well that we were hard up, for there was no risk of being seduced by the more exotic and evocative equipment on display. Much of it had a decidedly pre-war look, but it was all indisputably new; a portable metal hip bath with a strapped-down cover, equally suitable for floating across rivers or porterage atop some curly head; a range of khaki canvas tents with or without built-in mosquito screens, and furnished with a variety of folding and collapsible furniture constructed of plain varnished wood and green canvas; pressure and incandescent paraffin lamps and humble hurricane lamps; water filters of varying degrees of complexity, and water purifying tablets; a primitive snake-bite outfit – a metal cylinder the size on one's little finger with a sharp blade in one end to ensure a flow of blood, some potassium permanganate crystals in the other to rub into the wound;

canvas water containers; gadgets for discouraging or demolishing ants, mosquitoes, flies. It all combined to make the heart beat a little faster, but left our exiguous bank balance largely unscathed; our main purchases were half a dinner and tea service and a plywood 'cook's box' of heavy duty aluminium utensils; the colander still survives.

In the clothing department a clerkly assistant drew attention to an assortment of spine pads – obsolete and ludicrous even in 1952 – and solar topees or 'Bombay bowlers'. These two were faintly risible relics of an earlier age; yet they were, I believe, uniquely comfortable, extremely light in weight and well ventilated. And even then they were part of the wardrobe of expatriate officialdom in those territories – Kenya and Bechuanaland for example - where uniforms were regularly worn. I was tempted by a 'double felt terai' a broad-brimmed hat with two thicknesses of felt and hence rather heavy; but settled for an Australian-style bush hat which was lighter and a good deal cheaper. I was gently pressed to buy a white dress uniform, sun helmet and sword, bush jackets and baggy shorts, and a 'sharkskin' dinner jacket, but ended up with a white drill dinner jacket, a cummerbund, a budget-priced Palm Beach suit which was to last me the next ten years, and the snake-bite outfit.

The footwear department was an eye-opener for someone accustomed to buy shoes at Bata or Lilley and Skinner. I had not imagined that such a range of shoes, boots and riding boots existed – and at such outrageous prices! We chose a sensible pair of brogues each; mine were Tricker's at an extravagant £3 (£60)[8], and four years later I sold them for a few shillings to an envious and importunate chief. He will now be dead, but they may well still be in use; they were good shoes. Mosquito boots were urged upon us, but unavailingly. I bought some canvas and leather army surplus ones for 30p and Sylvia acquired an extraordinary thigh-length pair from her sister who had lately been with her husband in the Gold Coast (Ghana). She never wore them.

So far we felt that we were not conspicuously well kitted-out, and indeed all our purchases from the tropical outfitter, next seen in the Customs shed at Dar-es-Salaam, were neatly packed into a robust wooden box about three feet

---

[8] All contemporary monetary values should be multiplied by a factor of 20 to give approximate 2004 equivalents.

long and eighteen inches square. My final purchase did something to redress the balance, a single-barrelled folding shotgun of their own make from Cogswell and Harrison in Picadilly; I felt that I was really on the way.

Our wedding in July was followed by a short week's holiday in Somerset, a tour of my relations in Lancashire, and a few days with my parents and sister in Monmouthshire; then it was time for *me* to go, for Sylvia would not be accompanying me. At this time there was a regulation in force which prohibited a married cadet's wife from joining him until he had passed his law and lower Swahili examinations, which rarely took less than a year; and a wife would interfere with the process of getting to know the country, or at least the district. Fortunately for us, this rule had already been inadvertently breached, and with the benefit of precedent, Sylvia could expect to fly out later in the year.

We had a farewell night in London; it was hot and sultry following a blazing summer day full of exhaust fumes, a combination which makes London so good to get away from. The following afternoon, the heavy baggage having gone on in advance, a superannuated boat train from Liverpool Street carried us to Silvertown. Alighting, we turned our backs on the bulk of Tate and Lyle's sugar refinery to face a street of Victorian shop fronts and cottages; on one corner was a pub with prominent cornices round doors and windows. Two hundred yards to the rear, and parallel to the main road, was the dock boundary, and sandwiched in between were terraces of artisans' and dockworkers' houses – the older ones of mellowed yellow brick, Edwardian ones grimy red, a little grander, and with bay windows. A few minutes walk took us to the gates leading into the King George V Dock. Beyond a long low brick warehouse with a serrated roof was a row of perhaps a dozen cranes, and –more important – the top half of mv *Dunnottar Castle,* painted in distinctive Union Castle livery; the hull was a shade of dirty pink with a hint of slate blue, the superstructure white, and the funnel vermillion and black. It seems a little ironic that my last contact with England should be with this dockland village, as alien in its way as any huddle of huts I might encounter in East Africa. For the next twenty years or so Silvertown went quietly to seed as the London dock industry declined, and then lay semi-derelict for two decades, awaiting the next stage of Dockland reincarnation. Now, in an apt juxtaposition of old and new, London City Airport lies alongside the King George V Dock.

In 1952 the age of cheap air-travel was a decade or more ahead. Sea travel was commonplace, and the ports of Southampton, Liverpool and London carried a large passenger traffic. From Southampton there was a weekly Union Castle sailing direct to Cape Town; from London, more irregular sailings round Africa, through the Mediterranean, the Suez Canal and Red Sea, and down around the Cape and back to London.

There is an air of expectancy generated by anticipated departure, even on a channel ferry; but here in King George V dock there was a difference. This was not a ferry crossing or a cruise, and I was very conscious that at the other end was a new and very different way of life, a life of which I would become, or fail to become, a part. There were two parties of District Officer cadets on board; we had chosen a minority career for our own various reasons, but I imagine that most of us had similar reflections on the future between boarding and our last sight of the Lizard light.

The voyage.

Late in the afternoon those who were not sailing were hastened ashore, and Sylvia and I made our farewells; the sirens blew, hawsers were cast off, and the tugs manoeuvred us towards the dock gates. Amongst the crowd on the quay, vibrating with a hundred waving arms was Sylvia's blonde head and her black and white 'going-away' outfit. Ahead was the curve of the Thames below Woolwich, and across the river Plumstead Marshes and the terra incognita of south-east London. We moved slowly downstream on a murky turning tide; well down the estuary we dropped the pilot and gathered speed, and the ship began to move to the sea. By mid-evening we were halfway down the Channel and the eight of us destined for Tanganyika alternated between the bar and the ship's rail, the circumference of our circle occasionally touching that of a smaller group who were now employed by the Government of Uganda. A variety of reactions were apparent, but predominantly a relief that we were now on our way, lectures, seminars and essays behind us; and ahead, what ….. ? I wondered how much of Kenneth Bradley's diary was still relevant; it had been written half a generation and a war ago, and many things would have changed. We could not have guessed how short our careers would be.

The Bay of Biscay was unpleasant and the sunlit green hills of Galicia at the north-west corner of Spain the next morning were a reminder that Iberia is not all Castile and Andalucia. Down the Portuguese coast we passed sardine fishermen, their briskly bobbing boats an unwelcome reminder of the previous night. At Gibraltar we went ashore, climbed the rock, and had a ritual look at the Barbary apes. Thence to Marseilles, where there was just about time to visit the Chateau d'If, and we wondered whether the crowded troopship alongside our own was destined for Algeria or what was still French Indo-China.[9] At Genoa we explored the waterfront and the hills encompassing the town to the north. And then we were away again, past Stromboli and Elba, through the Straits of Messina, round the toe of Italy, and eastwards towards Port Said. Early one morning in the lee of the long mole projecting seawards, we slid past the statue of Ferdinand de Lesseps – later destroyed in a fit of patriotic enthusiasm – and came alongside just astern of a black and rust-coloured vessel, the *Ranchit*, home port Karachi, and exuding a perceptible odour of stale curry. Further along the quay was a French ship of the Messageries Maritimes, with numbers of troops aboard, bound for Djibouti or Madagascar, both French colonies; close behind us, all white with pale yellow funnels, a multi-deck P and O liner with a cargo of British immigrants for Australia.

At this time the British influence in Egypt was still strong, the Canal Zone occupied by British troops, largely National Servicemen doing two years obligatory service. However, Colonel Nasser had recently come to power, ex-King Farouk was in exile, and there was a noticeable sense of mixed uncertainty and expectation in the air. We ourselves, recollecting too vividly old soldiers' tales of the iniquities of Cairo and Port Said, did not venture far from the ship. Indeed there was probably not a great deal to see and we contented ourselves with a visit to Simon Arzt's famous emporium only a stone's throw or two from where the ship was berthed. Having begun the voyage with only ten pounds by way of spending money I contributed little to the Arzt family fortunes and left with a cheap straw hat, regretting my impecunious condition.

On board the *Dunnottar Castle* the bumboat men and other vendors had turned the main deck into an oriental bazaar. Here one could purchase from a

---

[9] Now Vietnam,Cambodia,Laos.

range of tropical fruits, and an infinite variety of camel leather goods, belts, purses, holdalls, suitcases, key rings, handbags, with or without motifs featuring the Sphinx, pyramids, and Pharaonic personalia; and many-hued carpets and wraps, most cheap and tawdry, some not. A gentleman with a cast in his eye urged me, unavailingly, to purchase a diamond ring which he demonstrated on a piece of glass which looked and sounded more like Perspex. On the side of the ship away from the quay the bumboats were ranged in a row, tied to the rail; below, the vendors would hold up their wares, and at the slightest hint of interest, an aide would haul them up on a piece of cord for closer inspection. In the non-stop haggling the passengers were invariably addressed as Mr. or Mrs. Mackintosh, the eponymous Briton of assumed thrifty habits.

There were also the 'gully gully' men; gathering an audience, these engaging conjurers delighted young and old alike with their skilful legerdemain, magicking away day-old chicks and making them reappear from mouth, pocket, bosom and handbag. Finishing off with a deliberate appeal to the children, contributions were generous when the hat was passed round. In the early evening preparations were made for departure of the southbound convoy. The hucksters were hustled over the side and down the gangways, and as the time to cast off approached the bargaining became keener and noisier. My own booty comprised a camel saddle which served for years as an occasional stool, and a plaited leather riding crop which came unravelled in no time at all. Intending neither to ride nor beat my future staff, I cannot think why I bought it in the first place.

At dusk we moved into the canal; the landscape was dull, but history stirred the imagination; this was the beginning of the Orient. Here things had changed little since Biblical times, but here also Napoleon's eastern adventure had ended, Lt.Waghorn had pioneered the Overland Route to India in pre-canal days, and not far away to the west Hitler's armies had been halted and turned back. The next morning we waited in the Bitter Lakes as a northbound convoy passed, and then entered the southern leg of the canal which led us into the Gulf of Sinai.

For most of a morning we sailed between ramparts of sun-blasted jagged mountains of bare rock, occasionally passing small fishing villages or encampments on the western shore. To the east Mount Sinai rose from an uncompromising landscape, an entirely appropriate milieu for an Old Testament prophet. If Moses found a spring in that bastion of rock it was a miracle indeed. An hour or two later Sinai was out of sight, the shore of the Red Sea dim on the starboard side.

It was about here that the heat and humidity began to be really unpleasant, and the significance and desirability of P O S H became clear; port out, starboard home. Four of us shared a cabin on the wrong –or starboard – side. Here, moving south, the ship's steel plates heated up for six hours or so from midday onwards, turning the cabin into an oven in which sleep later was almost impossible. There was no air conditioning, and the ventilators blew warm air. Some cabins had metal scoops which, when fitted to the portholes, directed the breeze inwards; some cabins, like ours, didn't. The Captain's concession to this was to zig-zag the ship now and again so that cabins on both sides of the ship caught some of the southerly wind which was blowing up the Red Sea. At night some passengers slept on deck on chairs and benches; others stayed below on towel-draped bunks and sweated, and became acquainted with prickly heat. At this stage of the voyage we uttered uncharitable thoughts about the thriftiness of the Colonial Office, which had booked us tourist class instead of the first class accommodation to which we were formally entitled.

We approached Port Sudan at five o'clock one morning and even at that hour the air burned its way down into the lungs; at noon the temperature was over 120F(50C), but it was a dry heat, and bearable. A few passengers went ashore to sample cold drinks and air-conditioning at the nearest hotel, and some of us took a trip in a glass-bottomed boat to have a brief look at the spectacular marine life. In the late afternoon the sky darkened in the west, and a sandstorm blew up - not a severe one, but enough to require us all to get under cover, with windows and portholes shut fast and ventilators closed down; it was dreadful. During the night we sailed for Aden.

Aden Colony itself had no natural raison d'etre, and was a creation of British imperial needs by now largely obsolete, a fuelling station and staging post on the route to India and the Far East. A splendid harbour was backed by a range of awesomely spiky mountains, cubic miles of solid rock; and on a promontory overlooking the harbour were Government House, and Flagstaff House wherein resided the C in C Indian Ocean station. Along the waterfront at Steamer Point were the offices of shipping firms and bunkering agents, and a few shops and banks. A long taxi- ride away and out of sight of the harbour was Crater, the commercial centre for Colony and Protectorate (both now part of Yemen); and round the headland, the air and army bases and oil installations which were then a thread, still intact, in the fabric of Britain's middle-eastern interests. At the time there was no hint to the passing traveller of the violence which was later to erupt and shatter the fragile confederation of sheikdoms in the Protectorate, and for some years leave the Russians established in force on Socotra island, and where the British bases used to be at Khormaksor and al-Mansoura.

From Aden we set course to round the Horn of Africa, and some days later, soon after sunrise, we approached a low, sandy, palm-edged coast, and slipped into Mombasa's Kilindini harbour. This was to be *our* Africa, and we walked into town, visited Nyali Beach and Fort Jesus, one of Portugal's outposts of empire three centuries earlier. One afternoon we hired a couple of sailing dinghies from the obliging manager of the Yacht Club, and another day Tom Moon and I borrowed a pair oar from the rowing club. But we were anxious to be on our way; the ship was an inferno, with no ventilation for most of the day. To heat and humidity was added the clatter of cargo being unloaded and our ears rang as local African labourers chipped old paint off the superstructure with steel hammers as a preliminary to repainting. On the slow route round Africa, passengers came a poor second to cargo.

Our stay in port was enlivened by Tom Moon's engagement to Pat, a newly-qualified nurse encountered on the voyage. This was not unexpected, and married myself for only five or six weeks I had been approached for a little avuncular advice somewhere off the coast of Italian Somaliland a few days earlier. It was a good excuse for a party when we needed one.

After an interminable week the ship sailed, made a brief stop at Tanga, and next morning we awoke off Zanzibar, with a fairy-tale view of the Sultan's palace, and dhows at anchor or hauled onto the beach. There was the smell of cloves drying in the sun, and cloves by the ton in sacks awaiting shipment. I did not go ashore, and spent most of the morning in the sick bay. I had an appointment with a surgeon in Dar-es-Salaam.

CHAPTER TWO

Dar es Salaam and Manyoni

An inauspicious start

The *Dunnottar Castle* had sailed from London on 13th August 1952, and dropped anchor in Dar-es-Salaam harbour on 13th September; I am not superstitious, but perhaps the dates were significant. From somewhere at the bottom end of the Red Sea, the ship's doctor had been treating me for gastroenteritis. The symptoms did not respond and by the time we reached Zanzibar he had decided I had acute appendicitis. He radioed Dar-es-Salaam, and hardly had we got there and manoeuvred into the inner harbour a few hours later when, clad in a dressing gown more appropriate to an English winter than the East African coast, I was hastened down the ship's ladder to a waiting motor launch. My fellow cadets were to see my baggage ashore and into the Customs shed. Our mutual goodbyes were necessarily brief, and I missed the shared round of appointments ashore and whatever celebration preceded their final dispersal to up-country districts; I saw none of them again in Tanganyika.

It was dusk when I came round in a six-bedded ward in the Ocean Road hospital. Only one of the other beds was occupied, by a police officer who was to leave the following day. I was still fuddled, but our initial brief exchange was not to be forgotten.

'Who operated on you, do you know?'

'Dr. X.......I think'

'God, you're lucky to be alive, he's usually stoned!'

The discomfort of the first couple of days was succeeded by boredom and an anxiety to get to my first post. Maudie Lee helped on both counts. She was a WAA[10] in the department of Local Government and Administration, the one to

---

[10] Woman Administrative Assistant; comparable to District Officer in status, but employed exclusively in HQ and Provincial offices, never in districts.

which I now belonged; her daily visits to cheer me up were greatly appreciated. On the first occasion she told me I was to go to Manyoni. There is a consolatory and self-consciously cheerful way of breaking bad news, and it was clear from Maudie's manner that Manyoni was not generally regarded as a plum posting. However, I was to be there for only a few months, and this was the least of my worries; it was all new, and there was much to learn. Of far greater concern was the unknown answer to the question – would I, after six relatively leisured years in the army and at university, be able to buckle down to a serious and demanding job?

Impressions of Dar-es-Salaam following discharge were fleeting. I spent a few days convalescing as the guest of a bachelor Administrative Officer, Geoffrey Allsebrook, who was serving in the Secretariat. Whilst he was at work I had a few undemanding duties of my own to perform. I walked round to Government House to sign the book recording the names of daily callers; His Excellency the Governor and Commander-in-Chief Sir Edward Twining, KCMG, now knew that I had arrived – or probably not, for in my ignorance, and following the example of the previous signatory, I entered the acronym 'p.p.c' (pour prendre congé) which announced my departure! This gaffe probably cost me an invitation to drinks, as HE usually made a point of meeting all newly-arrived cadets. Another walk took me to the office of Frederick Page-Jones, head of the Provincial Administration[11] of which I was now a member; this was located in a prefabricated one-storey building, its door opening on to the street. It all seemed very accessible and informal, as did the white shorts and short-sleeved shirt which he wore; the only concession to formality was a tie, a distinction which I was to discover separated the Secretariat sheep from the up-country goats. I also had to call on the Chief Secretary, who formally welcomed me to the Service, and administered the oath of allegiance

On a more mundane domestic errand I made my way to see Bill Mate, the Government Passages Agent, a friendly and obliging man whose main task was to assist officials moving themselves and their families into and out of and around the country between postings. On this occasion he got a berth for me on the next overnight train to Dodoma where I was to recuperate for a further week,

---

[11] Also member of the Executive & Legislative Councils, and responsible for local government and administration.

and undertook to have my heavy baggage freighted up to Manyoni . This now included a newly-purchased paraffin-operated Electrolux refrigerator against which the Accountant General had made me a loan. Our imported effects were all dutiable; there was no discretion, and I was allowed half a month's salary in advance – twenty five pounds – to clear our small wooden case and a few trunks through Customs; a mean beginning I thought.

Dar es Salaam harbour   NJB

During my brief stay in Dar-es-Salaam it was the street scenes and sounds which registered most strongly, particularly of course those which were distinctively African. The streets were ablaze with the deep orange blossoms of the flamboyant trees – a variety of acacia – and rarely was a mango tree or palm not visible. Also flanking the streets were open storm drains into which rubbish was apt to be thrown and where, in consequence, pi-dogs scavenged; and kites too, when not wheeling overhead, mewing like kittens. In shop doorways Indian traders stood, and on their verandahs black and brown-skinned tailors worked on their treadle sewing machines.

At the bottom of Acacia Avenue was the Askari Memorial, a life-size bronze of a soldier of the King's African Rifles, commemorating the service rendered by Tanganyikan *askaris* in two world wars. Along the beach edging the harbour fishermen landed their catches from outrigger canoes, loafers sat and laughed and chattered, and passengers from one of the anchored ships aimed their cameras. As well they might, for no-one who has been through Dar-es-Salaam could be indifferent to that curve of sand framing the harbour, edged by palm trees behind which are the white, red-roofed buildings of the German and British colonial periods, and the two cathedrals.

There were the smells too, not unpleasant, but certainly distinctive – a faint but predominant hot-house taste in the air, compounded of rotting vegetation, fruit and seaweed, drying refuse, and an occasional whiff of drains and diesel fuel from the harbour. It was a smell first encountered in more intense form at Port Said, and later in Port Sudan where the mid-day sun put a heat-tempered edge on it. Up-country the chemistry was different, a pot-pourri of hot dust and wood smoke, with a varying injection of evaporating animal urine and, at the right time of year, the scent of acacia blossom in the bush.

Journey Up-Country

My departure from Dar-es-Salaam railway station is not one of my more cherished memories. The train left at 9.30 at night; mosquitoes swarmed, and clouds of insects swirled round the dim overhead lights. It was hot, over ninety degrees (+30C), and clothes hung limp, clammy, and soaked with sweat. I had more hand-luggage than could comfortably be fitted into my sleeping compartment, a circumstance which my travelling companion, a Government doctor bound for Iringa, must have found tiresome. The wire gauze over the windows kept out air as well as mosquitoes; I felt, and smelled, like a newly wrung-out dishcloth.

By the middle of the following morning the discomforts of the night were forgotten. Up at the front, a wood-burning Garrett locomotive towed us along the metre-gauge track at a steady twenty-five miles an hour. One of the attractive features of the antiquated rolling-stock of East African Railways and Harbours at the time was a little open-air gallery at each end of the first-class cars. A wrought-iron balustrade prevented the traveller from falling off, and the extended roof kept the sun at bay. It was a delight to sit on the iron floor, arms looped round the upright rails, legs dangling in space, and watching Tanganyika unfold. In truth it was not a riveting landscape. An occasional line of low blue hills would advance, turn brown and recede to blue again, and little patches of cultivation showed up green but in general it was brown land, brown men, brown cattle, and brown houses. Two hundred miles or so of brown; we had passed the green bit and the Uluguru mountains during the night. It was a sunburnt brown, but if the sun burned the landscape to a uniformity of colour it also enriched it with a range of shades from bleached pale yellows to tawny and dusky browns – with black where the sun did not reach.

At Dodoma[12] I stayed a night or two with the Australian DC John Pearce and his wife, met my Provincial Commissioner, Leonard Heaney, and then moved for a few days into the Railway Hotel. In retrospect this was an undistinguished building, but it seemed wholly appropriate to its dry and harsh surroundings. It was square in plan with an internal courtyard. The rooms were cool and shaded, with dark polished wood floors and furniture, and each opened onto a small private balcony. Here, with the aid of a few rehearsed phrases of halting Swahili, I hired Athmani, our first cook. In the event he was not a great success and we parted company a few months later.

Early on the next Monday morning I was collected by the Dodoma Resident Magistrate (RM) in an Austin A40 pick-up; he had a civil case to hear in Manyoni. The journey was only eighty miles, but it was a poor road and the RM was a cautious driver. Athmani, sitting in the back, slept most of the way. It could not be said that the country through which we passed was beautiful; but, drier west of Dodoma than it had been to the east, it impressed by its sheer harshness. In fact it was semi-desert, punctuated visually by outcrops of rock and a scattering of baobab trees, thorn bush, and an occasional patch of withered millet. We dropped gradually down the eastern slope of the Rift Valley, and then drove for fifteen miles across the barren floor of the Bahi Depression. Around Saranda there was water, and an oasis of green trees; elsewhere just bare earth and dust, thorn thickets, and a clump of doum palms here and there. From time

---

[12] Then headquarters of Central Province, now the national capital.

to time we saw a Gogo[13] cattle herder accompanying a few tiny under-nourished beasts, sometimes a donkey amongst them carrying one or two leather panniers. Then we tackled the steeper western escarpment. The train needed two locomotives to push and pull it to the top at a good walking pace; the R.M's pick-up was somewhat faster, but its radiator was boiling by the time we reached the top. We rested awhile, and I took in the view to our rear, where the Rift Valley lay spread out below us, running north to south – and going on and on to the Dead Sea in one direction, and down to Nyasaland (Malawi) in the other.

The valley side was well-wooded, and I enjoyed my first sight of wildlife in the form of a flock of green and red parakeets squawking amongst the trees. From here onwards we climbed only very gently, and then levelled off, driving first through light *miombo* or open woodland and then through thorn bush until suddenly without warning, we were at Manyoni.

Manyoni

I was not disposed to be critical – it was all new and exciting; but by the end of the three months I was there, and although it had not begun to pall, I recognised its limitations in terms of experience and opportunity to learn. The learning began at once, sitting in with the RM as he dealt with the litigants in a civil case in the DC's office. At lunchtime I was told that the DC – Bill Helean, a New Zealander – had gone to Dodoma the previous day accompanied by his wife Ethel, for hospital treatment; I also learned that there was an outbreak of bubonic plague at Itigi, forty minutes drive to the west along the railway. Completely unsighted, I consulted the Provincial Medical Officer in Dodoma over the phone; he assured me that all I needed to do was ensure an adequate supply of gammaxane powder to the African public health staff at Itigi who were engaged in eliminating rat fleas. It was a relief when Bill Helean returned three or four days later.

There then began a more purposeful process of learning on the job. I was pitched into the Native Treasury for afternoons at a time – hot, sticky afternoons under a corrugated iron roof – where Hassan the Treasurer showed me how the

---

[13] The predominant local tribe.

accounts were kept; instruction was none the easier for being conducted in Swahili. A few weeks later I was assumed to be competent to carry out the monthly check on his books. As a Third Class Magistrate, and with the aid of an interpreter, I began at once to hear straightforward cases in the District Court; and within three weeks heard my first Preliminary Inquiry (PI), a process whereby a magistrate determines whether or not a person charged with serious crime beyond his jurisdiction should be discharged or sent for trial by the High Court; in this case a man had shot and killed a neighbour with a poisoned arrow. I was sent out to investigate and settle a minor boundary dispute between two adjoining chiefdoms; and on a similar occasion incurred Bill's displeasure by giving away a small piece of Manyoni to Singida district, whose delegation was led by Geoff Thirtle, a DO a year ahead of me in experience and fluency in Swahili. I uttered warnings to Fazal Ladha, a local trader who was selling weevily flour, not yet realising that most flour was infested to some degree, and best sieved before use; laid out the site for a new primary school; and annoyed Bill yet again by failing to arrest a man I had been specifically sent out to pick up for threatening violence to the outposted police corporal at Itigi Junction. The culprit was engaged on urgent locomotive maintenance, and the engineer in charge promised to send him in later, which – to my relief – he did.

On another occasion Bill required me to accompany Sub-Inspector Boniface and a few constables on what he described as a 'tax raid' in Manyoni settlement, which comprised no more than thirty or forty dwellings. This involved knocking up the occupants in the small hours and requiring adult males to show their tax receipts; bleary-eyed and grumbling, most of them did so. Defaulters were expected to show up next morning cash in hand, or face prosecution. I found the whole process demeaning and personally embarrassing; it achieved nothing which could not have been done conventionally by one or two tax clerks during the day. In the event this experience turned out to be irrelevant, and I never came across the practice anywhere else, nor ever initiated it.

A daily diversion was the five minutes or so spent with Rajabu, the imprecisely-designated Station Hand. A slight man, wearing a navy sweater, khaki shorts, and a military manner reinforced by a sergeant-major's swagger stick, he presented himself early every morning to consult me about the disposition of the current contingent of extra-mural prisoners. In stations where there was no prison, offenders given short sentences were required to undertake some form of public work until they had served their time. They slept in very basic dormitories, and during the day carried out a variety of tasks – typically cutting grass along the road verges, clearing ditches, watering plants, chopping firewood, and so on. Rajabu supervised them and dispensed their daily rations.

One afternoon, at their request, I tried to mediate in a domestic dispute between husband and wife. Mansur was a plump and prosperous middle-aged Arab timber merchant with a tuft of grey beard, and wearing an orange turban, white calf-length tunic, and sandals; in the sash around his waist was a curved dagger in a splendid silver sheath. His African wife was probably in her late teens, attractive, coquettish, and swathed in a pair of red and yellow patterned *kanga* – matching rectangles of cloth – one round her waist serving as a skirt, the other draped over her head. Formal appearances in a District Court were not unusual, especially where there were cultural or ethnic differences, or there was a conflict between local customary law and, say, Islamic law. But this was an informal affair; no doubt both parties had already consulted relatives and friends, and now they sought a neutral opinion and an indication of what would be involved in going to law. Listening carefully, and with the help of an interpreter I felt very inadequate in the rôle of Dutch uncle. At the end I could only hope that the voice of reason and authority carried some conviction, and that a divorce would be averted. I rather doubted it.

Medical provision in Manyoni was exiguous and came in the solitary form of John Kunsinda, a Rural Medical Aid with a year's training, limited diagnostic skills, and a range of very basic drugs at his small dispensary. John was a tall, cheerful, and kindly man in his mid-thirties. We never had to put his skills to the test, and our occasional conversations tended to revolve round public health matters. One singular personal characteristic lingers in the memory; he had a conspicuously ill-fitting set of false teeth which rattled and clacked when he spoke, and appeared to have a life of their own. We assumed that he had picked them up second-hand as a preferred option to toothlessness, but he quietly declined the offer to help him get a set that fitted.

Manyoni district was not very fruitful ground for missionary activity; there was a small Church Army mission at Kilimatinde, on the edge of the Rift, and below it, at Makutopora, a brace of CMS (Church Missionary Society) ladies ran a leprosarium. One of these was an Australian who turned up from time to time in a small Fordson van to seek assistance from the District Office;

perhaps she felt she had some special claim on a fellow-Antipodean. At any rate she had a certain facility for getting under Bill Helean's skin. He was a bluff and hearty man, and a bit of a bully, and it was a matter for surprise and amusement that he could be so easily rattled by this earnest spinster. She had recently wanted us to disperse discharged patients from the vicinity of the leprosarium where, she complained, they were seriously depleting the mission stocks of food. Bill had not unreasonably declined, suggesting that they stayed precisely because they *were* fed, and would drift off home if this largesse ceased. One afternoon I was working on some papers in my office when Bill dashed in through a connecting door, having spotted the Fordson van approaching; 'It's that bloody woman from Makutopora again…. tell her I'm on safari ….get rid of her and let me know when it's all clear'. With that he let himself out through a rear door leading to a small inner compound. I did my duty and basked in Bill's approval for the next day or two. For a man who was normally pretty robust in his dealings with the public, this was a new side to his persona.

Main Street – Manyoni

DB

The only other non-official Europeans in the district were the Robbie family; they eked out a precarious living on a small plantation, originally German-owned, but now leased from Government. I visited the family only once, and wondered how they could subsist in such an unpromising environment for agriculture; one could only admire their fortitude.

* * *

Most evenings were spent poring over the Laws of Tanganyika and A

21

Handbook for Magistrates, Local Government Memoranda[14], and my Swahili vocabulary. If law and language examinations were not passed within two years there would be no more salary increments. This compelling though scarcely generous carrot as a reward for diligence was reinforced by two sticks. A DO cadet in his first tour was not allowed a car loan as were his more senior colleagues; the idea was that he should be out and about on foot getting to know people and country. The second stick, the conditional ban on wives accompanying their husbands on first appointment, has already been referred to.

However, with the benefit of precedent, Sylvia was booked to fly out in November. The reasoning behind the tattered prohibition now became clear; less of my time was spent on books, more on preparations for Sylvia's arrival – having a bath installed and a privy built, staining the woodwork of our little thatched brick rondavels with a solution of potassium permanganate, and acquiring a few more sticks of furniture. There was nothing much I could do about our water supply, which came out of a shallow well five yards from the front door, and which was so muddy that the ceramic elements in our water filter rapidly clogged and had to be cleaned twice a day. Every expatriate household had a filter; these were upright cylinders about 2ft (.7m) high, of glazed earthenware or aluminium. Into the upper chamber went the boiled water, which was then filtered through 3 hollow porous 'candles' into the lower chamber, from which pure water was drawn by tap. The 'candles' normally needed cleaning only once a week. Rubber washers within the filter ensured that the water acquired a slight taste; this was partly dispelled by refrigeration, wholly so by the addition of fruit cordial or juice.

The kitchen did not lend itself to improvement; it was typical of the period, and assumed that the colonial wife was inept, idle, or both, and that cooking would be left exclusively to the cook. It was built at a distance from the house, and was equipped with an iron wood-burning stove, probably cast about the time of the Boer War, bought in bulk, and issued for the use of generations of colonial officials thereafter. In the capital and larger towns, electric cookers had begun to make their appearance; two years later we graduated to an indoor kitchen, but one still equipped with an iron stove; and for our last few months in the country

---

[14] Which described in some detail the policies, structures and practices of local government.

we enjoyed the luxury and decadence of a bottled gas cooker.

Sylvia duly arrived by the morning train. She had been accompanied on the last part of her journey by the DO, Geoff Thirtle, who had bested me in the boundary dispute, and who was on his way back to Singida after a visit to provincial headquarters. To Sylvia's credit she did not burst into tears when she saw her new home, for in truth it was very basic; two round rooms twelve or fifteen feet in diameter joined by a small mosquito-proofed verandah. Until I moved in it had been a rest-house, used by officials on tour; I rather resented being docked the regulation ten per cent of salary by way of rent. However, it was only a temporary home and we were to be transferred to Kondoa at the end of December. With this in prospect, and partly because we were still very new, we did not make any close friendships in the tiny expatriate community in Manyoni.

First home – Manyoni   DB

Apart from Bill and his delightful wife Ethel, this comprised Toby Reilly, a middle-aged Crop Supervisor, and Tony Mence, a young Game Ranger who always looked the part, and both bachelors; and there was Bertie Hall, the District Foreman, and his wife. We played tennis together, visited each other's houses for drinks or dinner, and went down to meet the train twice a week to see who was passing through. I enjoyed Manyoni, but was scarcely more permanent than the train passengers who passed in transit, thankful that *they* were not stationed there.

In retrospect I suppose Manyoni's reputation was justified. The district, with an area of just under 11,000 square miles and a population of only 59,000 was one of the largest and most sparsely populated in the country, and also one of the least developed; like most of Central Province it was extremely dry. Its eastern boundary lay in the Bahi Depression, its western part covered with almost impenetrable thorn bush described on the map as Itigi thicket. Between escarpment and thicket was mixed woodland and thorn bush, with patches of half-hearted cultivation, and occasional expanses of *mbuga* which were swampy in the brief rains, and approximated to parkland in the dry season. Apart from the escarpment, with its breathtaking vista to the east, the district was scenically extremely dull, epitomised by the view from our back door where, after twenty yards of bare sand and dust, the thorn bush began, and went on and on and on. In this inhospitable landscape lived the Gogo, a small tribe of pastoralists, still semi-nomadic, but becoming increasingly settled. They demanded little other than to be allowed to live as their tradition prescribed, with minimal interference from central authority; of Government they expected only that relief be provided in times of famine, and that rural medical services be extended into the remoter parts of the district; education was not a priority.

Manyoni settlement was wholly undistinguished. Fewer than a dozen decrepit *dukas* or shops huddled in the dust along two sides of a desiccated market place. The shops referred to here and elsewhere were indeed shops in the sense that goods were exchanged for cash; in other respects they were not quite the shops we know. Construction ranged from daub and wattle with earth floor, to cement block, with roofs of either grass or corrugated iron. Typically the sizeable front room of the building, usually windowless, was the shop; entry was by one or two wooden double doors, left open during business hours, which ran from early morning until late at night. Along the walls were plain wooden shelves carrying a range and quantity of commodities contingent upon the requirements of the local clientele and the credit-worthiness of the proprietor, who lived behind rather than above the shop. On the floor were 4 gallon tins of paraffin, ghee, sunflower and sesame oil, sacks of rice, flour, sugar and beans, bundles of hoe heads, *pangas,* (machetes), buckets, cooking pots and assorted hardware. There was usually a limited range of cheap fabrics and *kangas*, and there was sometimes a 'tailor' available who could run up simple garments. In the case of Manyoni, the few *dukas* peddled a severely limited range of goods, mostly of the poorest quality, for the Gogo domestic economy was not such as to

24

sustain a flourishing trade in even the most basic consumer commodities.

At the other end of the main street was the Boma[15], a ramshackle single-storey mud-brick building which an optimistic Greek had once owned and run as a hotel. At the other end the shops and houses soon thinned out, and a hundred yards or so beyond the market the road disappeared westwards into the bush, accompanied by a single telegraph wire suspended from metal poles, a symbol rather of isolation than communication.

Prior to Sylvia's arrival I had made a few rather inconsequential safaris, educational rather than useful. I accompanied Toby Reilly on one of his field trips, the better to understand the nature of his work. On another I was sent to make some assessment of food reserves in the remote south of the district, reached along dusty imperceptible tracks. On this occasion I just about preserved my savoir faire when, shortly after stepping out of the office Landrover, an apparently crazed old man about five feet in height rushed at me brandishing a spear and shouting incomprehensibly, stopping abruptly two or three paces away; this, it was solemnly explained, was by way of being a traditional greeting to strangers. It might easily have been misinterpreted.

It was possibly a commonplace with newcomers, but camping under canvas in the bush initially occasioned some anxiety regarding the habits of predatory carnivores, and on my first couple of outings I took precautions with deterrent fire and hurricane lamps, and carefully laced up the tent before sweatily and wakefully retiring. Within weeks, I concluded that this was nonsense; the risks were negligible, and an open tent was cooler, especially if open at both ends. Later I often dispensed with the tent and enjoyed the night sky.

Sylvia's first safari experience was not a happy one. We set off in the Native Authority (NA) truck; first stop Itigi, to check on the aftermath of the plague outbreak, and then south-west to carry out a routine check on the local court and dispensary at Ukimbu, where we were to spend the night. The domestic arrangements were primitive. A small daub and wattle structure purporting to be a rest-house had recently been thrown together; it comprised a single windowless room, with earth floor, about eight feet by six. Outside, a door was propped

---

[15] A *boma* was any kind of protective enclosure; German administrative centres pre-1918 also tended to be defensive installations, so the District Office everywhere came to be known as ' the Boma'.

against a wall, but the frame into which it would eventually fit had not yet been installed. Towards evening the sub-chief casually remarked that there was a man-eating lion in the vicinity, at which moment the lack of an effective door assumed a larger importance. It now seemed a mere trifle that Athmani had brought only one camp bed; thirty inches wide, this promised us an uncomfortable night rather than a cosy one. When it was time to turn in, I wedged the door into the aperture as best I could, loaded my shotgun with heavy SSG shot and put it under the bed, just in case. It was an unforgettably excruciating night.

This then was the background of our introduction to East Africa and of my own initiation into the craft of district administration. There was more than enough to engage the interest and energies of a raw cadet, but Kondoa already beckoned. It was by all accounts a more complex and developed district, politically more sophisticated, and with formidable problems of overgrazing and soil erosion. The DC was also said to be an able and thoughtful administrator, and such criticism as I heard inspired approbation rather than anxiety. Shortly before Christmas we set off in the Native Authority 3-ton Bedford, Athmani curled up amongst our goods and chattels in the back, and Sylvia with me in the cab, she nursing a recently acquired three-month old pup, Oliver Cromwell.

It was a good time to arrive, and we were pitched into the round of jollifications without any of the disadvantages of preparation. As if the Christmas and New Year festivities were not enough, the DO whom I was replacing was married during the few days of our overlap. We thus met all our colleagues in a relaxed holiday atmosphere, although the confrontation between their concentrated African experience and our own lack of it was a constant reminder of our shortcomings.

On New Year's Eve our next-door neighbour Douglas Turner threw a party for the rest of the station. Shortly after midnight the festive mood was dispelled when Douglas's cook came in with the news that the man who looked after the rest-house two hundred yards further up the hill had been found hanging by the neck from a beam. Jimmy and Douglas went to investigate, and the party petered out. A few days later I was deputed to conduct the inquest, and was grateful to have observed one of the East London coroners at work the previous year. It was a sad case, and suicide was the inevitable verdict; the cause of death was confirmed by the government doctor, and there was no evidence of foul play.

The caretaker had been a conscientious man, of a rather shy and retiring disposition, and it was reported that he had recently been taken to task for some minor dereliction of duty, which had upset him; but it was unlikely this alone had prompted him to take his own life, and his family could shed no further light. After this initiation I conducted perhaps half a dozen inquests a year; most unnatural deaths were clearly either accidental, murder, or manslaughter.

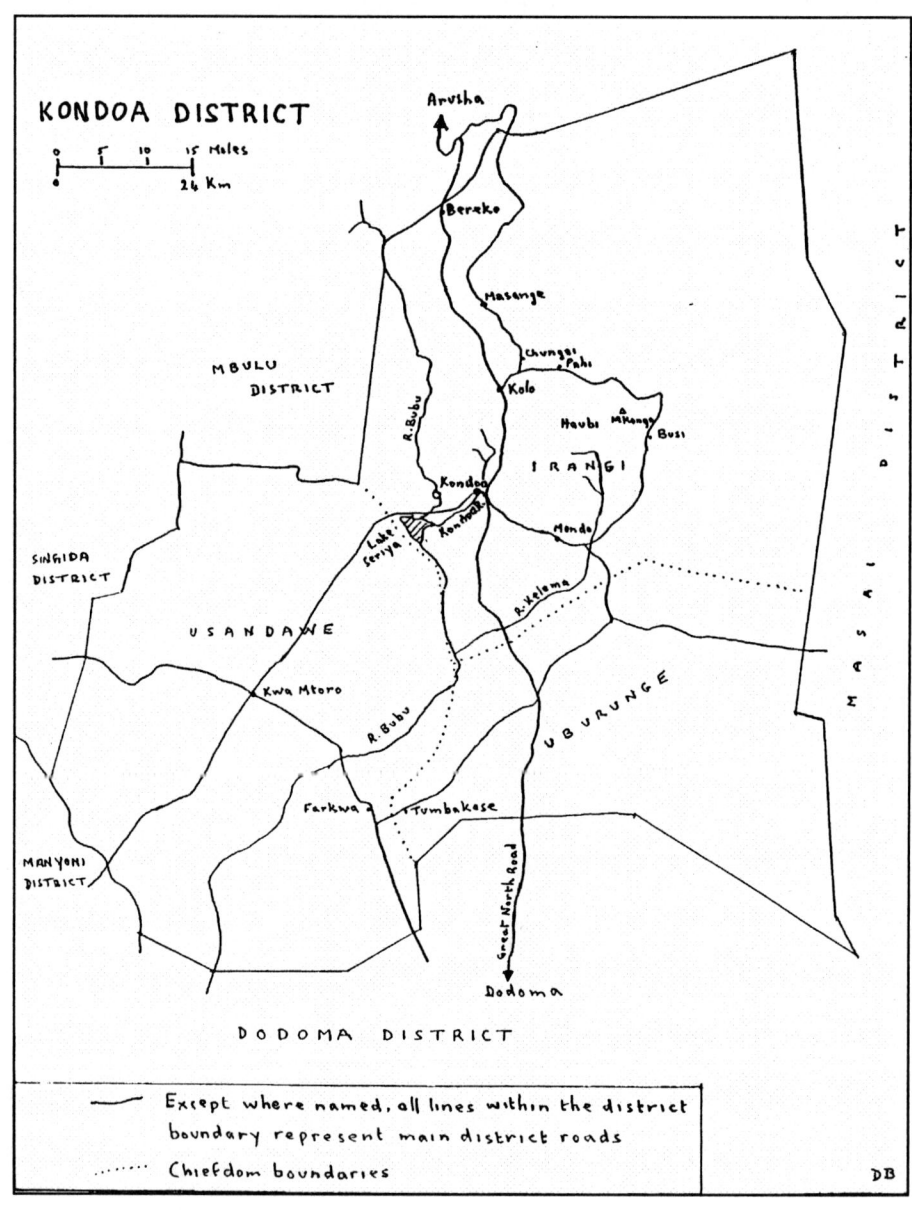

KONDOA DISTRICT

0 5 10 15 Miles

24 Km

Arusha

Bereko

Masange

Chungai
Pahi

MBULU
DISTRICT

R. Bubu

Kolo

Haubi

Mkongo

Busi

I R A N G I

Kondoa

Kondoa

Lake
Seriya

Kinihembe

Mondo

R. Keloma

SINGIDA
DISTRICT

U S A N D A W E

Kwa Mtoro

R. Bubu

U B U R U N G E

Farkwa

Tumbakose

MANYONI
DISTRICT

Great North Road

Dodoma

DODOMA   DISTRICT

M A S A I   D I S T R I C T

——— Except where named, all lines within the district
boundary represent main district roads

.... Chiefdom boundaries

DB

CHAPTER THREE

Kondoa

Background

The staffing of a district depended on its size, population, and the level of economic and political development; Kondoa was middle of the road in all respects. Less than half the size of Manyoni district, it had three times the population, and problems deriving specifically from localized overgrazing and overpopulation.

The team of expatriate officials was presided over by the DC, Cecil Winnington-Ingram, a bachelor in his late thirties. There were two DO's, Jimmy Hildesley, ex-Indian army, divorced but shortly to remarry, and myself. The only other bachelor on the station was Douglas Turner, the Provincial Tsetse Officer; he was, like me, in his mid-twenties, and although having provincial responsibilities had chosen to live in Kondoa rather than Dodoma. The others were all married, mostly with children either living with their parents or away at boarding school in Tanganyika. Jack Allen, the Settlement Officer, had been brought up in Tanganyika; he was there to ensure the medical treatment, rehabilitation and resettlement of a group of Sandawe from the western part of the district who had contracted sleeping sickness a year or two earlier. Mr. Tymkow, with an unpronounceable first name, was an excitable but congenial Pole who, with many of his compatriots, had been taken prisoner by the Russians in 1939; they were later allowed to leave via Iran on condition that they were not engaged as combatants by the Western Allies, and saw the war out camped in East Africa. Mr. Tymkow (he was always Mr.) was the District Foreman, responsible for all Government stores and the maintenance of buildings and district roads. David Goode, born and raised in India, was the able agricultural Field Officer, whose misanthropic manner disguised a generous and helpful nature; he was engaged primarily in agricultural extension work. The Veterinary Officer, Horst

Retzlaff, was a German married to a Swedish countess, and concerned with animal husbandry as well as health. The small and rather primitive government hospital was run by an Indian, Dr. Apte, assisted by an eccentric Scottish nursing sister, Marguerite Hartley, who later died prematurely in Nigeria. An African Schools Supervisor kept primary and middle schools up to scratch. Such was senior officialdom in Kondoa at the time of our arrival. Together and in collaboration with the Native Authorities[16], assisted by mainly African staff, they were responsible for the administration of the district, and insofar as limited budgets permitted, its development.

The ford - Kondoa   N T B

Set a little apart from the rest of us was the Seychellois Benoiton family. The husband was responsible to the Provincial Engineer in Dodoma for maintaining over 100 miles of the Great North Road, and was based in Kondoa purely for reasons of convenience; he had no special interest in the district. Of the local junior civil servants, there were three clerical staff working in the District Office, the senior of whom was Selemani, a Somali. He was efficient, but his officious manner, lack of humour and air of superiority did nothing for his popularity, and he must have been a very lonely man. The busy cash office was run by the quiet and self-effacing Mr. Padmanabhan, recruited from India, and assisted by an African clerk; the bulk of incoming revenue was collected by a contingent of tax clerks. There were

---

[16] These were variously district and chiefdom councils, chiefs and sub-chiefs, with a wide range of local responsibilities

perhaps twenty police constables, managed by Sub-Inspector Gurmuk Singh, a young Sikh, and an African sergeant. The prison was under the day to day control of a Head Warder, of warrant officer rank. Common to all Bomas were our messengers, of whom more anon; at this stage I did not appreciate their unique value.

The Government station was separated from the township by the Kondoa river, most of the buildings dating back to the time when Tanganyika was German East Africa. The Boma, approached by a tree-lined avenue, had been a combined administrative centre and fort, and on a hilltop ten miles or so to the southwest were the remains of an old heliograph station, part of a network covering the colony; weather permitting it had been possible to flash messages – over 700 miles – from the coast to Lake Tanganyika within hours. All but two or three of our bungalows were solidly Teutonic, with thick walls and wide verandahs; they were thus relatively cool, and we were glad to move into one after several months in cramped temporary quarters.

Kondoa had been the site of a major action between British and German forces in the 1914-18 war, during which a few hundred Germans leading African troops had tied down a much larger British, Dominion and Colonial army; they were still undefeated at the armistice. There was a further reminder of those days in the person of Paul Tchoepe, a diminutive German in his fifties, who had been chauffeur and orderly to General von Lettow-Vorbeck, the German commander-in

-chief. When invited to dinner, and with little encouragement, he would relate with glee how the quick-witted Germans regularly put one over on the plodding British. Now he was the proprietor and occupant of a small hotel which had been left high and dry when the main north-south road by-passed Kondoa two miles to the east. He earned a living doing a variety of contractual work for Government and the Native Authority.

Down near the river, opposite our tennis court, was a graveyard, shaded by mango and casuarina trees; the Commonwealth War Graves Commission remitted a small annual sum with which we employed a caretaker to keep it tidy. The war graves had been supplemented by that of a DC, Mr. Darling, who had come to an untimely end falling out of a tree sometime between the wars.

Just below the graveyard the road ran into a concrete drift or ford, beyond which was Kondoa township, a bustling place with tree-lined streets, and a busy market. Its population numbered little more than a thousand, including a number of Indian and Arab traders, two or three of whom specialised in supplying groceries to the expatriate community. Prominent amongst these were the smooth- talking Ali Hamad Amour, a handsome Arab, and Abdullah Sajan, a noisy and argumentative Gujarati, whose wife made the best samosas west of Bombay. The township also boasted a playing field, a small mosque, and two Christian missions tactfully located at opposite sides of the settlement. The sizeable Roman Catholic mission had several expatriate staff, and ran a dispensary and middle school; by contrast the small Anglican CMS (Church Missionary Society) church was presided over by a solo African pastor.

Kondoa district, like most others on the inland plateau, lay at an altitude varying between 3,000 and 4,000ft. (914-1,219m); days were warm to hot, and evenings cool. The south of the district shared some of the characteristics of Manyoni; dry and flat or gently undulating, it was covered in sparse thorn scrub and supported a scanty population. Some miles to the north of Kondoa township the land rose steeply to a well-defined plateau carved into rounded hills with natural but depleted open woodland, cultivation, and grazing. This wetter northern part was quite heavily populated, but much of it was also seriously eroded, with gullies twenty or thirty feet deep cut into the soil, and sometimes down to the bedrock. These highlands were part of the western escarpment of the Rift Valley, and a thousand feet (304m) below, as far as the eye could see, was spread the southern part of the Masai steppe, dry grassland with scattered thorn bush and acacia. A few miles west of Kondoa the Bubu river ran from north to south, separating Usandawe and Irangi chiefdoms; southwards it petered out in the Bahi Depression. West of the river was thick woodland with a variable distribution of thorn scrub, heavily infested with tsetse fly; as elsewhere the pattern of settlement was determined by availability of water from springs, wells, and permanent pools. Of the total population of about 150,000, the majority were Rangi who occupied the centre and the northern highlands, with the Sandawe to the west and south-west, and the much less numerous Burunge to the south-east. The Rangi and Burunge were both cultivators and stock owners, but the high incidence of tsetse fly and the risk of trypanosomiasis in Usandawe limited the areas in which cattle could be kept. The Sandawe are unusual in that they speak a 'click' language, as do the Xhosa in South Africa, and it is thought that they were descendents of an ethnic group which got left behind during the southward migrations centuries ago. It was no doubt the merest coincidence that the second name of our Sandawe Boma messenger, Gabrieli Tsotsi, is also the Xhosa word for an urban petty criminal. Gabrieli thought this highly amusing when I told him.

In both Irangi and Usandawe are to be found rock paintings indicating permanent settlement in prehistoric times; but preoccupied with the here and now these were of less interest to us than to the occasional visiting archaeologist and anthropologist.

* * *

About a week into January the rains began. I had thus far experienced little more than three months without rain, and could not have imagined the excitement it generated amongst the local people after some seven months without any. They danced in the streets, soaked to the skin, all smiles and jubilation. An instant by-product was the swarming of flying ants from their holes in the ground. They fluttered upwards, shed their wings, and fell to earth. Many survived long enough to create a new generation of termites, but it seemed that even more were swept up by enthusiastic women and children, a welcome supplement to their diet. Fried in their own fat, the ants made a tasty snack. When the rain slackened off the same women and children tapped the ground with sticks to simulate the sound of falling rain, thus enticing more flying ants to venture forth and contribute to the family cuisine.

That year the rains were exceptionally heavy during January, and the Kondoa river rose in flood. But by the end of the month most of the year's rain had fallen –some twenty inches (50cm) or thereabouts, but just about enough to produce an adequate harvest. In Usandawe it was markedly less, and soon became a cause for concern. Meanwhile the Kondoa river thundered through the township, carving cubic metres from the concave bends, and threatening to demolish the small CMS church if something wasn't done. The following dry season we sank a palisade of timbers into the river bed along the bank by way of protection, but it seemed likely that this would be only a temporary expedient.

Early safaris

Cecil was the most experienced of the four DC's with whom I worked, having gone to Tanganyika shortly before the outbreak of war in 1939; suffering from spondylitis, this condition precluded any liability to military call-up, and he had about fourteen years service under his belt. By contrast, the other three were ex-servicemen recruited to the Colonial Service after the war, and having no more than eight or nine. In his attitudes Cecil struck a nice balance between the conservative and the progressive, and judging by my own experience took very seriously the responsibility for training his DO cadets. It was not until my next tour that I appreciated how thoroughly and thoughtfully he had planned my own training. There were mandatory duties relating to Government and Native Authority administration, finances, and staff, with occasional sessions sitting in on council meetings, familiarisation with policing, running of the prison, and tax collection for example; and more time was spent in court hearing a greater variety of cases. Most rewarding were ad hoc duties in different parts of the district. In geographical terms Cecil assumed particular responsibility for Irangi and Uburunge, whilst Usandawe was allocated to Jimmy. I perhaps got the best of it and was sent into all chiefdoms to undertake a variety of tasks which were intended to broaden my experience,

My first extended *safari*[17], accompanied by Sylvia, was typical of many which were to follow. One Monday morning the heavy canvas tent and other camping gear were hoisted into the back of the NA Bedford three-tonner together with our domestic impedimenta and a forty-four gallon drum of water, and we set off for Farkwa in the south of Usandawe chiefdom. On arrival we unloaded and the driver departed; he would to return to pick us up on Saturday morning. Gabrieli Tsotsi, the Boma messenger (who would also interpret Swahili-Sandawe for the week) supervised erection of the old-fashioned but robust canvas tent and the ingenious X-pattern beds, table and washstand. In the meantime Sylvia sat under a tree and read whilst I went to make myself known to the *Jumbe* or sub-chief at the nearby Native Court or

---

[17] Simply a journey, by whatever means.

Baraza[18] which was his place of work. He was a tall man who on this occasion wore a khaki jacket over a long white gown or *kanzu,* the ensemble topped off with a red fez. I never got to know him well; he was a rather aloof man with little sense of humour and a strong sense of his own dignity – or perhaps he was just reserved and a little wary. I outlined the purpose of my visit and spent the rest of the morning checking the sub-chiefdom accounts and court records, and laboriously discussing the contents of selected case files.

Meanwhile back at camp the customary gift of chickens and eggs had been delivered to Athmani by one of the *Jumbe's* underlings. This apparently charming and courteous tradition, ostensibly reflecting the good nature of the local chief or headman, was often in practice a form of extortion which I was not aware of at the time; the *Jumbe* could easily have seized the chickens and eggs from neighbouring households. In Kondoa at any rate, reform was imminent, and shortly after this Cecil instructed that in future these offerings were to be delivered up to us by the actual donors, and paid for on the spot at the going rate – which was derisory enough in all conscience at the equivalent of 2 1/2p for a chicken and 1p for 10 eggs. By way of comparison, my own salary at the time was £610 a year, an African clerk or tradesman could expect about £80 a year, an unskilled labourer 5p a day, and an African adult male paid poll tax of about 50p a year.

The week was a long one for Sylvia, effectively confined to camp and the immediate vicinity by heat and lack of transport. I on the other hand was out from dawn to mid-day, and again in the cool of the evening, tramping round the landscape, primarily to assess the food situation and, more particularly, to form an impression regarding the state of the recently planted maize and sorghum crop. There had been heavy rains in January, but these had tailed off, and whilst there was continuing intermittent rain in the Irangi highlands, we were already seriously concerned at the prospect of a failed harvest in drier Usandawe. The first morning's walk was agony. I had woken before sunrise for an early breakfast, and the sun was still not up when I set off for Tumbakose in Uburunge chiefdom, where I was to meet *Jumbe* Salim and attend a village meeting.

---

[18] Also a public meeting.

Our guide was a wiry little man, all muscle and sinew, and he evidently saw it as his duty to get us from Farkwa to Tumbakose as swiftly as possible. He set off at a spanking pace, followed by me, with Gabrieli bringing up the rear. I normally walked pretty briskly myself, at about four miles an hour, but our guide must have been stepping it out half as fast again – a forty mile a day man! I could not easily keep up at a walk, but was determined to avoid the ignominy of asking Gabrieli to tell our guide to slow down. Instead I motioned Gabrieli to go in front of me, and let the two of them draw seventy or eighty yards ahead. Thereafter by alternately walking and trotting I was able to keep them in view. The sun rose, but the pace did not slacken, and thoughts went back to the sweat and lather of army assault courses, of Eights Week and Henley, the familiar ache in legs and chest, the rivers of sweat. The map is not very helpful in determining the distance between Farkwa and Tumbakose. It is probably not more than five or six miles, but it seemed a great deal longer, the time interminable. The subsequent village meeting was a welcome respite, and when Gabrieli – who had a good eye for country – reassured me that he could retrace our footsteps without difficulty, I paid off the guide and sent him home. He went off as swiftly as he had done at dawn, and I was glad to see him go. Whether it was fortuitous or part of Cecil's design, my week of walking round the Farkwa area marked the beginning of one particular concern with Usandawe chiefdom; if there was not more rain during the next three or four months I would be deputed to deal with the resulting food shortage.

These few days also brought a bonus in the form of Father Valentino, a member of the Passionist Fathers order – irreverently known to us as the Passionate Pops – who had a substantial presence in the district. He was a somewhat over-weight, extrovert, and irrepressibly cheerful Italian, whose forté was a home-made alcoholic distillation which he jocularly described as 'Farkwa water'. Some months later he was transferred to Isololo below the Irangi escarpment; here he demonstrated his versatility by turning his hand to cheese-making, and he produced a range of cheeses of different shapes, sizes, and flavours approximating to native Italian varieties. His visitors – whether at Farkwa or Isololo – could be assured of a warm welcome, good conversation, and a liberal offering of his specialities.

During most of January and early February I was out a good deal, mostly trips to collect tax from the several sub-chiefdom headquarters in Irangi. These local *Barazas* comprised a small office and store built behind an open courtroom, which served also for village meetings and other communal events. Despite the sturdy independence of the Rangi they were, on the whole, prompt in the payment of their taxes, and during the first two or three months of the year money came rolling in faster than tax clerks could bring it in to the Boma. So I went out and gathered it in. The cash would be hauled out of the court safe, and I would count it and check it against the counterfoils retained by the tax clerks. This chore could take three or four hours, with several thousand pounds worth of coin and notes, mostly in small denominations. Dirty currency has a smell of its own, and there was invariably rapid recourse to soap, water, and scrubbing brush after depositing the booty in the Boma strong room. Another indelible memory of those tax-gathering circuits was the smell of bats. In all the courthouses visited they roosted in the space between the ceiling and the corrugated iron roof. The soft-board or hessian ceilings retained their droppings and absorbed their urine, and the heat generated by the tin roof brought out the smell in all its acrid intensity. More than once I had to break off for a few minutes worth of fresh air whilst counting the cash or checking court records.

My next *safari* was with Cecil, and mainly on foot. I accompanied him so that I could observe his conduct of public meetings, and be introduced to a wider range of the tasks which sustained the links between the Boma and village, between central government and NA. On this occasion we were dumped somewhere off the main road south of Kolo, Cecil having an embarrassingly large quantity of personal baggage which absorbed the lion's share of the carrying capacity of the fifteen or so porters assembled to carry our loads. That night I began to revise my ideas as I downed a bottle of beer, a case of which Cecil had thoughtfully included in his commissariat.

Our first stop was at a village in the highlands where soil erosion was particularly severe. Here a group of perhaps forty to sixty peasant farmers had been gathered by their headman. They were dressed mainly in black *kaniki,* a cotton cloth draped diagonally across the body and knotted at one shoulder. The prevailing black was punctuated by a sprinkling of white caps, and the *kanga* of the few women present provided a welcome splash of colour. Cecil sat and talked about anti-erosion measures, resettlement, and local government representation, with Malesa, the most amiable of our office messengers interpreting from Swahili into Rangi, and vice versa. Much of it was beyond my comprehension, and repeatedly I was left wrestling with the meaning of a word as the dialogue moved on. However it was possible to observe, and to identify a model for the future; seriousness of purpose, but with an element of humour, light-heartedness and sympathy, and with a mutual appreciation of wit and repartee.

The porters had meanwhile gone on ahead, and in the afternoon we followed along the track which led down the escarpment to Pahi. From the hillside Cecil pointed out the block of bush which was to be cleared later in the year, and settled with colonists from the over-grazed and overpopulated highlands. A spur jutted from the escarpment at Kinyasi; below and a little to the right and beyond it ran a tongue of bush, dark against the sandy brown of the flanking grassland. This was the Maweni ridge, which over a period of two or three years was to be cleared of bush and tsetse fly, opening up many square miles of land for settlement and grazing. Further to the right, beyond Masangasi hill, the plains of Masailand stretched northwards up to and beyond the Kenya border. Looming behind us, the mass of Mkonga mountain rose several hundred feet (ca.200m) above the general level of the escarpment; the extra altitude brought additional rain to the mountain, and unlike the landscape below it, the upper slopes were covered in thick rain-forest where a few buffalo dwelt in isolation and relative safety. At Pahi Cecil immediately went into a long private session with *Jumbe* Yusufu, leaving me to check the accounts and as many court case files as I could get through during the rest of the afternoon. That evening, outside the stuffy little mud-built rest-house Cecil revealed, in addition to the beer, another of his little *safari* extravagances – a gramophone and records. It was a wind-up affair with a horn, but meticulously cared for; the Mozart with a fibre needle provided a welcome if incongruous accompaniment to our chicken, potatoes, and bottles of Tusker IPA.

The next day we trudged back up the escarpment to Haubi, held another *baraza,* or public meeting, inspected the local primary school, and called at the Passionist mission, where we conversed with the resident Italian Father in Swahili. And then down the escarpment to Busi, *Jumbe* Juma's headquarters, where we spent the night. An important item on Busi's modest list of requirements was some sort of water supply. There was a small spring which trickled out of the hillside five hundred feet up and a mile or so away. Was it practicable to bring the water down to the village? Next morning, as he immersed himself in deep conversation with *Jumbe* Juma, Cecil sent me off to investigate and to calculate the rate of flow. I had little idea of what this might involve but took along an empty four-gallon (18 litre) paraffin container, the ubiquitous *debe*; it might come in useful.

At the spring was a small pool which dribbled over a rim of rock and earth at half a dozen points. How did one calculate the total rate of dribble? The first thing to do was to get all the water flowing from one point in such a way that I could catch it in the *debe* . With Malesa's assistance I built up the rim with mud, and embedded in it a short section of split bamboo hacked from a nearby thicket. The water rose, and eventually began to run down the bamboo gutter. I filled the *debe* a few times, noting the time it took to fill, and converting this to 2,400 gallons of water an hour. Having ascertained that the spring did not fail during the dry season, this was more than enough to supply a stand-pipe for domestic use and a trough for watering cattle.

The following day was Saturday, and in mid-morning Mohamed arrived in the NA Bedford. It was a blistering drive back, for Cecil introduced me to a novel but very effective way of viewing the countryside, standing in the back of an open lorry; and later sitting somewhat precariously in our wood and canvas camp chairs. Between Tandala and Mondo Cecil pointed out a mile length of road which needed realigning and straightening, avoiding a particularly bad stretch of sandy river bed with excessively steep approaches. We got back to Kondo, uncomfortably sunburned, for a very late lunch.

A few months later work began on clearing the bush at Kinyasi, and before I left Kondoa the following year, boreholes had been sunk for water and dozens of familes resettled. On the basis of my figures and a rough sketch the Water Development and Irrigation Department designed a small water supply for Busi, and towards the end of the year the tap was turned on in the market place. As for the road, Cecil sent me out to survey and demarcates a new line; and though he subsequently amended it a little to reduce the costs, the exercise was useful practice for the future. There would be other roads to construct and maintain. For the uninitiated it should be explained that at the time there were only about 200 miles of surfaced road in the territory. All others, many thousands of miles of them, were dirt roads; the main trunk roads were tolerably well-maintained, whilst district roads attracted less funding, and were variously good, poor, and indifferent.

Soil erosion and resettlement

The problem of overstocking in Irangi has been alluded to. It is on record that in German times Irangi had regularly exported quantities of grain to the less favoured and drier districts of Dodoma and Manyoni to the south, but by the 1950's this was no longer the case. Population growth and the associated increase in livestock had led to deforestation, overgrazing, the reduction of natural vegetation in the hilly northern areas of the chiefdom, and increased pressure on cultivable land. This resulted in widespread and severe soil erosion, a reduction in the area of land available for agriculture, and declining fertility. It was scarcely a matter for pride that agronomists and land use experts came from far afield – including a party from Bechuanaland (Botswana) – to shake their heads at the despoiled hills of Irangi. The district remained generally self-sufficient in grain production, but if there was insufficient rain in any part of the district, Irangi rarely had a significant surplus for local redistribution. And of course cash incomes dependent on surpluses were affected.

Our chosen remedial measures were several, none of them welcome, since they involved some inconvenience, hard work, a departure from custom, and in a few cases real deprivation. Certain hilly areas had been completely closed to settlement, cultivation, and grazing, and the people moved down to the plains below the escarpment, where bush was cleared and wells dug to await the new settlers.The clearing of more land for resettlement was now in progress, with additional selective clearing further afield to eliminate tsetse fly and open up country for grazing. Similar work, but on a smaller scale, was initiated during the current year in the extreme south-west of the chiefdom along the Bubu river. As for the actual clearing, this was largely dependent for its execution on the use of compulsory communal labour. The concept is now viewed with distaste, but then the practice was hallowed by long usage and in any case had the justification of necessity; indeed, in some districts the practice could be attributed to local custom pre-dating colonial rule.

Our rationale, rightly or wrongly, was that in a country with exiguous revenues where the annual poll tax was about fifty pence, it was a convenient substitute for additional taxation, and what could not be paid in cash was paid in sweat; every able bodied male adult was required to put in a month's toil a year, ten days of this being unpaid. In exchange they received free rations including meat, which was generally lacking in a normal diet; with free beer thrown in, the clearing camps were not seriously unpopular, and they often had something of a holiday air. Nevertheless, the colonial government eventually gave way to United Nations pressure, and the 'tribal turnout' was discontinued. Its merits were recognised after independence, when it was reintroduced as voluntary self-help.

The other element in our campaign was compulsory destocking; the grazing capacity of each village area was assessed in stock units of sheep, goats, and cattle; animals in excess of this were required to be sold. Individual liability was determined by reference to a sliding scale so that large stockowners had to sell proportionately more, whilst the poorer peasant might not have to sell any animals at all. To the pastoral African the ownership of livestock represents social as well as economic wealth; his esteem is measured in terms of cattle as also is often the value of his womenfolk when a marriage contract is made and cattle change hands by way of surety. The obligatory sale of stock involved some loss of status, but the indignity was equitably spread on the whole, and the additional cash income was some consolation. That said, it also provided our local critics with a source of grievance. None of these measures was, or could be, exactly popular, and all were open to the risk of abuse or unfairness. It was all very pragmatic, but it was also reasonably effective in view of the slender resources at our disposal; refinement costs money and time, and we had little of either. The obligatory sale of stock was the feature which trespassed most on tradition and custom, and yet paradoxically the cattle market was soon established as a popular social occasion, as it is all over the world – a place where wits are sharpened, guile exercised, and gossip exchanged. And of course it provided a legitimate excuse to get away from the field, wife, screaming children, or all three.

I couldn't pretend that the Rangi were enthusiastic about the means devised for their well-being and the rehabilitation of their eroded hills. There had been consultation, and the ground had been prepared at numerous public meetings, the general response being one of reluctant acceptance; this was probably as much as could be hoped for. There was a certain amount of agitation by a disaffected minority, and after the formation of TANU (Tanganyika African National Union) in 1954, the district was visited by its founder and leader, Julius Nyerere; perhaps surprisingly, he broadly endorsed what we were doing. The resettlement programme went reasonably smoothly, but during my period in Kondoa two related incidents occurred which merit mention.

* * *

Jimmy Hildesley and I were sitting in Cecil's office late one afternoon discussing the season's bush-clearing programme in the Bubu valley. Jimmy was to be out supervising operations for two months, whilst Cecil and I were to share his normal duties at the Boma and his touring. We were just about ready to call it a day when a visiting Livestock Marketing Officer based in Dodoma, and whom we knew only by sight, burst in and at once began to unburden himself.

He had been overseeing a cattle market near the Kelema river halfway between Mondo and Goima, about twenty miles distant along an execrable road. Little over an hour earlier he had, he said, been set upon by a crowd of hostile Africans. They had pursued him to his Landrover and he had made his getaway amid a hail of clods and sticks and lumps of dried cattle dung. No, there had been no provocation. Whatever the facts of the matter, it must have been an alarming experience, and our caller was still visibly agitated. However, sympathy was tinged with a certain defensiveness; 'our' Rangi could be difficult, but they were not unreasonable.

I was deputed to go out and investigate the following morning, for the sun would be down in half an hour; the livestock marketing man declined to stay and accompany me, preferring to hotfoot it back to Dodoma and report the incident to his departmental senior. I was off shortly after breakfast the next morning with a police constable in attendance. The road to Mondo was the worst in the district and though easily negotiable by short-wheelbase Landrover, the journey was extremely uncomfortable; Landrovers in Africa had much to do with the increased incidence of a hitherto unknown but subsequently fashionable complaint, slipped disc. At Mondo I caught *Jumbe*

Goronya at his breakfast. The Sub-Chief was an old rogue, probably about sixty, with outsized yellow teeth; yes, he had heard about yesterday's incident, and those responsible would be punished. This wasn't necessarily what I wanted; I was not confident that he would either take the trouble to investigate properly, or that if he did the real culprits would be traced, or that if they were they would be culpable anyway, or that if they were they were the ones who would actually be punished – though no doubt it would all look very tidy in the local court records. I said I would rather look into it myself, and asked him for a messenger who could take me to the village headman concerned.

We bumped away down the road leading downhill and south-eastwards away from Mondo, and forty minutes and several dried-out river beds later reached the headman's home. He was sitting at his doorway, on one of the ubiquitous little folding wooden chairs which could be bought almost anywhere for two shillings.

We ran through the formalities:

'Is nothing the matter?'

'Yes, nothing is the matter'

'What health have you?'

'My health is good.'

'What is the news?'

'The news is good, but ……'

And so on. The routine was at its most impressive on the road, when two travellers approaching each other on foot would begin the greetings when they were two hundred yards or more apart; and would still be going strong as they passed out of earshot in opposite directions. All this without voices apparently being raised.

The headman was expecting a visit and was clearly anxious. He had witnessed the incident, and the substance of the Marketing Officer's story was true. What he had omitted to mention was that he had himself provoked the crowd by his rude and aggressive demeanour, and the free use of a *kiboko* or hippo-hide whip to hasten business and add point to his abusive language. No, he had not actually hit anyone with the whip, but he had threatened people with it. Some of the young men – and the Rangi were not without self-respect and spirit – had lost their tempers; remonstrance having failed they began to shout, and had underlined their annoyance by flinging whatever missiles came

43

most readily to hand. The official had taken fright and made off. Obviously there was no certainty of getting at the whole truth, and I was only too aware that my function was to go through the motions and issue some sort of reprimand. The headman's story rang true and I was disposed to accept it.

However, I suspended belief and said I wanted to see as many of his people who had been at the market as could be speedily assembled. He sent word around, and we then settled down to discuss more general matters; tax collection, prospects for the season's harvest, whether there had been any trouble recently with Baraguyu cattle thieves from over the district border. I also asked whether the previous day's demonstration represented a general resentment of stock culling or was primarily a specific reaction to one man's behaviour and attitudes. He insisted it was the last, and this view was reinforced by the comments which came out at the ensuing discussion with the villagers. Those assembled were a cheerful bunch, and came no nearer to apology than pride and self-righteousness could permit. Yes they had done wrong but the *Bwana* had not behaved as a *Bwana* should. I delivered the necessary lecture and admonishment, and departed to a round of clapping which I thought had scarcely been earned.

The constable was grinning, though whether at my gullibility or in approval I could not know. On the way back I managed to convince myself that I'd been far too soft and that I should have made at least a token arrest. I was, after all, still in my first year, and a cadet was a very lowly form of colonial life. In the event Cecil was not critical, though to him fell the more difficult task of conveying to the Provincial Veterinary Officer that we had taken appropriate measures against our malefactors – and furthermore that his Marketing Officer should watch his manners. It was all too easy to develop a proprietary and possessive view of one's 'parishioners'; several years later in Ukerewe, I felt a distinct surge of pride when some of 'my' islanders successfully broke into the strong room of a bank in the Provincial capital; their failure lay not in the execution but in their subsequent free spending. It seemed almost a betrayal to send them for trial and subsequent imprisonment.

* * *

The next upset was rather more serious. Well into the 1954 clearing programme, Cecil was hosting an evening party for all expatriates and the

African staff from the Boma and District Council when the convivial atmosphere was disturbed by the arrival of the senior clearing supervisor, one Nassoro Seifu – affectionately known as *Kichwamaji,* literally waterhead. In a private conversation with Cecil he explained that earlier in the day Chief Heri Salim had visited the clearing camp below the escarpment and been chased off by an angry mob of labourers. Cecil and Douglas excused themselves from the party, and set off for the camp, some 20 odd miles distant.

On arrival they found it apparently deserted, but after some minutes figures began to emerge from the bush into the light of hurricane lamps and dying camp fires. The workers had not decamped as feared, and they gathered round to engage in the customary discussion or *baraza.* It emerged that the incident had in fact been provoked by *Mtemi* (Chief) Heri, who had turned up just as work for the day was finishing. He would have done himself a lot of good had he circulated amongst his fellow Rangi and commended them on a hard day's work well done. However, he tried to bully them into doing some more clearing, notwithstanding that the day's allocated tasks had been completed. Whether he thought that this would reinforce his increasingly shaky authority or would please us was never established, but whatever the reason it was an ill-judged decision; he was lucky to get away unscathed, except that his local standing slipped a little further. Cecil's reaction to the event was much the same as mine to the incident at the cattle market, except that his command of Swahili permitted a more profound dialogue as well as a more emphatic expression of displeasure, and a warning that recourse to violence could not be tolerated. His greater wrath was reserved for *Mtemi* Heri the next day.

The combined conservation, culling, and resettlement project was known as the Irangi Development Scheme. Its objective was 'to bring new land into use, to make the best use of both the new land and of land at present occupied, and to rehabilitate lands which have been partly destroyed. It is hoped both to raise the standard of living of the residents of Irangi Chiefdom....while at some time preserving and improving the land for posterity.' Insofar as it represented a valid response to specific problems it was largely successful over a period of some years, and even by the time I left towards the end of 1954 the eroded areas, closed to settlement a few years earlier, were beginning to recover, and the farmers then displaced were established below

45

the escarpment. However the development aspect was, and continued to be, hamstrung by shortage of funds, and earlier expectations were not in the event realised.[19]

Coronation

I was to discover that organising famine avoidance measures, a population census, or an election, required a certain amount of native ability and acquired skill. But nothing which was to come in the future seemed significantly more complicated than organising the Coronation celebrations, which in 1953 subsumed the annual Empire day school sports. It would, Cecil assured me, be useful training. It was, and I learned a great deal, including the fact there is not necessarily any direct relationship between the complexity of an occasion and its importance.

The first – and easiest – task was to order the fireworks, several months in advance, through the Crown Agents[20]. After much discussion of the merits of the various combinations and displays offered by Messrs Paine, we eventually settled on a £270 package with a bias towards rocketry.

Ahead lay a good deal of sheer tedium. All primary schoolchildren in the district were to be brought in for the day and provided with one meal, and there were something like forty schools. The girls and boys from the several middle schools were to come in for inter-school sports, and would stay in Kondoa overnight. Transport, food, accommodation, cooking facilities had to be provided, the sports events planned, and the field laid out; Chiefs and other dignitaries were invited, together with groups of tribal dancers. During the week before the 2nd June, one or other of the folders labelled Transport, Sports, Programme, and Accommodation was rarely out of my hands. All the loose ends had been brought together on paper, though it could safely be

---

[19] I understand that the problem of overgrazing and erosion in the hills recurred in the 1960's and 1970's and that more radical measures had to be taken by Government.

[20] A British Government agency, located in London, which purchased and forwarded materials and equipment ordered by Colonial Governments.

predicted that they would become frayed and tangled on the day. It was a relief that Douglas, the Tsetse Officer, would be largely responsible for running the sports.

In England it would have been recorded as a matter of surprise and satisfaction that Coronation Day dawned clear and bright. In Kondoa in the middle of the hot dry season, almost rainless since February, it could not have been other than clear and bright. By ten o'clock, when the festivities began and the first contests were being run, jumped, and skipped on the sports field, the sun was beating down from a nearly cloudless sky, the cool blueness of which seemed inconsistent with the heat down below. Cecil, wearing his white ceremonial uniform and sword gave a formal speech in impeccable Swahili, the police contingent under Sub-Inspector Gurmuk Singh let off a somewhat ragged *feu de joie,* but were otherwise immaculate in their dress and evolutions. The sports were declared open, and Cecil swiftly changed into his customary shirt and shorts.

They were about as chaotic as might have been expected, a concern for punctuality not featuring very significantly in rural African life. Events were delayed as children went missing, usually because their teachers, nominally in charge, tended to wander off on their own business. Still, the momentum was maintained, though not entirely without incident. The winner of the race in which girls ran with bottles of water on their heads was found to have cheated, and had to be disqualified. More serious was the frequency of personal intervention by Father Emidio, the Italian head of the Passionist Fathers mission, who saw it as his duty to ensure that the mainly Muslim competitors from the Native Authority middle schools were beaten – preferably soundly beaten – by the enlightened Christian youth of his own schools.

In fact the results were a foregone conclusion. The senior mission boys were anything up to four years older than the lads from the NA schools; indeed we suspected that a number of those competing had already left school. Moreover they had expatriate teachers, one of whom had been subjecting his boys to rigorous coaching; when we got wind of this, Douglas and I thought it not quite sporting, and engaged in a little amateurish counter-coaching in the evenings. The clincher was the fact that many of the NA competitors were fasting. Her Majesty's advisers had clearly not consulted representatives of the Muslim faith before fixing on a date for the Coronation, and that date fell in the month of Ramadhan. In consequence millions of her loyal subjects were celebrating on an empty stomach, unable to eat between dawn and sunset.

We had expected a degree of religious rivalry. What we had not expected was active participation by the local representative of the Bishop of Rome. After all, his faction was going to win, and in the circumstances it could reasonably be expected that, as a prominent guest, he would sit and watch, perhaps a little smugly, secure in the knowledge of victory to come. In the event, or more accurately during the course of many events, we were disabused of this expectation. He was at the winning post, the jumping pit, the high jump, challenging the judges' decision whenever one of the NA boys won, applauding when one of his own flock did so. And if he was unable to be at the finish of everything it was not for the want of trying. In vain did we attempt to curb his meddling; he was divinely inspired and the light of battle gleamed in his eye. This was all extremely tiresome, and Douglas and I in particular heartily wished him elsewhere.

Meanwhile, away from the sports field, local traders had set up their little stalls for the sale of tawdry gimcrack novelties to the unsophisticated, tea, fizzy drinks, sweetmeats, peanuts, and cigarettes to those in need of refreshment. Below the Boma half a dozen groups of dancers stamped, jumped, and chanted to the accompaniment of drums, and the police whistles which had long ago become an essential feature of any dance. There were teams from each chiefdom, the most spectacular being those from Tumbakose, whose colourful traditional garb of skins, feathers and beads was set off by a head-dress embellished with a corona of brightly painted old electric light bulbs. Like so many African traditional dances the movements were on the whole rhythmically slow, conservative of energy, and with a quality of regularity verging on the hypnotic. Sweat poured down the drummers' faces, and less profusely down the dancers'; dust, stirred by the shuffling feet, rose in a fine haze, registering on the taste buds, and lingering in the nose and throat.

And everywhere were the sightseers, townspeople in their rather sombre festive best, predominantly black and white, with a few suits which were the uniform of clerks and junior officials; Hatibu Mohamed, the District Council Secretary, dazzled with a yellow and red striped blazer which – with a boater instead of a fez – would not have disgraced Henley. And there was a throng of peasants in from the country, some blasé, some bemused, most of them sober, a few drunk, all curious. They came up the avenue of trees to the Boma, stood in critical appraisal of the dancers, moved on to the sports field, then back again, a slowly eddying, swirling tide of people not so very different from the thousands of other crowds assembled that day in England and over much of the world.

Late in the afternoon the sports ended, by which time the less hardy spectators had retired to rest, prepare their evening meal, or refresh themselves in anticipation of further celebration. The prizes were distributed by Marguerite, the Nursing Sister; and Father Emidio was exuberant at the mission schools' handsome win over the heathen, clearly attributing this to divine dispensation rather than the effects of fasting on the opposition. At this point, tired as we were, Douglas and I had another engagement. A football match had been arranged in the township between the Mission middle school and its NA rival. This was to be a 'friendly' match, but in view of the good Father's performance earlier in the day and his probable attendance at the match, we thought we had better be there too. The standard of play was not noteworthy, and was characterised by enthusiasm rather than skill; to my untutored eye there appeared to be a good deal of random kicking and wasted effort as bare black feet met leather and raised clouds of dust. The referee was Sylvester, an amiable and usually capable Boma clerk, but occasionally rendered less capable by his fondness for the bottle. He was also cross-eyed and bespectacled.

On this occasion it could not fairly be said that he was drunk, but had drink taken. Whether his judgment was impaired is neither here nor there, but in a closely fought game which was nearing its close at 0-0, he allowed an NA goal against the Mission team, from a kick which was arguably off-side. At once Father Emidio on the opposite touchline leapt to his feet in protest, and led a crowd of partisan supporters onto the field, shaking his fist and shouting at the bewildered referee. Douglas and I, concerned that there should be no broken heads, dashed across the field to restrain the church militant. With a combination of persuasion and discreetly applied main force, we accompanied him, one on either side, off the field. Out of consideration for Sylvester, we declared the match abandoned, thanked the contestants and sent them home, bundled Sylvester into Douglas's Landrover, and after watching everyone drift away, departed.

A two-hour break before the firework display allowed the Muslims to eat after a long foodless day, whilst we officials foregathered by the light of pressure lamps on some open ground near our homes for a picnic, the main feature of which was a sheep which had been slowly roasting all day in a pit full of hot wood-ash and charcoal.

By this time the sole remaining duty fell to Jimmy who, as a former regular soldier, had volunteered to take charge of the pyrotechnics. We followed him to the appointed location, and were happy to let him get on with it. The crowd was delighted, and were not to know until later that Jimmy had nearly knocked an eye out with a delayed-action rocket in a dark corner of the field. He was lucky to get away with a blistered cheek as he examined the touch-paper. Meanwhile, beyond the crowd and near the dried up Kondoa river, the carcass of a cow was being roasted whole, and forty-four gallon drums of freshly brewed *pombe* or beer awaited distribution to the multitude. The fireworks over, we circulated briefly to bid goodnight to African colleagues and friends and then withdrew to have a leisurely communal drink with Cecil. Down the slope the tower and crenellations of the Boma were silhouetted against the steady red glow of dying fires, and the noise continued unabated. Sylvia, three months pregnant, was exhausted and I was pretty weary myself. Oblivious to the drumming, we were asleep within minutes of return to our own quarters.

Bereko

Cecil had decided that I needed a break from the office and to get out on tour. There were a few tasks to be done at Bereko, and it would be useful for one of us to see how things were along the Bubu valley. Bereko is a small trading centre lying about thirty-five miles to the north of Kondoa along that bone-shaking ribbon of earth, dust, sand, rock and mud grandly known as the Great North Road. Northwards it was said to go on to Cairo, and southwards it certainly reached Cape Town. The settlement was pleasingly situated on a hilltop, with the main road running downhill to north and south. It comprised a huddle of whitewashed shops encompassing a dusty market place, and built with mud brick or daub-and-wattle; there was a dispensary and primary school, and a local court and administrative centre, presided over by *Jumbe* Mohamed Heri, younger brother of *Mtemi* Heri. The village sat on a broad hilltop at an altitude of about 4,000 feet (ca.1,300m), so was relatively cool, and at night chilly enough to justify the chimney and fireplace in the little rest-house which we had built there for £150 or so.

Grain silos - Bereko   DB

There were two ways of getting to Bereko. Usually I went in the elderly 3 ton Bedford truck belonging to the District Council, and driven by Mohamed, a good-natured middle-aged Rangi. On these occasions he taught me to drive; he must often have thought me a poor pupil as I wrestled with the crash gearbox, double-declutching furiously – occasionally with success – whilst negotiating the hairpin bends on the escarpment above Kolo.

Over a period of some months I shared a good deal of time with Mohamed in the cab of his truck, and our conversations had become easier and less superficial as my Swahili improved. He was a gentle man, thoughtful, and conscientious, and not afraid to speak his mind. It was a surprise to hear, shortly after one of our *safaris,* that he was in the district hospital following an attempt to disembowel himself; I visited him at once, and we talked at some length. He seemed perfectly normal, with no hint that anything was amiss; and before leaving I insisted that I needed him to carry on with my driving lessons. During the night he tore off his dressing, reopened the wound and bled to death. His widow seemed comforted by her assumption that it was *shauri ya Mungu,* the will of God.

The other way of getting to Bereko was by a rough track up the Bubu river valley for perhaps twenty-five miles, then north east for another fifteen miles by foot. On this occasion I was to walk all the way, and hold a couple of village meetings, assess the state of the harvest, and form some impression about the movement of grain from the north of the district into neighbouring Mbulu district. This trade was not yet prohibited, but it was certainly unwelcome in view of likely food shortages in Usandawe chiefdom later in the year; if it became serious, this local export would have to be banned.

A preliminary to any foot *safari* was to get word to Mohamed Sadala, the town *Jumbe* or Headman. He was a man of uncertain age, somewhere between forty and sixty, small of stature, wrinkled of skin, and short of teeth. And in the gnome-like face, his yellowed malarial eyes always held a twinkle and a hint of laughter. He was conservative by nature, and had no truck with intrusive manifestations of progress. Into this category came the local *wahuni,* layabout youths who wore fancy shirts and tight ragged trousers, and sat around chattering and gambling all day. He was also pretty hot on tax collection – a not unrelated observation, for the *wahuni* tended also to be tax defaulters. If the *Bwana* was going on *safari* he would need some porters; it would be unjust to impress honest toilers in the fields – or even tempt them away – for this purpose, but the *wahuni* were fair game. The pay they would receive for this honest if involuntary labour would go some way to paying their current year's poll tax.

A few days later I set off, preceded by a guide and a motley collection of inappropriately dressed youngsters bearing my camping gear, cook box, food and drinking water; they were more cheerful than perhaps they had reason to be, in view of the miles of hard slog ahead. I brought up the rear with Malesa, who was my favourite amongst the younger Boma messengers; invariably cheerful, with a ready grin, he was reliable, knowledgeable about local matters, and a good companion on tour. Mzee our new cook, tagged along a few paces behind, round white cap perched on his head; in the eight years we were together I rarely saw him without it. We had recently parted company from Athmani and Mohamed, our first cook and houseboy. Athmani was apt to be surly, whilst Mohamed was too often drunk and had an obstreperous and raucous wife. The two men were prone to squabble, and some weeks earlier Sylvia, whilst inside the house, heard them quarrelling and shouting at each other sufficiently loudly to make her go and see what was going on in the outside kitchen; they were brandishing knives at each other and mayhem seemed imminent. She shouted at them to stop, and to her surprise and relief they did so. She was still shaken when I strolled up to the house for lunch. The culprits were later paid off and replacements sought. This was my first *safari* accompanied by Mzee Hamsini.

Leaving the house, we walked down the dusty road, which was flanked by flamboyant trees with their bright vermillion blossoms and pale green lacework of leaves; on past the prison and a row of mauve-flowered jacarandas and a dark clump of mango trees; then left down to the Kondoa river, now reduced to a trickle in the dry season. There was a slight but noticeable smell of maturing urine in the air, for at this time of year the river bed was a convenient cattle track; a small boy with a dingy calico wrap and a stick taller than himself wandered along behind a few diminutive humped cattle. We crossed the drift, leaving the suspension footbridge upstream; this was rarely used except when the river was in spate in January, when it was the only means of access to the township.

We went on along the main street, and as we passed the store of Hilal Mohamed I stopped to buy a packet of biscuits; his shop was one of the archetypal kind already described. The wide doorway was the only source of light, so the interior was gloomy. On the rickety wooden shelves behind the counter were long bars of unwrapped blue and white mottled soap, tins of varying age, hurricane lamps, ancient jars of Brylcreem, a selection of cheap toiletries, packeted sweetmeats and confectionery, bottles of sauce – in short a variety of essential and inessential commodities; and over all, a thin layer of dust. I exchanged greetings with Hilal, a hawk-nosed aloof Arab who was decidedly casual in his customer relations, for a transport business, wholesale trade, and a little discreet black marketeering were his main sources of income. I bought my biscuits, first opening the packet to ensure that they were free of weevils and not unacceptably stale. As I turned to leave I spotted a solitary bottle of Mackeson's Milk Stout on one of the upper shelves. I have long outgrown Mackeson's, but then it was like meeting an old friend; so I bought it, and Mzee popped it into his cook's box for my future refreshment.

We rejoined the porters, who had taken the opportunity of stopping in the market-place, hub of commercial and social activity in Kondoa township; here they were engaged in exchanging robust ribaldries with their more fortunate fellows as the serious business of the market-place went on about them. Just as I caught up, Mohamed Sadala appeared round a corner; he had his *wahuni* on their feet with a few well-chosen but unrepeatable epithets. Whilst the others made off out of range, we went off up the gentle incline of the road heading westwards towards Usandawe; the road from Kondoa intersects the Bubu river about four miles out of town. Depending on the time of year it rages or trickles from north to south; just below the wooden road bridge it widens into a shallow lake, Seriya, fringed with papyrus and reeds, its fish and waterfowl a useful addition to the pockets and diet of the peasant households in the vicinity. Further south again, the river peters out in the arid desolation of the Bahi Depression in Manyoni district, where the floor of the Rift Valley is virtually semidesert. That morning we bore away to the right a mile or two before Seriya, skirting the smaller and more attractive lake Dalamatai. We walked up the valley, the rising mid-morning temperature moderated by a slight breeze. But it was a hot and dusty business, worse of course for the porters; but they at least had the advantage of taking the shortest route to our agreed meeting place whilst I wandered about the landscape with Malesa to talk with the occupants of little farmsteads and farmers in the fields, a process which added a few miles to my morning's walk.

Early in the afternoon I caught up with the porters; some of them were dozing in the shade, others eating roast maize cobs or cassava root, and chatting desultorily. I was pretty dozy myself, but resisted the temptation to lie down – it is then always an effort to get moving again. Having got into the habit of not eating when out on foot I also declined offers of food; whether my travelling companions were impressed more with my fortitude or my folly I don't know. After twenty minutes or so we agreed on our next rendezvous up in the hills to the north-east. Here we were to spend the night, and it was my expectation that when I got to camp that evening the tent would be up, a fire going, and a meal half-cooked.

Again I had to make a detour to attend a village meeting accompanied by Malesa to show me the way. After a mile or two we turned eastwards up a small tributary valley. The effort left little breath for talking, but we chatted fitfully on the lesser inclines; it diluted my awareness of the increasing discomfort of the climb, and it was useful practice, for my Swahili, though much improved, was still less then fluent. We discussed his schoolboy eldest son's future career. No, he was not going to be a *karani* or clerk – this said emphatically and with some contempt – but a mason or carpenter; at all events an artisan of some sort. We also reflected on the performance of Roger Bannister who had recently done the first four-minute mile; and jointly shook our heads over recent attempts to get a satellite into space – we shared a perhaps unadventurous view that what went on 'out there' was best left alone, and that we had problems enough to be going on with down here.

The meeting with a group of villagers provided a welcome break. It was not a long one and we were soon on our way, the sun at our back, Malesa seemingly tireless, myself a little weary. It was about then that I began to think of my bottle of Mackeson's, which I had impressed upon Mzee was to be put into the canvas washbasin with water, to await my arrival. The thought recurred with increasing frequency as the afternoon wore on and the ache in thighs and calves intensified. To distract attention from this, and conversation exhausted, I mentally composed a variety of appreciative letters to Mr. Mackeson, detailing the circumstances in which I had enjoyed this particular bottle of his stout, and thinking that it might be good for a complimentary crate by courtesy of his agent in Tanganyika.

Half an hour or so before sundown we reached our appointed camp-site, where the village headman was waiting for us. Below, a pattern of spurs and ridges dropped down toward the Bubu, where a thin mist was already rising and a Bateleur eagle sailed along on its black wedge of wing, making its last sortie of the day; westward lay Usandawe, with miles of tsetse bush stretching to the horizon, where the sky was now spectacularly ablaze as the sun rapidly dropped. So much for the view, but here there was no promised tent, no bed or bath, no clean shirt, no roasting chicken. A rock to sit on was the extent of home comfort. Within minutes the sun went down, the valley filled with mist, the moon came up, and the temperature dropped. In fact it was bloody cold, and somewhere down there were those bloody porters; and with them a tin box with a sweater and trousers – and my Mackeson's.

Malesa and the headman whispered earnestly for a few minutes in Rangi;

the headman disappeared whilst Malesa came over to explain that something was being arranged. It was, and shortly afterwards we were led to a hut a short distance away where the owner greeted us and said that I was welcome to spend the night. He was a friendly man, amused yet also politely concerned with my predicament. Just as I accepted his invitation a figure appeared from the direction of the Bubu. It was a messenger with the unwelcome intelligence that the porters had gone on strike down in the valley. The day was longer than they had expected and they wanted more pay; not an unreasonable proposition, but it would have made more sense to have staged their protest where and when I could have responded. Clearly it would have to wait for the morrow; I sent word that I would meet them at Bereko and sort it out then – and if they didn't turn up, not only no pay but I'd have Mohamed Sadala down on them like a ton of bricks.

My host's home was a daub and wattle hut with the traditional flat *tembe* roof – a platform of poles, virtually flat, laid across a stouter central ridge pole which gave the roof a slight curve; then a layer of dried grass, the whole topped off with six or seven inches of earth. The theory, or at least the practice, was that even the heaviest rain was absorbed; it then evaporated to leave the *tembe* dry for the next downpour. In the heat, it was also reasonably effective insulation.

The householder was one of nature's gentleman, and we all sat round and talked, mostly of agricultural and local dynastic matters – this always a subject of consuming interest, for Chief Heri Salim of Irangi was not a popular man, and there were many who would have liked to see him go. We ate a heavy, stiff porridge which was the main staple – and an extremely dull one – of the Rangi diet; the water was tempting but suspect, so I went thirsty. It was hot and airless in the hut, a half-hearted fire of wood and dried cattle dung and a dim kerosene lamp filling it with smoke that settled on the stomach and hurt the eyes. It did not appear to discourage the mosquitoes though, and they whined savagely at the ear and drew blood silently near floor level. The conversation died as, mercifully, did the fire, and my host and his family withdrew into the smoke-blackened recesses beyond the lamp. Swathed from head to toe in a borrowed length of decidedly off-white cotton cloth as a defence against the mosquitoes, I got what sleep I could on a rope bed which I took to be marginally less uncomfortable than the beaten earth floor.

It seemed a long night, and sleep was elusive; soon after dawn, and after thanking our host and accepting a piece of roast cassava root for breakfast, we overcame his reluctance to accept payment and set off for Bereko, now some ten miles away and more or less on the level. Muscles groaned and the early morning damp clung, and the dew was cold and wet on ankles and shins, but as the sun got higher the aches diminished and we got into gear; at least I did, for Malesa never seemed to be out of gear – he could do 40 miles a day and think nothing of it.

It was only a three hour walk or so to Bereko, but with my detours and diversions, followed by a formal call on *Jumbe* Mohamed at Bereko itself, it was mid-afternoon before we pitched up at the rest-house. It was a warm day, all blue and gold, with a drift of dazzling white clouds, and a light wind moved the tops of the tall umbrella-shaped trees which dotted the three hundred yards between village and rest-house. In the shade of one of these was my wood and canvas camp table, set for breakfast, lunch or dinner as the case might be. Mzee was there, grinning, a four-gallon *debe* full of water on the fire, and preparations in hand for a meal; and there was the bottle of Mackeson's cooling in the washbasin

I luxuriated as far as was possible in the three feet square canvas bath; then followed a lazy shave, and a positively sybaritic appreciation of the texture and smell of a clean shirt and shorts. I had already taken the edge off my thirst with two glasses of squash, my first drink for over twenty-four hours, so the Mackeson's could wait its turn and be properly enjoyed. The porters were in a little huddle behind the kitchen, looking variously sheepish, anxious and truculent. I was to be collected by lorry later in the day, and they would get a ride back to Kondoa. I gave them a ritual choking off with greater good humour than I had felt the night before, reminded them of my amicable relationship with Mohamed Sadala, and paid them off at the rate agreed before we left Kondoa.

It was time to turn to the camp chair and enjoy the Mackeson's. Glass ready, bottle opener out, off with the cap. No anticipated hiss of escaping air. I poured – it was flat; and not only flat but a little sour.

* * *

By road Bereko is an hour's drive north of Kondoa township. A little less than halfway lay Kolo, headquarters of Irangi chiefdom and home of Chief Heri Salim. Like many other chiefs he epitomised a rôle which was in the early nineteen-fifties already being overtaken by political events and the gradual modernisation of local government. It was nevertheless one which was still essential for purposes of getting things done on the ground. Chiefs were hereditary, elected or appointed, and commanded varying degrees of respect; this depended increasingly on personality and conduct rather than status.

Bereko was 20 miles beyond Kolo and several hundred feet higher. It was a pleasant if undistinguished place, in rolling upland country where the red soil, badly scarred here and there by gullies, supported fields of maize and millet, and small herds of tiny ill-nourished cattle. Villages, though not unknown, were not a feature of traditional East African society, and here as elsewhere, homesteads were scattered over the landscape, each with two or three acres of cultivation.

Bereko itself was an artificial settlement and administrative centre; a row of shops faced each side of the market square, owned and run by Indians and Arabs, the latter a relic and reminder of slave trading days a century earlier. One of the shops belonged to an elderly and friendly Indian, Mr. Pardhan, who on our first visit to Bereko was only reluctantly persuaded that Sylvia, a year younger than I, was not in fact my daughter. Convinced or not, she was thereafter his sister, and he was sixty if he was a day.

On one of my many visits I was to lay out some new building plots, this time exclusively for Africans – an intention which was viewed favourably by the locals, although few if any were potential shopkeepers; but no doubt some had their dreams and there was no shortage of helpers as I moved around with my tape-measure, cord, and pegs, getting the corners right with dim recollections of Pythagoras and the instructions of Mr.Longland. Eventually the job was done, and my sketch map of the area, replete not only with trading plots and access roads, but a few residential plots as well, was examined, discussed, and endorsed by the idle and curious. For good measure I took the names of a few people who expressed an interest in taking up a plot. Chatting with some bystanders on the main road I was struck by the sound of a vehicle approaching unseen from the north. It was certainly not the engine of a typical truck or car, and yet it struck a chord in the memory; there then appeared an early 1930's supercharged 41/2 litre Bentley open tourer in British racing green, the engine emitting its distinctive robust growl. The driver was dressed à la mode, tweed cap back to front, goggles, and a scarf flying behind him, altogether an incongruous but cheering sight. We exchanged waves, and he was gone.

Turning back to my companions, I learned that there was a lake nearby, just over the border in Mbulu district. I made enquiries, borrowed a bike, and late in the afternoon set off with my shotgun tied to the crossbar with a piece of string, a handful of cartridges in my pocket. The first bit was easy, and I freewheeled down the main road leading northwards, bumping over the sun-baked corrugations. Then off down a lesser road to the left, where after a mile or so it levelled off to cross a little stream named the Yere Awak on the map, but described by the inhabitants of Bereko as a *kijito tu* – just a little stream. I was now over the district border, in Ufiome chiefdom; the Fiome are a very small tribe, and the men were said to be particularly handsome, the women attractive to match, and both disinclined to dress from the waist up. But I met no men or women along the road, and after two or three miles there was still no sign of the lake, described as having been *karibu* or nearby. I was beginning to learn that *karibu* was relative in Swahili, and that it was used more as a word of encouragement to the traveller who still had perhaps several weary miles ahead of him, than as a statement of proximity. Still, if the lake was elusive, it was nevertheless an evening to be enjoyed. Beyond a low wooded ridge to the north-west rose the massive flattened cone of Hanang mountain, home of the Mbulu, and although thirty or forty miles away it seemed much closer. Then, just over a gentle rise, there was the lake, glassy, calm, and fringed with reeds, with *miombo* woodland beyond the far shore. The sun was low and a thin haze of mist already hung over the water. There were black and white ibis or rainbirds flapping slowly in, the lower ones in silhouette, those a little higher catching the last of the sun. There were flighting ducks too, but mostly on the far side. However, I managed to bag one, but thoughts of roast duck were rapidly dispelled as the depth of water and tangle of weeds prevented me getting at it. I was wet and cold, for by now the sun had gone, and I headed back to Bereko, gently uphill all the way. As darkness fell I had a thought; what else was it that I had heard about Ufiome apart from the bare-breasted women? Then I remembered.

There had been a man-eating leopard about for some weeks with a dozen or more kills to its credit, and it was still on the loose. The ride back seemed interminable. Spirits lifted a little as the moon came up; it would at least allow me to see the leopard and either throw the bike at it or beat it over the head with my shotgun – I had taken only a few cartridges, and these had all gone. Meanwhile, behind every rock and bush there lurked an imagined leopard, each breath of wind amid the maize stalks was a *chui* accelerating for the final leap. The bush and fields along the track were positively alive with invisible leopards. Back at Bereko and on the right side of a bottle of beer, washed, and relaxed in front of a wood fire in the rest-house, it all seemed rather silly. After dinner and a chat with Mzee I pulled on a sweater and strolled over to the shops; most were still open, pressure lamps burning within the wide doorways. Remembering Ali Salehe's coffee, rendered nauseating by cardamon seeds, I declined the Arab's invitation to step inside. We exchanged social pleasantries on the verandah of his shop whilst a multitude of bugs battered themselves to unconsciousness or death against his hissing Petromax lamp. He sympathised over my lost duck, and lamented the state of his business; it was a bad year – but then it always was.

Negotiating the unseen pitfalls of the market place, I next called on Mr. Pardhan. He was pressing with his hospitality, and politeness required that I at least sample the ghastly tea favoured by East African Indians – the basic brew being boiled up with quantities of sugar, condensed milk and oriental spices. The formalities required the exercise of a good deal of self-control, but on this occasion early rescue was at hand. Sporadic drumming beyond the market indicated that drums were being warmed up in preparation for an *ngoma* or dance; for this purpose the skins are held close to a fire until they are dry and taut, and the apparently random tapping with hands and sticks is analogous to a European orchestra tuning up. I made my excuses, and walked towards the two grain silos adjacent to the market place; brick-built, these were cylindrical in shape, about twenty feet high and fifteen in diameter (6m x 4.6m). Kept full of maize or millet, they were our first line of defence against local famine. A small crowd had gathered, and as I approached, the drummers, four or five in number, settled into their separate rhythms; it is a characteristic of African drumming that each drummer pursues his own theme independently of the others – hence the irregularities of beat which can delight or sometimes frighten the foreigner.

I climbed up the wooden steps of the nearest silo to enjoy an uninterrupted view. The dancers were Fiome from over the border, an equal number of young men and women alternating in a circle perhaps twenty five feet across. They were remarkably good-looking – a generalisation which could not be made at all such gatherings, or indeed at an average Saturday night hop in rural England. The men wore shorts, the women somewhat longer skirts, and that was all, men and women alternating in a wide circle. The movements of the dance were rather dull and repetitive to European eyes, but the evident pleasure of the participants was infectious as they circled to the insistent beat of the drums. From time to time they burst into a song which, unlike most African music, had a melody which seemed not entirely alien to European ears, and which induced a whistle just as surely as the drums activated my feet.

As for myself, I just sat and took it in, with some slight regret that it was not possible or appropriate to join in the uncomplicated proceedings round the fire; shortly I left them and walked back to the rest house. The evening had been real enough but it was a part of Africa to which we intruders did not and could not belong. It would have been presumptuous to pretend otherwise; *my* workaday reality had been the trading plots earlier in the day, and the practicalities of district administration. Tomorrow there would be the Bereko court records to check, and judgments to review, for local court holders were not invariably objective; drugs stocks to be checked at the dispensary; and the primary school to inspect, with the pleasurable prospect of a chat with the excellent head, Robert Pirmin, an inspirational teacher far from his home in the extreme southwest of the country.

Even now tomorrow intruded, and the cicadas in the foreground competing with the drums in the background, I settled at my slatted wood and canvas camp table to re-read some court case files which on first perusal had seemed suspect, and which in the morning would have to be discussed with *Jumbe* Mohamed Salim. There were not to be many more discussions with *Jumbe* Mohamed on these or any other matters; several months later he killed himself with a shotgun, though whether this was accidentally or with intent we never found out. Some local opinion attributed his death to witchcraft, a view which was reinforced when a short time later, his other brother Ali, *Jumbe* of Suruke, was murdered. I heard the Preliminary Inquiry, a chore which if possible was allocated to the most junior DO. There had been nothing supernatural about the knife which killed Ali, but it may have been significant that the murderer, Mohamed Nyakusa, had been mixed up in a rather nasty case involving witchcraft and death some years earlier. This time he was convicted and subsequently hanged[21].

* * *

A little over a year after our arrival in Kondoa I unexpectedly found myself, nominally at least, in charge of the district. Cecil had driven down to Southern Rhodesia (Zimbabwe) to study some African co-operative farming schemes, combining duty and local leave; he was away for a month. Concurrently Jimmy Hildesley was transferred at short notice to take over Manyoni district. It was comforting to know that Cecil did not visualise the district descending into chaos during his absence.

On my own, I again had cause to visit Bereko, always a pleasure whatever the purpose. On the return journey I made a detour from Kolo down the escarpment to Masange to call on Johanes, manager of a small experimental farm where trials were in progress with a view to introducing millet with a shorter growing season and hence greater tolerance of drought. On the way back to Kondoa in the late afternoon, I stopped to spend a little time with Hugh and Ros Lamprey, recently arrived, and living in a little rest-house at Chungai; this was perfectly sited on a little rocky knoll commanding views north and south along the escarpment, and eastwards over southern Masailand. I had known Hugh at Oxford, where we rowed for our colleges and were members of the OU Exploration Club; he was also a mountaineer. He was now the Game Department biologist, charged with devising humane forms of game control and crop protection. Early trials of electric fencing were in progress.

Sitting outside and reminiscing over a pot of tea we were puzzled to see two sizeable elongated clouds to the east, perhaps four or five miles away, visibly changing shape. Clearly they were *not* clouds; what then? The Bubu valley had the previous year been ravaged by flocks of Sudan diochs, so birds perhaps? Then the advance party arrived in the shape of a sprinkling of red

---

[21] The death penalty still existed in Britain at the time.

locusts. With the new season's crops in growth this could be serious, and I hastened back to the Boma as fast as a short-wheelbase Landrover could safely be driven; from here I phoned my Provincial Commissioner, Leonard Heaney, with the unwelcome news. I optimistically assumed that an insecticide-spraying aircraft would be despatched from Northern Province or even Kenya, to deal with the invaders. I was mistaken. In mid-evening, after some long-distance phoning on his own account, the PC called me back; no material assistance would be forthcoming, and the only feasible action was to keep the swarms moving over or away from areas of cultivation and into the bush where they could munch away to their hearts' content. This could be achieved by mobilising farmers to light smoky fires and kick up a row by beating tin cans, cooking pots, and so on.

I summoned my colleagues and explained the situation. It was agreed that we would all set off at crack of dawn next day, each to a different part of the district, with appropriate instructions to chiefs, sub-chiefs, and such village headmen as we could get to. Meanwhile the locust swarms, having spent the late afternoon in the shade of the escarpment, and following a relatively chilly night, were in a state of torpor; they would need a spell of warm sunshine to galvanise them into action, in the event halfway through the morning. By this time the word had been spread, and bonfires laid with plenty of green wood and leaf; and farmers were at the ready to raise a racket if and when need arose. As I drove back from my corner of the district I passed through part of a swarm, and my windscreen was spattered with locust body-parts and goo; and it was gratifying to see clouds of smoke drifting across the landscape, and peasant families beating their pots and pans. Unsurprisingly, these simple measures were not wholly successful; but the public response was good, and comparatively little damage was done to growing crops. By nightfall the swarms had disappeared westwards into unoccupied bush.

* * *

By the time I was due to leave Kondoa I had established a familiar and friendly rapport with the people living in and around Bereko, and my farewell visit was primarily a social occasion. The previous year I had helped a group of enthusiastic villagers to set up a rudimentary community association, and had been able to put some basic furniture and equipment their way. Its committee had now organised a tea-party, whilst Robert Pirmin the headmaster conducted a small concert; prominent amongst the performers was a boy with an outsize grin, appropriately nicknamed *Chura,* Swahili for frog. It was a modest but heart-warming affair, and I responded to the valedictory speeches in my best Swahili and a few carefully rehearsed phrases of Rangi. It was with some sadness that I climbed into the Landrover and drove away downhill, knowing that I would never return.

Lake Tanganyika: local leave

Home leave every two to three years was arguably overgenerous at five days per month of service, and invariably I found the time began to drag. At the start of my career this was in addition to travelling time by sea, but by the end of my first tour flying was the standard mode of travel; we could still go by sea, but quite reasonably it then came out of our leave entitlement. In addition to this we were allowed two weeks a year local leave to recharge batteries and simply 'get away';[22] in practice it wasn't always possible to take advantage of this opportunity, and in my nine years service I had local leave only twice. The first occasion was the most memorable.

There were not many perquisites attached to working for the Government of Tanganyika, but one of them was free first-class travel on local leave by East African Railways and Harbours (EAR & H). This was of little avail if you were remote from their network, which embraced rail, road and lake transport; but in Kondoa we were well placed to make the most of it. The prospect was particularly welcome, as by mid-tour Sylvia was pregnant with our first child; a restful leave was indicated.

The first leg of our trip was by railway bus down to Dodoma, the journey enlivened by conversation with a Canadian DO, John Cairns, and his wife, who were themselves returning from a spell of local leave in the north. From Dodoma the train took us westwards to Lake Tanganyika, the deepest in Africa; we approached the lake port of Kigoma soon after sunrise, running

---

[22] It should be remembered that the standard working week then included Saturday mornings which, up-country, ran from 8-12.30.

gently downhill alongside the sluggish Malagarasi river and its attendant swamp. We were fortunate with our connection; the lake steamer *Liemba* was due to leave in the evening, so we had time to take a taxi to Ujiji, where Livingstone's meeting with Stanley in 1871 is commemorated by a substantial carved granite pillar and plaque. This meeting was not as peremptory as is commonly supposed and the two men explored Lake Tanganyika together, after which Livingstone accompanied Stanley as far as Tabora, over 200 miles to the east; the journalist then left for the coast to report his having found the 'missing' explorer and missionary.

'Liemba' at Mpulungu

NJB

Back in Kigoma we boarded the *Liemba*. The vessel had a singular history; prefabricated in Germany before the first world war, it had been shipped out to German East Africa in segments, transported up to the lake, and reassembled as the *Götzen*. Sunk during the war, it had been salvaged after Britain assumed responsibility for Tanganyika, and later incorporated in the EAR & H fleet – most of which was to be found on Lake Victoria – and renamed *Liemba*. The vessel was brought to the attention of a wider public when it featured in the television series in which Michael Palin made his way from North to South Pole in the 1990's; it then seemed sadly neglected compared with its relatively spruce and shipshape condition in 1953.

Our cabin was generous in size and comfortable, deck space adequate, the stewards obliging and cheerful, and the food excellent. The only discordant note was struck by the captain, a loud-mouthed bully of an Englishman. By contrast, the First Officer was a most congenial companion; sadly he lost his life a few years later when, sent to secure a laden lighter in tow during a storm, the hawser snapped, whipped back, and killed him.

We left Kigoma after dark, by which time fishermen were out on the lake in their canoes, each of which had a pressure lamp placed in the bows to attract *dagaa,* a small fish very like whitebait. The visual effect was magical – little pools of light scattered across the lake, with the canoes and their occupants silhouetted against the glow. As the unobtrusive sounds of a sleepy lake port receded, the silence was broken only by occasional exchanged greetings and banter between the fishermen, and the muted throb of *Liemba's* engine. The next two days were a delight and wholly restorative, as we made our way southwards; we stopped at several lakeside villages, went ashore to stretch our legs and chat with local bystanders, always curious to know where strangers had come from. The only jarring note occurred when our captain ran us aground in the small hours whilst manoeuvring into Kipili Port, an event followed by a good deal of swearing and bellowed instructions.

On the third morning we anchored at Mpulungu, a small port at the extreme southern end of the lake, and located in Northern Rhodesia (now Zambia). There was nothing to detain us, and we took a service bus into Abercorn (now Mbala), where we paid a courtesy call at the District Office, and sought advice about getting to the Kalambo Falls. These were at no great distance, and we took a taxi. Our approach to the falls was not heralded by the sound of rushing water or clouds of spray; we had got the timing wrong, and towards the end of the dry season, a modest stream no more than a metre wide tumbled quietly over a rocky ledge and disappeared. But what a vista. The Kalambo Falls are the second highest in Africa, with a dizzying vertical drop of 725feet (221m), twice that of the Victoria Falls; beyond the flanking cliffs, miles of Africa faded away into the distance. As for the water, we could not tell how much of it, if any, reached the bottom, or whether it was vaporised on the long way down.

Northbound on the *Liemba* our passengers included several young white Southern Rhodesians, men and women. Otherwise well-mannered and behaved, they spoke of Africans in general in the most offensive and disparaging way. On this small piece of evidence we were glad that we were living in Tanganyika, where there was little racial tension and relations were on the whole relaxed and amicable. This encounter had a particular personal relevance, for had I not been selected for the Colonial Service I had a broadly similar job lined up in the Southern Rhodesia Civil Service; it would probably have been a brief career, ending in resignation.

Bwana Shauri

The Boma at Kondoa was a splendid and romantic-looking affair; a relic of the German occupation, it was the surviving part of what had been an enclosed fort. Originally there had been a perimeter wall embracing living quarters, stores, stables and administrative offices. Whatever *our* offices had once been, the building itself came straight out of a film set. It had two storeys, with massive stone walls held together with rock-hard lime mortar, and rendered with whitewashed plaster. A verandah ran the greater part of the length of the upper storey, supported by neo-Gothic arches. Where the straight stone steps reached the first floor, the verandah was uncovered, and edged by a low parapet; to the right, and separate from the main bulk of the upper storey was a square tower with crenellated battlements and a flagpole. Its interior was ventilated and illuminated by two small arched windows and an ever-open door. This was the office of the junior DO – myself.

As already mentioned, allocation of work between DOs was a matter for the DC, and this could always be changed at short notice. For 2-3 months in 1953 Jimmy Hildesley was engaged exclusively in planning and supervising a bush-clearing programme in the Bubu valley; during this period half his normal workload was transferred to me, and my resultant list of duties read as follows:-

DO II

Day to day oversight of
- Police and Prison
- Government cash office
- Native Authority (i.e. District Council) treasury and stores

Land matters, excluding native tenure and resettlement

Schools and education

District Court returns

Township water supply

Dispensaries, health and medical (excluding sleeping sickness)

Game and crop protection

Social welfare, games, and sport

Minor settlements and trading centres

Labour matters and payment of labour

Relations with Post Office and East African Railways and Harbours (re the daily bus service to Arusha and Dodoma)

Few of the tasks arising required close daily attention, and it was a joy to have a stab at the variety of problems thrown up, especially with the reassurance that Cecil was there to provide guidance, instruction, and when necessary, correction. On Jimmy's return he took back those duties temporarily transferred to me, and I was given responsibility for dealing with the looming food shortage in Usandawe.

Despite variations in the division of work between DOs, there was one component in the daily round which was common to all throughout the territory; this was the *shauri*, an imprecise but useful Swahili word embracing problems, matters of concern, complaints, petitions, and so on. Anyone with something on his mind – it was usually him – and which he thought 'the Government' could do something about, had open access to the district office; in practice he was normally seen by a DO, universally known therefore as *Bwana Shauri*. He might have to wait, or even be asked to return next day; but he *would* be seen, listened to, and whenever practicable and reasonable, helped. A caller might have domestic problems involving wife or children, a grievance about a neighbour, official, or Chief; he might seek tax exemption or resolution of a land dispute, or question whether he had received his proper gratuity following military service in Burma, or whether the requirement for him to sell some of his cattle had been correctly calculated; or he could be wanting advice on education, an agricultural loan, purchase of a piece of machinery – *anything*. There could be five callers a day, or a dozen, or twenty, but rarely none at all.

The most bizarre – and wholly inconsequential – *shauri* which came to my door in Kondoa afforded me half an hour of mixed exasperation and entertainment; exasperating because I was otherwise engrossed in plans for dealing with an imminent food shortage, and entertaining because it was so preposterously surreal. The incident went something like this.......

'*Hodi*' – announcing arrival.

'*Karibu*' – come in.

'*Starehe*' – don't disturb yourself.

The ritual civilities exchanged, my caller stepped out of the sunlight into the room. He was an Arab, his face long, lugubrious, and dusty light brown; his dress was the usual loose white collarless cotton shirt and baggy pyjama trousers, and open leather sandals. On his head he wore a round white cotton hat subtly embroidered with gold thread; this he removed, revealing a clean-shaven head. I waved him to a chair, and as he sat he rummaged in the folds of his pyjamas and produced a small flat tin; it might once have held tobacco, but the colours and design were largely worn away. He wrestled with it, the top flew off, and half a dozen tattered and grubby pieces of paper fell to the floor. These he recovered, selected one which was markedly fresher than the others, and passed it over.

Kondoa Boma

It was a letter from the Tanganyika Red Cross Society in Dar es Salaam announcing that Salim bin Salehe had won the fifteenth prize in a raffle; the prize was a permanent wave. I glanced at his head, suppressed a smile, and prepared for the inevitable tussle; the situation was itself comical enough, and I had little confidence that my Swahili would be equal to the occasion. Salim was aware that he had won something, but was not clear as to what it was. This I endeavoured to explain, a task not made any easier by the fact that the prize was redeemable only at Maison Chloe, a ladies' hairdresser in Dar es Salaam. After listening intently to my fractured Swahili, Salim's face lit up. 'Ah, so I am to receive this machine which folds the hair'.

'No *Bwana* Salim, you are *not* to get a machine, you are to get what the machine *does*... it is a *process* ... you see ...' This was less than lucid, and he did not. 'Anyway' I said, 'you will have to go down to Dar to have this permanent wave...' 'How it that? Why cannot it be sent?' I explained, and he began to get heated. 'But that is a swindle. Why should I have to spend time and money travelling to Dar es Salaam?' Why indeed! The capital was a two to three day journey away, a hundred miles by bus followed by another three hundred or so by rail. Absurd.....I commiserated.

'Then why cannot this machine for bending the hair be sent to Kondoa to save me trouble?' 'Ah *Bwana* Salim, that would not do, as there is no electricity here in Kondoa, and electricity is necessary to make it hot.' Too late I recognised the blind alley into which I had inadvertently stepped. Salim pounced.

'But are there no such machines which work with charcoal or kerosene?' Conscious of this glaring gap in western technology, I explained, somewhat apologetically, that there weren't. Salim sniffed; these Europeans weren't so clever after all.

We carried on in this vein for some time, getting nowhere. Finally I played my trump card. 'Now listen *Bwana* Salim, this isn't really a man's sort of thing... it is more for women, and besides, you have no hair for this machine to bend...' Unwarily I rambled on...... 'Now your wife....'

At this Salim bridled.

'My wife? What has my wife got to do with it? It is *I* who have won this prize, not my wife, and here you are trying to give it to her.... and as for my hair, why do these people offer prizes which a man cannot use?'

I wished Salim had won the first prize, a Hillman Minx saloon car; it would have been much simpler. Finally, with a sort of inspired resignation, I hit on the home perm. I got the message across, and assured Salim that I would write to the Red Cross regretting his inability to collect his prize and asking them if they would supply a home perm outfit instead. Somewhat mollified, Salim departed, and I was able to resume work on contingency planning for the expected food shortage in Usandawe chiefdom.

Some time later the home perm arrived; 'Twink' I think it was called, or some such manifestation of the advertiser's art. I sent word to Salim bin Salehe, who came along later in the day to collect it, as hairless as on the previous occasion. We traded the usual courtesies, and after a decent interval Salim took the box off to investigate its contents. That, I assumed, was that. A few minutes later he was back holding out the instruction leaflet. Could the *Bwana* translate? The manufacturers had been both conscientious and optimistic, and the leaflet was printed in a number of languages, but not, alas, in Arabic or Swahili. Enough was enough I thought, and besides, my own Swahili wasn't yet up to it. I ushered Salim out of my office and into that of Selemani, our efficient but officious Somali chief clerk; *he* could have a go at it. I had had my fill of permanent waves.

I could hardly bring myself to believe that this was the end of the matter and that there would be no occasion for a further visit. But Selemani had evidently done his job well – or intimidated Salim into not returning; or perhaps Salim drank the contents of the two little bottles which constituted the kit. At all events I never saw him again.

* * *

Often serving as interpreter or intermediary when a *shauri* was being dealt with was one of the local complement of district office messengers, or *tarishis*, an indispensable component of local administration. Their uniform was common throughout the territory, khaki drill shorts and jumper, this last sporting a large oval brass badge with the letters DO (District Office) stamped into it; completing the ensemble was a red fez or tarboosh, but without the familiar black tassel. Footwear was optional but generally absent.

The messenger was very much the DC's man. Implicit in his designation was the requirement to deliver messages, written or oral, to chiefs, sub-chiefs and other members of the local government hierarchy; but also, in a district where there was but one post office and no postal deliveries, to traders, mission stations, schools, and so on. They were rarely fully occupied, but were always available to set off at a moment's notice, or to interpret, to advise or inform the latest DO cadet, to attend a public meeting and report on what took place, to investigate informally the substance of complaints which, conducted by the police, would have drawn a blank, or – again informally – to bring someone in for questioning or to be given information or advice by one of the Administrative Officers. They also had limited powers of arrest, but normally only on instruction. As with many of our junior African staff, the messenger was apt to be taken for granted; no doubt he sometimes succumbed to the temptation to take advantage of his position at the Boma, but by and large he gave conscientious and loyal service for small reward. He might from time to time be found dozing on the Boma verandah in the heat of the day; but he could be on the road at five in the morning, or well after sundown.

Famine Avoidance

Central Province was dry. The winds which blew inland from the Indian Ocean and those which spilled eastwards from the steamy Congo basin had little rain left over for central Tanganyika. Every five years or so the rains failed completely, and there was severe famine in Manyoni and Dodoma districts, an area largely occupied by the Gogo people. The Irangi highlands ensured a higher and somewhat more reliable rainfall over much of Kondoa district, but Usandawe was drier, and we were concerned that the area would have a negligible harvest in 1953. There were national strategic reserves of grain against serious famine, most of it imported from South Africa and Southern Rhodesia (Zimbabwe). To cope with localised famine, the expectation was that this would normally be dealt with by the redistribution of surpluses elsewhere in the district. However, this year it was clear that there would be very little surplus in Irangi, as only an average harvest was likely. Against this contingency we had local reserves in brick or concrete silos in the three chiefdoms; these were maintained by the Native Authorities, with surplus grain purchased direct from the producers in good years. In 1953 it seemed certain that these reserves would not meet Usandawe's needs. Cecil thought it would be useful training and experience for me to assume responsibility for the detailed planning of famine avoidance measures. Files dealing with previous food shortages were withheld until I had worked out an outline scheme of my own; this I then revised and subsequently discussed and agreed with Cecil. With the threat of partial famine looming, it was crucial that we should not lose any of the small surpluses generated in Irangi. Yet we *were* losing it, and there was a thriving black market export trade in grain. Opportunist traders, mainly in Dodoma, were buying clandestinely in the less hard-hit parts of the Province; they were prepared to pay something over the market price – at least enough to persuade the peasant farmer to part with what surplus he might have – in expectation of worthwhile profits in the drier areas of Manyoni and Dodoma districts when the famine began to bite.

Kondoa was one of the districts where some buying was taking place. Both the purchase and movement of food crops in time of shortage were controlled by legislation, and were theoretically possible only on issue of a permit from the exporting district. But legislation was one thing, practice another. We did not have a very extensive road network, but with our twenty or so policemen to cover four thousand square miles of country we were manifestly unable to control every motorable track leading out of the district. And of course there was collusion between buyers and willing sellers. Almost daily we heard from Dodoma that Naranjan Singh or Ali Nassoro or R.J. Patel[23] had run in a load of millet from Kondoa the previous night. So far we had drawn a complete blank at our end, and Cecil was hopping mad – the more so because if this went on we would end up buying in unnecessarily large supplies of grain ourselves, at inflated prices.

Then we got a tip-off, and I was sent out to make the necessary interception. I set off about dusk with half a dozen constables in the worn-out police Landrover. We had a pole and a couple of trestles in the back to set up a road block. The *askaris* were excited, laughing and joking behind me as we drove out of the police lines; the hunting instinct had asserted itself, and I was not immune myself. By midnight, parked just off the main road close to the Dodoma district border, and the barrier in position, it had worn a bit thin. It was chilly, and without fire or light, we were all a little forlorn. We had stopped a couple of lorries, but their commerce was innocent. At the coldest and darkest hour the first cock crowed in a nearby homestead, and later a second and third time, by when the sky had begun to lighten and my watch read four o'clock. Then there came from the north the unmistakeable sound of a throaty diesel engine, and hope revived. We gathered at the barrier and waited. A few minutes later, headlights appeared along the road, and a heavy Mercedes lorry bore down on us at about fifty as I stepped forward with a torch to wave it down. The gesture was disregarded, engine speed increased, and the lorry crashed through our flimsy barrier. Peeved, and without further thought, I snatched a .303 Lee Enfield from

---

[23] Fictitious names.

one of the *askaris* and let off a couple of rounds, aiming a little below the disappearing tail-light in hope of puncturing a tyre; I missed. Pursuit was useless; there was no way in which our decrepit Landrover could match the Mercedes for speed, and with a good start, the lorry driver would get off the road into the bush, switch off his lights and sit tight. After we had passed and abandoned a necessarily desultory search, he would disappear down a bush track and make his way on to Dodoma.

Reluctantly I resigned myself to this minor failure. The sun would soon be up, and I ordered my companions back into the pick-up for the return journey. Eyes flickered, and the stale, sour aura of a sleepless unwashed night hung in the cab. We had not been on the move very long when the sun jumped up over the Uburunge skyline. There is nothing more cheering than the sun after a long dispiriting night, and it brought us an additional bonus. At the other end of a long straight stretch of corrugated road that set the teeth rattling, a lorry approached; it was slow, and heavily loaded. When it was about 300 yards away I pulled the Landrover across the road and stopped it. The lorry, plainly in some distress, with sagging springs and boiling radiator, came to a halt.

Behind the wheel was an African driver, at his side a middle-aged Indian who scrambled out through the wooden half-door and stood wringing his hands. Once the bloom of youth has faded, an Indian's complexion is apt to turn a dusty grey, and this man's face was positively ashen. The lorry was piled high with sacks of grain, not mere millet, but maize; this meant that it had probably come from Mbulu district to the north of Kondoa, but this made no difference – he had no permit. I said he must accompany me back to Kondoa where he would be charged and tried; his driver was to follow along behind with one of the *askaris*. At this the poor man collapsed completely, sank to his knees, clasped my legs, and poured out a litany of pleas and excuses as the tears rolled down his face. The *askaris* sniggered, perhaps more out of embarrassment than malice, and I brusquely shut them up, for *I* was embarrassed too, both for the trader and on my own account. He was probably not a rich man, and this could ruin him; there was no excuse for his offence, which was to make a useful profit out of approaching famine conditions, but it was difficult not to feel a twinge of sympathy.

We drove back to the Boma in uncomfortable silence, broken occasionally as my passenger began to speak, only to tail off as he realised the futility of it.

By the time we arrived I almost wished we hadn't caught him; I would certainly rather have nabbed the new Mercedes that had eluded us. Cecil on the other hand was delighted; the Indian was formally charged, and half an hour later was in court being tried. Cecil was hard on him I thought, but I also knew he was not an unjust man, so perhaps my own judgment was lacking. The penalty was confiscation of both the load of maize and the lorry; the latter had little life left in it, and several months passed before we were able to sell it. The maize we bought on the Native Treasury account for famine relief work, crediting 'court fees and fines' with the revenue.

Later in the day I walked along to the police lines and asked Gurmuk Singh for the armoury records; guiltily I entered the two rounds of .303 ammunition as having been used for target practice, and Gurmuk smiled his complicity. As I returned to the Boma I passed the lorry park and bus station adjoining the prison. The railway bus from Arusha to Dodoma was due, and a few passengers were gathered with their calico-wrapped bundles, baskets tied with string, and a chicken or two. Amongst them, but a little apart, were the Indian trader and his driver. I averted my eyes and went on to inspect the prison, where at the time there was a trio of Barabaig cattle thieves.

These enterprising young men had raided across the border from Mbulu district, with the laudable aim, in their view, of stealing a few cattle to prove their manhood. Unfortunately they had killed one of our Sandawe farmers in the process, and so had been charged with murder. I had recently heard the Preliminary Inquiry, and committed them for trial by the High Court in Dodoma; they were now awaiting the arrival of transport and an escort to take them away. As it happened, they contrived to escape, but in their innocence made their way back home across country and were later arrested and sent on to Dodoma. The PI had been a gruelling affair; knowing the possible outcome of murder trials, conducting the inquiry was usually a melancholy business, and I did not enjoy it. On this occasion there had been an additional dimension in the form of fifty or sixty of the defendants' friends and relations who had hired a couple of trucks to bring them the eighty or more miles from Mbulu. Our little courthouse, open on three sides, was far too small to accommodate them, so proceedings were shifted to the larger Native Authority council chamber which was ventilated on one side only by a few wooden windows. Now the Barabaig at the time dressed in home-made badly cured leather, and achieved an attractive highly burnished sheen to their own skins by the application of ghee, a cooking fat derived from milk. The atmosphere in the court may be imagined and my conduct of the enquiry was punctuated by the frequent need to step outside and gulp in some fresh air.

At about this time I passed my law examination and graduated from Third to Second Class Magistrate, with enhanced sentencing powers; and not long afterwards I made the satisfying discovery that I could dispense with the services of a Swahili-English interpreter in court. I confess that I did not greatly enjoy court work, partly because it kept me away from more interesting and, as I saw it, useful tasks. Routine cases could be extremely boring, whilst more serious ones often had elements of personal tragedy and sadness. There was some compensating satisfaction in convicting the rare serious and unpleasant malefactor, or in putting a bewildered defendant at ease, perhaps challenging a prosecution witness or curbing the enthusiasm of the prosecuting Police Inspector. From time to time there were also moments which were conducive to momentary merriment. One such instance was the prosecution of an elderly Arab for 'illegal possession of a game trophy', the item in question being a rhino horn. It was, he explained, for purely personal medicinal purposes, which observation provoked an outburst of mirth amongst those assembled; I could not resist a quick smile myself, and ordered confiscation of the trophy, itself of considerable value, and a rather derisory fine in acknowledgement of the unintended light relief.

* * *

Plans for dealing with the food shortage were in essence straightforward. Arrangements were made for the purchase of any small surpluses in Irangi; later there would be the need to organize its transport to centres in Usandawe, together with the contents of the Irangi silos which would have to be bagged before being moved. The more immediate problem was to estimate whether we would need to import grain from that part of the national reserve held in Northern Province, and if so how much. To this end I was to spend a week in Usandawe to assess how much of the previous year's harvest was held by peasant households.

At the end of a particularly busy week during which Sylvia had been more than usually neglected, Cecil uncharacteristically suggested that I make a start after work on Saturday. This I resisted, and said I'd go down to Kwa Mtoro on Sunday evening, ready for an early start on Monday. Accompanied by Issa, the good-natured houseboy who had joined us at the same time as Mzee, I drove off in the office Landrover into the westering sun. The road to Kwa Mtoro was worse than most, and it was a dull journey at the best of times. Much of Irangi had been denuded of bush, but in eastern Usandawe it came down to the road which ran like a tunnel through the thorn and open *miombo* woodland on either side; it was, moreover, infested with tsetse fly, so that for twenty-odd miles there was a choice between driving with the windows closed and stifling, or with them open and being assailed by upwards of 20 bloodthirsty tsetse flies. I didn't really much care on this occasion, for by the time we were a few miles down the road I had a crashing headache.

An hour later, in the little thatched rest-house at Kwa Mtoro, and shivering violently, I realised I had malaria, crawled into bed, swallowed some aspirin and the recommended dose of Paludrine tablets plus one for luck, and waited for sleep. It was elusive, and later on I sought to relieve the monotony by taking my temperature. By the light of an exhausted Tilley pressure lamp I reckoned that the mercury had reached the top of the glass tube, which made it 44°C or so. In retrospect it was obviously wrong, but at the time adrenaline began to flow as I speculated whether I really ought to be dead. By morning, in a sodden and dishevelled bed, I was very much more alive, but the determination to be up and about waned when my legs collapsed on contact with the floor. I spent the day in bed swallowing pints of boiled water laced with orange squash, and reading 'Westward Ho!' by way of diversion. Issa did his best, but I was a bad patient, and most of the food he tried to tempt me with he probably ended up eating, or throwing away.

By Tuesday evening I was tottering about and called on *Mtemi* Issa, the hard man amongst our trio of local chiefs. He was a stern and uncompromising man who in many respects served us and his people well; but like some other chiefs he was prone to take advantage of his office to an unacceptable extent, and a few years later he was jailed, and dismissed for corruption. The same fate befell his successor Gabrieli Tsotsi, the former Boma messenger who during my time invariably accompanied me on my *safaris* in Usandawe. The sequence of events was in part attributable to the fact that the Sandawe did not have a traditional and hereditary chief; the office was a colonial, probably German creation, so that appointees did not have quite the same relationship with their people as was the case in traditional chiefdoms. As for Gabrieli, he had been a good messenger, but his appointment as a chief was not a wise one. That evening I explained the purpose of my visit, and asked for a guide to accompany me the next day. I proposed to walk round the nearest parts of the chiefdom, calling on individual households to establish an average time some months ahead when the domestic store of grain and cassava would be exhausted. This would give us so many weeks to the next season's harvest during which additional food would be needed; multiply this by the estimated consumption a head weekly, and again by the presumed population of the chiefdom at four and a half mouths to each taxpayer, and you ended up with a very rough estimate of extra food required. Subtract the known amount of reserves in the district, and you had some idea of the quantity to be imported from outside.

Wednesday was a tiring day, but I could not pretend to have covered much ground. Thursday was better, and Friday a long hard day from dawn to dusk. In all I suppose I walked no more than twenty five miles and called on perhaps forty or fifty households, far less than originally intended. Not entirely recovered from fever, the usual pleasures of being out on foot did not register; physically, foot safaris were not occasions of unalloyed enjoyment, however mellow one's subsequent recollections, and there was a constant awareness of heat, dust (or in the rains, mud),sweat, aching limbs, and persistent flies. The pleasure lay in an awareness of a useful job being done, and often rewarding encounters and discussions with local farmers, particularly when a few of them turned up at the tent or rest-house in the evening to join in the conversation round the camp-fire. Then there were the unexpected delights – the memorable view or incident, a sudden cooling breeze on an otherwise baking day, the sight of a kudu or impala, or perhaps a hornbill or a pair of pale green bee-eaters picking their prey out of the air; and sometimes a troop of baboons squatting on a rocky outcrop or raiding a maize plot, or the smile-inducing spectacle of a family of wild pig trotting along in single file, tails erect, and looking neither to right nor left. At the end of the day there was a recuperative bath, change of clothes and a bottle of beer to accompany supper.

On this occasion, in the wake of my mild bout of malaria, I trudged round the Kwa Mtoro area in a bit of a daze, paying little heed to the parched and withered landscape, and giving less attention than I would normally have done to the peasant families who were the object of my enquiries and perambulations. Back at the Boma the following week, I did my sums. We had about three hundred tons of grain, mostly millet and sorghum stored in silos throughout the district. I calculated that we would need another hundred and fifty tons or so, about fifty lorry-loads. Several months later when it was all over it was demonstrated that I had overestimated, and we had about twenty or thirty tons of grain left over. What I had not reckoned with was inherent peasant suspicion; *they* were not going to reveal the full extent of their food stocks, and in general these were rather larger than they had admitted during my *safari* in Usandawe. However it did not matter; the surplus was stored, treated with gammaxane to discourage weevils, and it became the first reserve against the next bad harvest. Meanwhile, in 1953-4, although there may have been some hungry stomachs in Usandawe, there were no deaths from starvation; indeed the diet of most Sandawe was very little affected. Of course, all this is small beer compared with the scale of famines which ravaged parts of Africa in the last decades of the century; but without planning and forethought there would have been severe hunger and probably some fatalities.

The measures we took were of famine avoidance rather than relief, designed to ensure the availability of food; this had to be paid for, and so we arranged employment for the impecunious. Funds were made available for improving the road from Kwa Mtoro into neighbouring Singida district to the west, and labourers accommodated in temporary shelters; payment was made in the form of vouchers issued to their families for redemption in the form of grain. It was a rather crude system, but it was both expedient and effective.

I paid periodic visits to monitor progress on the road works, chat with the workers, and deal with any complaints. On one such occasion I was woken in the small hours by the noise of a muzzle-loading *gobore* or musket going off, followed by the trumpeting of an alarmed elephant which had stumbled across the labourers' bivouac. The sound of it crashing through the scrub receded; no need to get up, and still whacked after a tiring day I was asleep again in moments. Next morning I was assured that the *gobore* had been fired into the air to scare the intruder off, so there was no danger from a wounded elephant on the rampage. There were estimated to be upwards of a hundred elephant in Usandawe, but this was the nearest I ever came to seeing one.

* * *

It was one of Cecil's successors who deposed Chiefs Issa and Gabrieli for corruption. I do not know the circumstances of their removal, but the events in themselves were illustrative of a problem. I have no idea of the extent to which Chiefs and Sub-Chiefs abused their power, or how much serious corruption went undetected. Occasional notorious cases came to light, as when the Nyamwezi Chief Nassoro Fundikira shot himself when about to be arrested for misappropriating one of his subject's inheritance of several thousand pounds; there had also been complaints of rape and the ordering of several murders, but there was no firm evidence of this.

More typical were lesser but nevertheless serious dishonesties; accepting a bribe for the 'right' judgment in a civil case in which, quite possibly, the same judgment would have been reached without the financial inducement; extracting free labour, a goat or chicken from a local farmer; exempting a taxpayer from the annual 'tribal turnout' upon payment of a fee; allowing personal considerations to influence public decisions – and so on. These were all things which would not show up in case files or cash books, and tended to be reported as rumour rather than in the form of hard evidence. When there *was* evidence it was not always expedient or desirable to do more than give a warning, and keep the culprit under scrutiny; a chief guilty of dishonesty, corruption or misconduct might otherwise be a very effective agent of local government, and not easily replaced. If he was popular or was a traditional chief who embodied tribal identity and pride, prosecution or removal could cause such a public uproar that it was not worth the candle; and when instances *did* occur, it also provided a convenient rod for the new breed of politician to beat our backs with. Both circumstances applied in Chief Fundikira's case, and Government was accused of having driven him to his death.

It would be wrong to suggest that corruption was endemic or universal; and whilst we tried to prevent it or at worst limit it, there is one respect in which it was, ironically, partially a consequence of colonial rule. In many indigenous societies there had been structures which imposed curbs on the power of their leaders. During the colonial period hereditary chiefs ceased to be accountable exclusively to their people, whilst appointed chiefs were never accountable in this way; all became primarily answerable to Government through the DC. By the same token they were apt to be seen by their people as creatures of the

Government. Thus anything they did could be thought to be approved *by* Government, with the concomitant assumption that there was no point in complaining *to* Government. This was not of course a universal scenario; people could and did complain, sometimes vociferously, but more usually sotto voce and in hope that word would not get back to the chief. Whether or not disciplinary or criminal proceedings were initiated was very much a matter of judgment by the incumbent DC.

Hospital Visits

High standards beget high expectations, and it was always a matter for surprise and dismay how the small handful of scoundrels, incompetents, and wastrels amongst us ever came to be recruited, and retained once found out. This view was perhaps priggish, and it was in any case unrealistic to suppose that even a carefully chosen sample of English society deposited in foreign parts would not contain its quota of bad hats. However it often seemed in practice that the damage done by the racially prejudiced, the bullies, and the dishonest amongst us, was disproportionate to their small numbers – especially as local politics took on markedly racial overtones in the middle to late Fifties.

One such was Ivor[24]. He had been a cattle dealer somewhere along the Welsh border, where he was well known to the police and magistracy for a range of dubious activities which straddled the dividing line between sharp practice and downright crime. Ivor was no fool and he certainly had the wit to gull the Colonial Office into taking him on as a Livestock Marketing Officer. In this capacity he was based at Dodoma, our Provincial Headquarters, whence he made forays into the outlying districts. His function, like that of the South African LMO who featured earlier in this chapter, was to organise and conduct stock markets, thereby supporting, in Kondoa district, our efforts to reduce the domestic animal population. I was unaware of the full extent of Ivor's malpractices, but certainly he engaged in some private trade in sheep and cattle; and made a bit on the side by charging buyers and sellers a small commission for changing notes into coin. He was loud, uncouth, and in

---

[24] Not his real name.

appearance he could have stepped right out of one of Breughel's more bucolic paintings.

We did not see a great deal of Ivor, but on one rare occasion early in 1953 I was thankful that he was in the vicinity. I was on tour at Bereko again, this time with Sylvia and Oliver Cromwell, our dog. I had work in the area which would occupy me for the best part of a week, and since we had no transport of our own, we had been dumped there as usual with our baggage, and with Mzee to do the cooking. We would be picked up on Saturday. On the second day Sylvia complained of pains in her abdomen; they persisted through the night and were still there the next morning. We tended to be rather blasé about aches and pains, but it *could* be appendicitis. We were just about half way between two hospitals which were suitably equipped, one at Dodoma 140 miles to the south, and the other at Arusha 140 miles to the north in the next Province. We preferred Arusha; it was cooler, and we had yet to go there. But how to get there? If we waited at the roadside a bus or lorry would come along sooner or later, but it would be slow and uncomfortable.

Then I remembered that a cattle market was due to be held that day, just a mile or so down the road towards Kondoa. There could have been any one of several LMO's manning it, but in the event it turned out to be Ivor. I explained our predicament, and with only brief hesitation he kindly offered to run us up to Arusha in his Standard Vanguard pick-up. Whilst we waited for him to settle his business I entertained the curious by putting Oliver through his paces. He had only one trick, but it was infallible; no matter how prolonged the temptation he would never eat without permission. The onlookers were greatly impressed, one of them so much so that he offered £2.50 in cash for our hoodlum dog, nearly double the going rate for a cow that day. I felt Oliver would have been proud had he known how highly his comprehension and obedience had been valued; the offer was politely declined.

The journey to Arusha was hair-raising; more than once we wished we had taken our chance on a bus. There was so little traffic on the road that it could not fairly be said that Ivor drove with a total disregard for other road users. But he certainly drove with a total disregard for his own vehicle and for the safety of its occupants. We hurtled along trailing a cloud of dust, crashing into potholes, sliding into ruts, rattling over corrugations, thudding into the concrete drifts let into the road to take water across during the rains. It was a relief to reach the tarmac on the outskirts of Arusha three hours later.

At the hospital we described the symptoms to a decidedly offhand fellow-countryman. He suggested we return in the morning. At that I retorted that we hadn't come tearing all the way up from Kondoa in someone else's car to be fobbed off with such a casual response. He took the point, and admitted Sylvia immediately. A short time later, having examined her, he returned looking rather sheepish; they would take her appendix out immediately.

With that reassurance I had to be content; Ivor was champing at the bit, and anxious to get back to Dodoma. The return journey was no less terrifying than the afternoon's progress. We set off into the late afternoon sun, but soon swung southwards leaving the sun to our right and the road ahead clearer in consequence. As we charged across Masailand darkness fell and the temperature with it; apprehension was suppressed by the cold. Anxiety returned as five or six pairs of eyes caught the pickup's headlights a hundred yards ahead. Ivor was not a cautious driver, and our onward rush did not slacken. As we drew abreast of the eyes, an impala launched itself in a graceful slow-motion arc across the road. We caught it on the cab, killing it outright; the roof of the driving compartment was badly dented, which was less than Ivor deserved.

At Bereko we stopped briefly to pick up Mzee and our kit, and were back in Kondoa by ten. I thanked Ivor, and paid him for the petrol. He accelerated away with another hundred miles to go, leaving us choking in a cloud of dust. I walked up the front steps, still vibrating from the journey and clutching a bloody leg unceremoniously hacked from the impala, whilst Mzee and Issa humped the other boxes and bundles inside. Next morning a phone call to the Boma announced that Sylvia was well. A week later I took the office Landrover up to collect her from the home of a new-found friend; by one of those small and happy coincidences, the other occupant of her two-bed ward came from Basingstoke, her own home town.

Our next expedition to Arusha 10 months later also had a medical flavour, but this time there was no urgency. Our first child was due early in January 1954, and Dr. Apte recommended delivery at the better-equipped Arusha hospital. Having an eye to the station's New Year's Eve party, we settled on 1st January for our journey. A short-wheelbase Landrover was not the ideal mode of transport in which to take a heavily expectant mother a hundred and seventy miles on a road which differed from an average English farm track only in being worse and wider. However, we derived some assurance from the presence of a Rover Scout who had fortuitously arrived in Kondoa on New Year's Eve. He was hitchhiking from Cape Town to Cairo, and whether or not he had a badge in midwifery it struck us that he would be a useful travelling companion. Apart from the numbing discomfort and the need to stop at frequent intervals in response to Sylvia's recurring bouts of nausea, the journey was uneventful, and the Scout's assumed skills were not put to the test. Indeed the shaking and bumping along the road seemed to have knocked into the unborn Nicola a determination to stay put. She arrived three weeks late.

Some time afterwards a paragraph in an airmail edition of The Guardian caught my eye. The women of Cheam in Surrey were lobbying the Minister of Health because their nearest maternity hospital – nine miles distant – was too far away.

Domestic Life

The appearance of Nicola on the scene may serve as a convenient peg on which to hang a brief description of domestic and social life in a rural district; even a narrative describing the varied work of a DO would be unbalanced without it, and would also be unfair to our wives, who bore the brunt of the deficiencies in both. With young Nicola to look after, much of Sylvia's time was devoted to the responsibilities of motherhood, for which she showed conspicuous aptitude, and from which she derived much satisfaction. There had, of course, been no ante-natal clinic, nor was there any post-natal care; this was the norm. We had earlier jointly dismissed Dr. Benjamin Spock as subversive, and when instinct failed, Sylvia fell back on a single rather conservative 'owners manual' sent out from England, supplemented by occasional advice from neighbouring mothers. As might be expected, the local shops did not cater for the needs of expatriate infants; the pram came down from Nairobi, clothes, nappies and gripe water from our parents in UK, whilst a regular supply of powdered milk was brought by Harchand Singh's bus from Arusha, together with our weekly order of fresh perishable foodstuffs not available in Kondoa.

Mention has been made of housing; in Kondoa the airy German dwellings were supplemented by three or four inferior houses built since the end of the second world war. This mix was not uncommon, whilst some of the old German Bomas incorporated a flat for the DC. On many stations there were modern bungalows, roofed with Mangalore tiles imported from India, or corrugated iron, and generally just one room deep so that every room benefited from a through draught when there was even the hint of a breeze. The older houses usually had outside kitchens and pit or bucket latrines. If you were lucky your house was equipped with a 'Tanganyika boiler', an old oil drum mounted horizontally on a head-high plinth outside the house; a fire was lit underneath it late in the afternoon, and hot water was piped through to the bathroom. Alternatively, you had a galvanised steel bath for which water was heated on the kitchen range. Floors were of smooth cement, and were treated with red or green Cardinal polish by the occupants – or left bare. Heavy furniture was provided; this could be pre-war or modern, and was rarely replaced. The newer items were made to standard designs by the Public Works Department and the furniture of DC and his District Foreman came out of the same workshops; it was all very egalitarian. As for the eclectic mixes of office furniture, its origin was a mystery – I have no recollection of any of it ever being replaced in the five District Offices in which I served. My office chair was always of the upright kitchen variety, rendered slightly less uncomfortable by a kapok-filled cushion.

On the wider domestic front our rather primitive cooking arrangements have already been mentioned; after a few months trial and error, and with advice from Mzee, Sylvia had mastered the wood-burning stove and was familiar with the burning characteristics of different kinds of wood. There was no electricity, and light was provided by the soft glow of an Aladdin lamp, or the harsher, brighter, hotter and noisy Tilley pressure lamp. The piped water supply in Kondoa was relatively clean and clear; flowing from a spring in the township, it was directed along an open concrete furrow to the river bank where a combination of velocity and volume powered a Blake's Hydram which pushed a proportion of the flow up the hill to an elevated water tank, whence it was distributed to government premises and the township. As elsewhere, drinking water had to be boiled and filtered.

Earlier mention of paraffin refrigerators may have provoked passing curiosity. I have no more idea now than I had then as to how or why they worked, but they did. A fuel container in the base fed a wick contained within a small glass chimney which protected the flame from draughts and enabled one to see that it was burning correctly. A narrow flue ran up the back, and this was cleaned out every two or three days with a small brush at the end of a long wire. The wick had to be trimmed frequently to ensure even and reliable burning. Inside the 'fridge, below the ice compartment, was a drip tray which had to be emptied every few days. Provided that the routine maintenance was carried out and the tank kept topped up, these refrigerators were quite as efficient as electric ones, though there was always a slight smell of burning kerosene. Another minor marvel of paraffin technology was the Tilley iron; this worked on the same principle as the pressure lamp, burning vaporised fuel – in this case to generate heat rather than light. It was more manageable than the cumbersome charcoal iron with which we were all equipped.

Our house – Kondoa

It was usual to employ a brace of servants, although to some extent it went against the grain; however, with no electricity there were no labour-saving devices, and without servants, keeping house solo would have verged on drudgery. Our employment of Mzee and Issa after a few months in Kondoa was particularly felicitous, and they very soon promoted Sylvia from *memsabu* (madam) to *mama* or mother, which she much preferred; they

86

became friends with whom we kept in touch until their deaths in the 1980's.

Choice and availability of food was limited. Milk, usually with a slight bluish tinge, was delivered daily in a calabash by arrangement with a nearby cattle-owner; it had to be boiled. Eggs were similarly supplied, and tipped into a bowl of water to confirm freshness – or otherwise – before purchase. There was a small abattoir in the town, and meat of one's choice was roughly hacked or sliced from the carcass by a butcher in the market. Chickens not much larger than woodpigeons were purchased live and dealt with by the cook. In Kondoa, one of our predecessors had established a sizeable carp pond, and this provided us – and the townsfolk – with a little variety, although the local people more commonly enjoyed mudfish from the Bubu river. The range of vegetables in the market was small, rarely more than tomatoes, squashes, egg-plant, and *mchicha,* which after cooking approximated to spinach.

The commoner fruits were oranges, limes, pawpaw, mangoes, and diminutive bananas. In addition we had a small communal vegetable patch, irrigated by water from the furrow, and we clubbed together to pay the gardener, who was supervised in turn by one of the wives. Thus, from time to time we were able to enjoy a salad, French and broad beans, carrots, and – more rarely – strawberries and asparagus.

For basic groceries – and they *were* basic – we had recourse to the *dukas* of Ali Hamad and Abdullah Sajan; flour, cooking oil, tea, coffee, sugar, tinned butter, jam, fruit and vegetables, and packeted soup and condiments, and our essential supply of Tusker IPA and, at long intervals, a bottle of Scotch or brandy. A fairly clear picture should now be emerging of a necessarily rather frugal way of life in which luxuries were few; it will therefore come as no surprise to learn that there were no bars, cafés, restaurants, cinemas, hairdressing salons or other familiar amenities. As was the case in Kondoa, there was usually no garage. Petrol came out of a hand-pump screwed into a 44 gallon drum, and we serviced our own cars; the uninitiated such as myself, when we aspired to a car ownership, were helped and instructed by more experienced colleagues; as a rule repairs and replacements were adequately carried out.

'The Club', lampooned in literature, was to be found only in the capital and larger provincial towns; it did not feature in small up-country districts.

Our social round was less a whirl than a recycling of familiar, relaxed, and comfortable pleasures with colleagues and friends. A daily hour or two of tennis was usual, followed by drinks at one of our homes; if the mood was conducive this sometimes ran on into supper, when a hapless cook would be asked to prepare food for a few extra mouths. And we regularly invited each other in for an informal evening meal or, on Saturday, a curry lunch. We were always glad to see and entertain visitors, and from time to time one of us would throw a party, often multi-racial. It was at the first such party, hosted by Cecil, that we got to know Mganga Kingu; he was the District Council's clerk of works, a quietly-spoken, conscientious, and intelligent young Rangi with a ready smile and a nice sense of humour. On this occasion he explained to Sylvia and me that, as Muslims sometimes did, he was about to take a second wife; the first was now helping him choose, with a view to avoiding future domestic discord. On longer acquaintance I thought that given the opportunity he would make a good DO; I was glad to hear, many years later, that he had become Comptroller of State House, the Presidential residence.

If our social life sounds unexciting, that is probably a fair assessment; but it was friendly and familiar, and there was always plenty to talk about. Large stations could be very cliquey, with mutually hostile factions; no doubt some smaller stations were riven with personality clashes, but in our own experience the small community thrown upon its own modest resources, was a happy one. *Not* to get on would have been too awful to contemplate.

There were other diversions. Sylvia took up collecting butterflies and moths, but soon abandoned it for humanitarian reasons. Then three of us briefly tried our hand at making kites but found that flying them soon palled. Prompted by this aeronautical experience Douglas and I introduced the art of making paper darts and gliders to boys at the Native Authority middle school; we then held a competition and presented a balsa glider to the boy whose paper version stayed aloft longest. Then there were occasional weekend picnics, and sallies to nearby Bicha lake to try for a duck or two. To my chagrin, having been designated a marksman in the army, I was a hopeless performer with a shotgun, and replaced it with a .22 rifle which I found more productive. The shotgun I sold to Sylvester, referee at the Coronation football match; shortly afterwards he appeared at our front door one Sunday with five ducks which he had bagged sitting with a single cartridge. He generously handed one over in appreciation of his new acquisition.

Some officials engaged in big game hunting and took out the requisite game licences; it was not unusual to supplement a modest income by shooting an elephant a year and selling the ivory to Government, which in turn auctioned it off to boost national revenues. A contempory fellow-cadet, Jerry Nettleton, was a keen hunter; he was trampled to death by an imperfectly-shot elephant whilst hunting on local leave.

For some officials and their wives, gardening was something of a passion; we were never amongst them, and the climate in Central Province in particular was not conducive to successful horticulture. Most garden compounds were enlivened by a few bougainvilleas, frangipani, and perhaps oleander and lantana, with a high probability of the climber golden shower along the verandah. Apart from this *we* never got beyond a row of canna lilies and some half-hearted zinnias wherever we were located. In the more favoured districts flower gardens colourfully and exuberantly rewarded the effort put into them.

We were not slow to seize opportunities for modest entertainment; thus it seemed a good idea at the time for three cars-full of us to drive from Kondoa to Dodoma, a round trip of 200 miles, to see the film of the Coronation. I was deputed to stay behind and hold the fort, and Sylvia chose to keep me company. On another occasion, a much publicised dash from Nairobi in Kenya to Salisbury (Harare) in Southern Rhodesia was being undertaken to demonstrate the robustness of the latest Morris Minor, not normally the vehicle of choice for African roads. We thought the driver might like some encouragement, and following his progress by radio, we assembled on the Great North Road at around midnight and hung about for an hour or more with a Tilley lamp and a crate of IPA to cheer him on his way and offer brief refreshment. He was running late, and not at all appreciative of the delay.

Most evenings were, as in UK, spent at home in unexciting domesticity. We had a weekly airmail newspaper from London, and magazines sent by Sylvia's mother; there was a brisk exchange of books between households, and the monthly offering from World Books was always welcome. Short-wave reception on our radios was appalling, ensuring minimum pleasure with maximum frustration; and having the battery recharged was a chore. There was, of course, no television. Long-play gramophone records had arrived, albeit not yet in rural Tanganyika, and we decided to await the advent of battery-driven LP turntables. Evenings could be particularly tiresome for our wives. The men often had some work best done at home without interruption by colleagues or *shauri*, so that there was less companionship at home than there should have been. Absorbed in my work, and married to an uncomplaining wife, I was blithely unaware of this consideration at the time. It was often a lonely life for wives, most of whom had not after all chosen to live in rural Africa; it was their husbands who had made this rather odd, and for them satisfying, career choice. Some wives revelled in Africa and were immune to its shortcomings. But by and large even those who would have preferred a more conventional life in their home countries were supportive of their husbands in their various rôles; and like them, were always 'on call' in one capacity or another.

Nor was there, up-country, much opportunity for employment; there were no commercial concerns, and Government, rightly, would not employ expatriate wives to do work which could be done by Africans. It was sometimes possible to do voluntary work for an existing organisation, but to initiate it required fluency in Swahili, and a temperament for which the colonial wife has often been unfairly caricatured.

Domestic life embraced a kaleidoscope of features absent in north-west Europe; the range of intrusive creepy-crawlies; the daily spraying with insecticide to control mosquitoes – an insecticide laced with DDT, long since banned; the pantomime of getting half a bitter Paludrine tablet into a squalling infant every breakfast time; mosquito nets, the unavailing battle with the ineradicable cockroaches with which all our kitchens were alive. Then there were poisonous snakes, which although rarely encountered, kept one on the qui vive; and hyenas rummaging through the contents of the dustbin were a common nocturnal event. Brief reference has been made to medical facilities; these were as good as a cash-strapped Government could afford. Most of us were basically fit anyway, in consequence of the thorough medical examination prior to appointment; Government did not want us expiring in service, nor to incur the cost of invalidity pensions. In Kondoa Sylvia had malaria once, quite badly, and a prolonged bout of amoebic dysentery; my second dose of malaria was contracted concurrently with the variety of hepatitis then known as yellow jaundice, a combination which kept me off work for a month. Two years later, in Masasi, the year-old child of an Italian colleague working on a water pipeline died of cerebral malaria.

In short, domestic life was generally simple, uncluttered, unrushed, and blissfully quiet – a combination not invariably appreciated.

* * *

Oliver Cromwell has been mentioned earlier; Sylvia fell for him shortly after her own arrival in Manyoni when feeling the first pangs of homesickness. He was a nondescript dog, and his name, we thought, gave him a dignity and stature which he otherwise lacked. It turned out to be an ill-chosen one, for he was never remotely puritanical.

At three months or so he came with us when we were transferred to Kondoa, and it was here that he began to show signs of juvenile delinquency. His talents in this direction were considerable, and in due course we resigned ourselves to ownership of a permanently disorderly adult dog. His trick of not eating without permission has already been described. On one occasion, having put a plate of food under his nose in the kitchen, I held up a finger and withdrew, intending to check on his resolution through another door to the rear. At this juncture our attention was diverted by a caller and Oliver was forgotten. Half an hour or more later, when re-discovered, he was still sitting there looking at his plate, a large pool of saliva on the floor under his chops. This of course was not the act of a wholly undisciplined dog; it was his Dr.Jekyll. His Mr. Hyde was manifested in his occasional disappearances for two or three days at a time; he would return from these expeditions with a torn ear or stiffened blood-clotted limb, and either full of bounce or thoroughly exhausted. One of his less engaging activities was to raid the local abattoir, from which he would return proudly dragging some unmentionable piece of offal, and invariably smelling to high heaven. On these occasions Issa would be deputed to dispose of the cow's tail or length of intestine or whatever it was, whilst I would drag Oliver to the tap outside the kitchen door and give him a good dousing, finishing off with a bucket of weak Dettol solution to mask any lingering odour of decay.

After some weeks in Kondoa Oliver developed delusions of grandeur, or claustrophobia – we were never sure which. He either thought he was human and entitled to be wherever *we* were, or else he simply disliked being locked up. Now life up-country was relatively informal and relaxed, but on the whole dogs did not accompany their owners to dinner parties. We were therefore mortified on the first such occasion to find Oliver scratching and whining at our hosts' door; to conserve peace and quiet he was admitted. Later investigations revealed that he had torn his way out through the copper mosquito gauze of our front door – no great feat this, though he must have burned his claws in the process.

The next time we went out in the evening I chained him to the leg of our dining table, a substantial piece of furniture which it took two people to move. From our neighbour's house we could hear him yowling, and on our return we found that he had torn the cane seat out of one of the dining chairs and chewed his alumininium bowl into a shapeless lump. He was delighted to see us.

At the time we lived in one of the substantial German-built bungalows. The inner core of the house consisted of a gloomy sitting room and bedroom; round this ran a seven-foot verandah, partitioned off in one rear corner to form a kitchen. One side was used as a dining room and the rest was just unused and unfurnished space. After some months of occupation we were excited and cheered by the news that we were to have an internal W.C. instead of the outside privy with its 'thunderbox' or bucket latrine which was emptied daily; moreover, a real bathroom with a full-length plumbed-in bath was to replace the portable tin one. The verandah would have sliding glazed windows as well as mosquito gauze. The relevance of all this to Oliver's social behaviour will soon be apparent. The workmen came in and filled the house with dust. A section of the verandah adjacent to the bedroom at the rear was walled off and took shape as a bathroom. Here, as work neared completion, a cast iron bath was placed prior to installation; in the outside wall a hole had been knocked to take out the waste pipe.

A week or two after Oliver had demolished the cane chair we were invited to dinner with the Goodes; this time I was determined that Oliver should be both secure and unheard, and took him into the new bathroom. Here I pushed an eighteen inch cement block across the hole in the outer wall and chained Oliver to one of the legs of the bath. I left through the robust door with its heavy brass handle and locked it. We had been at the Goodes for perhaps ten minutes when Oliver appeared through the door from the kitchen, his chain trailing behind him, tail waving furiously. Almost immediately he went to sleep under Sylvia's chair. Thereafter it was accepted that when we went out in the evening Oliver came too.

In similar fashion he established his right to accompany us on safari on the occasions when Sylvia joined me. Precedent was established thus: going out for the day in the Boma Landrover – to Bereko again! – I instructed Issa to hang on to Oliver's lead for five minutes following our departure; by then I reckoned we would be well away, even allowing for our sluggish progress over the heavily corrugated road out of Kondoa. This ran straight as a ruler out to its junction with the Great North Road at Bicha; there, before turning northwards, we stopped to make sure. Our own dust had been blown away from the road, and we were able to see clearly behind us for a little over a mile before it swung right into Kondoa. And there, on the straight, was a small puff of dust coming towards us. It could only be Oliver, although it was a minute or two before he was identifiable. We could not go on, and chose not to take him back. A very dusty dog came with us to Bereko; when we were fifteen miles north he was still panting.

During our leave in England Oliver stayed with Mzee. Five months later we met again in Dar-es-Salaam, and went on to Lindi and later Masasi. Here Oliver came to an untimely end, and one which was inappropriate to his character. He got a canker in his ear, and there being no vet, a mission doctor removed it; but knowing nothing about animal anaesthetics she overdid the chloroform. When I carried him home he was still alive, but he never came round; and when we saw the ants walking in and out of his mouth we realised he never would. His life had been a short one, but vigorously and joyfully spent; it seemed not quite right that he departed it with a whimper rather than a bang.

Departure

Our first tour turned out to be a short one of only two years; having passed my law and lower Swahili examinations, and demonstrated that I was not a complete duffer, I was confirmed in my appointment, and so would be returning to Tanganyika after a spell of home leave. Sylvia preceded me by a month, and at our farewell party we were told that our home for the previous fifteen months was allegedly haunted by the ghost of a German officer who had committed suicide there forty or fifty years earlier. There had been a collective decision not to tell us lest either of us were superstitious. We never saw any spectral manifestations, though there were occasional nocturnal bumps in our roof space; these I attributed to bats or the acrobatics of the colony of bushy-tailed mice which shared our quarters.

Burdened by suitcase and capacious carrycot which doubled as the top half of a pram, Sylvia took the daily bus to Dodoma, a bumpy 100 mile journey, thence the train to Dar es Salaam, and finally a BOAC [25]'Hermes' to London.

By the day of my own departure all that remained was a bachelor lunch with Cecil and Douglas prior to arrival of the bus. The meal was a leisurely affair, its progress determined by a temperamental wood-burning stove and a temperamental cook. The bus was due to leave at two o'clock, and at ten to, with the pudding not yet arrived, Cecil sensed my agitation and sent his houseboy or steward to await arrival of the bus and ask the driver to come up to the house to collect me. The bus pulled up outside just as we were polishing off a plum pie. I prepared to make a move, but Cecil insisted on coffee; the antique fine china cans in silver holders contrasted with the ample but crude house, and pre-war Government issue furniture which a suburban English housewife might well have turned up her nose at.

In fact we probably held up the bus by no more than ten minutes, and road conditions or breakdown could have delayed it a good deal longer anywhere along the 270 miles between Arusha and Dodoma; during the rains it sometimes didn't arrive at all. My baggage already stowed, I climbed aboard light-headedly, a condition induced by a combination of a couple of bottles of Tusker beer and an awareness that a chapter in my personal history was closing. Cecil was to be transferred to Nyasaland (Malawi) on promotion, so it was unlikely that we would ever work together again; it really *was* goodbye to a fine DC who had also been a forbearing guide, mentor and friend. During our next tour of duty in Southern Province, he wrote to announce his marriage

---

[25] British Overseas Airways Corporation; the Handley Page 'Hermes' was the first four-engined British airliner after the Second World War which was not a converted military aircraft.

to Maudie Lee, whose visits had brightened my week in hospital in Dar es Salaam. Our wedding present, in the form of a cheque, provided them with an evening at Glyndebourne. When next we met some fifteen years later, Cecil was Finance Director of the Royal Society for the Protection of Birds. Douglas I was to meet again sooner than I had expected.

Also at the bus to see me off were Mzee and Issa who, paid several months' retainer, would be looking after Oliver Cromwell, and joining us again when we returned from leave. And there was Kisoi Sogoi, the elderly senior Boma messenger; he was a gentle and thoughtful man from whom I, latest in a succession of cadets, had learned much, with his knowledge of local custom, history, and personalities. He died not long after independence, respected in his home village, and probably never wholly aware of the regard we birds of passage had had for him.A short tour meant a relatively short leave; this soon passed, and notification of my next posting prompted the wish for an even earlier return to Tanganyika.

The Irangi escarpment

Street scene, Kondoa

Kondoa river in the dry season

Kondoa market

Sylvia; on safari, Farkwa

Soil erosion, Irangi highlands

Farewell party, Bereko

Giant baobab, Kondoa

On tour, Lindi district

Main trunk road inland during rains, Lindi district

Our household staff, Mzee Hamsini and Issa Saidi

Main street, Masasi

Mr Sharif's superior shop, Masasi

On tour, Masasi district

Author in village baraza, Masasi district

Playing 'bao'

Mbangala river in flood, Masasi district

Liwali Mohamed with messenger and bystanders outside his court

Police constable at colleague's grave

The prison band at Masasi

CHAPTER FOUR

Lindi and Masasi

Lindi

On my first tour of duty I had sailed on 13th August; now at the end of four months leave we departed from Tilbury in the *Warwick Castle* on 13th January,1955.

The passenger list was made up very largely of the prosperous elderly and middle-aged intent on escaping the rigours of an English winter by taking the two-month voyage round Africa. Prominent amongst them was the Cockney owner of a Blackpool snack bar who was anxious to be back before Easter Week; he reckoned to make several thousand pounds over the Bank Holiday weekend, and wanted to make sure that none of it went astray.

He was not a shy man and with his strong Anglo-Saxon ethnocentricity was a rich source of quiet amusement as we progressed beyond the Straits of Gibraltar, reacting with hostility or indignation to the customs of French, Italians, and Egyptians in turn. In Kenya, avoiding the boredom of a week in Kilindini harbour, he and his wife embarked on a brief safari up-country with one of the local tour firms. He returned in a state of high dudgeon, having discovered that the real Africa did not conform with the sanitised version promoted by the tour operators. The substance of his complaint was that Africa was Africa, lacking the most rudimentary amenities. The last straw occurred when their vehicle became bogged down following a prolonged and heavy downpour, and all passengers had been required to get out and push, ankle deep in mud. He was still going on about it when we reached Dar es Salaam a week later.

Here we were met by Mzee and Issa, with Oliver Cromwell in attendance. I called on my head of department to be briefed about my new posting, and signed the visitors' book at Government House. Thereafter we were free to explore and gather a few supplies pending the arrival of the coastal steamer

106

which was to bear us southwards. The *Mombasa*, a tubby little black and white vessel belonging to the British India Line, was due two days later. The overnight journey with three of us and our baggage crammed into a diminutive cabin was not a comfortable one; next day we anchored at Lindi, the old port and former Provincial Headquarters in Southern Province, which had been upstaged in both capacities by Mtwara, built to meet the needs of the Nachingwea part of the ill-conceived Groundnut Scheme which was even then tottering to failure.

Dhow – Lindi   DB

Expecting to go on to Mtwara to meet my new Provincial Commissioner, alarm bells sounded when a DO came aboard and told us that we were to disembark at Lindi; he took us ashore and to the DC's house where, he said, we were to spend a few nights.

Some of his casual observations aroused further misgivings, which were later confirmed by the DC, Tony Golding. Whilst on leave I had received a letter from the Secretariat to say that I was to go to Newala as DC; this was something I might reasonably have aspired to several years later, and the prospect was therefore one which, with only two years under my belt, I viewed with both satisfaction and trepidation. The posting had been confirmed in Dar, where I had been told the problems and personalities of the district, and we were promised a marvellous view from the combined Boma and quarters on the edge of the Makonde escarpment, overlooking the Ruvuma valley and Portuguese East Africa. But it was not to be, and we stayed in Lindi where, with some mortification, I found myself the junior of two DOs. Why and how my posting had been changed was never revealed; Tony Golding did not know, and only just confirmed in my appointment, I was too junior to kick up a fuss. The only person to whom I could have made representations was my PC, Donald Troup, and it was presumably he who had engineered my diversion to Lindi. I only ever met him once, and did not warm to him; I was perhaps prejudiced.

It was some consolation that Tony Golding was a good DC to work with. Quite fortuitously his senior DO was not characterised by either zeal or competence, so Tony shared the more responsible duties with me, leaving my fellow DO with routine tasks of lesser importance. Fortunately DOs did not stand in a hierarchical relationship to each other, and both or all were answerable to the DC for their allocated duties; there was therefore no question of the senior DO pulling rank, and he seemed well content with the distribution of work between us. Tony Golding had had a colourful life. Born in India, and brought up there, in Britain, New Zealand and Kenya, he had served in the King's African Rifles in the campaign against the Italians in Ethiopia and the Horn of Africa, then in the Somaliland Gendarmerie and finally as a Political Officer in the Military Administration of Italian Somaliland.

Lindi was a rather run-down but bustling and pleasant little town with a population of perhaps ten or eleven thousand, mostly African of course, but with many Asians, and enough Europeans to support a club. In the vicinity were a number of sisal estates, a European-owned dairy farm, and the Steel Brothers timber concession managed by a Mr. Lovat-Campbell, who had rather old-fashioned colonial ideas. Some weeks after arrival I was sent off to investigate his claim that Africans were illegally extracting some of his timber, which involved an adrenaline-inducing flight in his light aircraft from his base on the Rondo plateau. We spotted one log being removed and I took what action I could through the Native Authority; it was not practicable to police the whole concession, but we managed a couple of prosecutions by way of a deterrent.

Lindi was set on the inner curve of a wide, sweeping bay with superb beaches which ran for miles to the north. On the harbour overlooking the estuary of the Lukuledi river was a pleasant but faded hotel which served memorable prawns, and two or three miles to the north at Ras Bura was a rustic bar cum restaurant; here were a secluded beach and several wooden cabins built for the recreation of the Nachingwea groundnutters a hundred miles inland. The short-lived Groundnut Scheme had been initiated by the Ministry of Food in Britain shortly after the war, to make good the severe shortage of edible oil. Two sites were selected, and large swathes of bush were cleared at great cost and with inadequate equipment in Central and Southern Provinces. By the early 1950s the projects were already being wound up, the assets disposed of, and the land intended for large-scale groundnut (peanut) production being put to other use.

A little way up the estuary were salt-pans which flooded at every tide, and where mounds of dazzlingly white salt awaited bagging and transport, and provided the Indian licensees with a handsome income. Close by was a seasonal anchorage for Arab dhows which traded across the Arabian Sea. An eclectic mix of products was imported, from carpets to Mangalore roofing tiles from India; and mangrove poles were a typical return cargo for the Arabian peninsula.

Our home in Lindi was a one-bedroom pre-war bungalow once belonging to Imperial Airways[26], and occupied by one of their radio operators. It sat on Wireless Hill overlooking the bay, though none of its gloomy rooms did; to enjoy the view and the sea breeze we had to go outside. For want of a second bedroom, Nicola slept on a verandah protected by mosquito gauze. But at least we had electricity, a fan, and clean mains water, and there was an excellent hospital should need arise.

In the circumstances of my arrival in Lindi I always felt a little detached, and was slow to immerse myself in the social round. However, there were events recollected with pleasure and amusement; one such was a tiring but enjoyable three-day foot safari with Martin Simmonds the Agricultural Officer, to check on the progress of cassava-planting in a remote corner of the district. One day it rained almost continuously, and on arrival at our camp site we were soaked. Dried out and rain stopped, we discussed matters of local concern with the village headman, enjoyed the watery sunset, and settled down to the usual safari fare of desiccated chicken and potatoes. A little later, the headman enquired if we would like to see some traditional dancing, and of course we concurred. It was then about eight o'clock. By ten the promised dancers had still not appeared,

---

[26] Later British Overseas Airways Corporation, and British Airways.

the camp fire had burned down to embers, and we turned in.

At about three in the morning we were woken by some tentative tapping as drum-skins were tautened over a revived fire, and then we were treated to the full monty. Martin and I were less appreciative than we would have been five hours earlier, but felt obliged to give half an hour's attention, and a few shillings pourboire; then back to bed. The dancers never turned up. In the morning the headman confessed that there were no musicians or dancers in the immediate vicinity, and had summoned the unfortunate drummers from several miles away. We hoped that our payment was adequate compensation for their trouble.

Lindi was a low-lying district, with rainfall spread over several months; unlike Kondoa, the landscape was one of lush vegetation, with coconut palms, cashew and mango trees in the settled areas. It was whilst strolling through the bush after carrying out a school inspection that I fell foul of the buffalo bean. It grows wild, and has a hairy pod; when dry the hairs drop off at the slightest provocation, in this case at the unwitting touch of an unobservant DO. Suddenly, for no reason that I could immediately discern, my upper body and legs burst into flames – or so it seemed. I sprinted back to camp, tearing off my shirt, and shouted to Issa to throw a bucket of water over me. This helped, and after a more leisurely bath and a change of clothes, I felt more or less restored; but discomfort lingered for another day or two.

The following day the local headman produced a group of parents – all fathers – and their truant children, in expectation that I would give them a severe rollicking. Duty required me to go through the motions, but the headman must have been disappointed at my inability to muster the hoped-for degree of wrath. When I'd finished my lecture there was some shuffling of feet in the dust, and a spokesman rather sheepishly admitted their collective failure to ensure their children's attendance at school. He then suggested that I give each of them a beating, an invitation which I declined, with a recommendation that they do their own dirty work. School attendance was variable throughout the country, and in this predominantly Muslim area attitudes to education were very ambivalent, whilst anywhere the needs of the family farmstead could take precedence over school. Shortly before independence, when I was in Lake Province, the Provincial Education Officer reported an enrolment of only about 80% in one of his secondary schools; this despite the small number of places then available.

Over a period of four or five months I began familiarising myself with the district, with the usual routine visits to local courts to review cases, hear an occasional appeal, check the accounts, relieve clerks of poll tax and market dues which they had collected, and get to know the local Native Authorities, here called *Liwalis*. The conventional European view of Africa expected indigenous societies to have chiefs with whom to negotiate, and later through whom to rule. Where they did not exist, as in the coastal region of Tanganyika, they were created. And so the Germans appointed the *Liwalis* as substitutes for non-existent chiefs; they were to a limited extent repositories of Islamic and tribal tradition, but were essentially an administrative device, lacking the authority and respect of traditional chiefs. The British inherited this arrangement and saw no reason to change it. As with Native Authorities elsewhere the *Liwalis* were responsible, with their councils and staff, for public order, the administration of native law and custom, the enforcement of local bye-laws, the collection of revenue, and the implementation of a range of minor public works.

On to Masasi

After six months in Lindi, just as we were beginning to feel at home and with some sense of belonging, I was transferred to Masasi, a hundred miles inland. The DC there wanted a married DO to replace a recently-departed bachelor, and I was succeeded by an unmarried Maltese DO in Lindi. It was disappointing to leave the amenities of Lindi behind, the sea, and newly-made friends; Sylvia felt this more acutely than I, and whilst in Masasi we drove down to Lindi for a weekend three or four times a year, staying with friends or in one of the groundnutters' chalets at Ras Bura. We had not accumulated many possessions, but repacking our trunks and crates again after such a short interval was tiresome. We saw our baggage off by road transport, with Mzee and Issa also on board, and then set off westwards in our new Opel station-waggon which had accompanied us from UK. The road took us through Mingoyo and Mtama, where there was a major grain storage depot, insurance against serious food shortages; this was supervised part-time by the likeable father of our rather academic Provincial Agricultural Officer. He also owned and ran the little bar perched above the beach at Ras Bura. Just beyond Mtama was a small and melancholy graveyard of imperial troops, mainly British, who died in the 1914-18 East African campaign.

War cemetery — Mtama

Another thirty miles, and we were in Masasi District. Wholly rural, and with a township of perhaps a thousand souls, Masasi boasted a small Native Authority dairy farm, a mission hospital and middle school, a piped water supply from a nearby dam, and a prison dating back to German times. The district's spiritual needs were catered for by two major Christian institutions; the Universities' Mission to Central Africa (UMCA) which had a cathedral and Bishop at Mtandi just down the road from the township, and the Benedictines (OSB) who had an even larger establishment twelve or fifteen miles along the road to Lindi. In addition to a Bishop and cathedral, they had a hospital, leprosarium, agricultural school, boys' and girls' secondary schools, and their own private printing press. This concentration of missionary activity was further manifested in a number of outlying mission stations, another leprosy outpatient clinic and two hospitals, four secondary schools and over fifty primary schools of one denomination or the other[27]; education and health provision was, by Tanganyika standards, very good.

---

[27] This in addition to Native Authority schools.

Masasi district was low-lying, and either flat or gently undulating, enlivened by a scattering of dramatic inselbergs, rocky outcrops varying in height from about a hundred to two or three hundred feet (30-90m). To the south east was the Makonde plateau, comprising most of Newala District, and to the south the Ruvuma river. Natural vegetation was not as lush as on the coast, but the general impression was of well-wooded country, green rather than brown for most of the year; on a misty morning at dawn, the aspect from our verandah was not unlike English parkland. Rainfall was generally reliable and plentiful; food shortages were rare, and consistent surpluses augmented by cash crops provided peasant households with modest incomes.

Masasi's 3500 square miles had a population of some 150,000, mainly Makua and Yao, but also Makonde, Mawia, and Mwera. They had much in common, and by the 1940's were so thoroughly mixed on the ground that the typical connection of tribe to locality had gone. This detracted from the rôle and effectiveness of the traditional chiefs, and to improve local government the district had been divided into six administrative areas, each with a *Liwali* appointed on merit. These were now well established; the oldest was Mohamed, a wise and urbane sixty-year-old, the newest Benedict Achimpota, an educated youngster in his thirties.

Most of the expatriate official households in Masasi were accommodated in bungalows of standard post-war construction, with Mangalore tile roofs. Ours backed onto a rocky kopje, with a vista of flat farmland to the south and east, and granite inselbergs pressing close to the north. This was to be home for the next two and a half years.

As in Kondoa and Lindi I was fortunate with my DC, Ronald Neath; he and his wife Jill and their two children were next-door neighbours. Ron had served in the RNVR during the war, latterly on the battleship *Duke of York;* like most, though by no means all, post-war entrants to the Colonial Service, he held liberal views which were in tune with moderate and thoughtful African opinion. We got on well together, and saw eye to eye on most local matters.

113

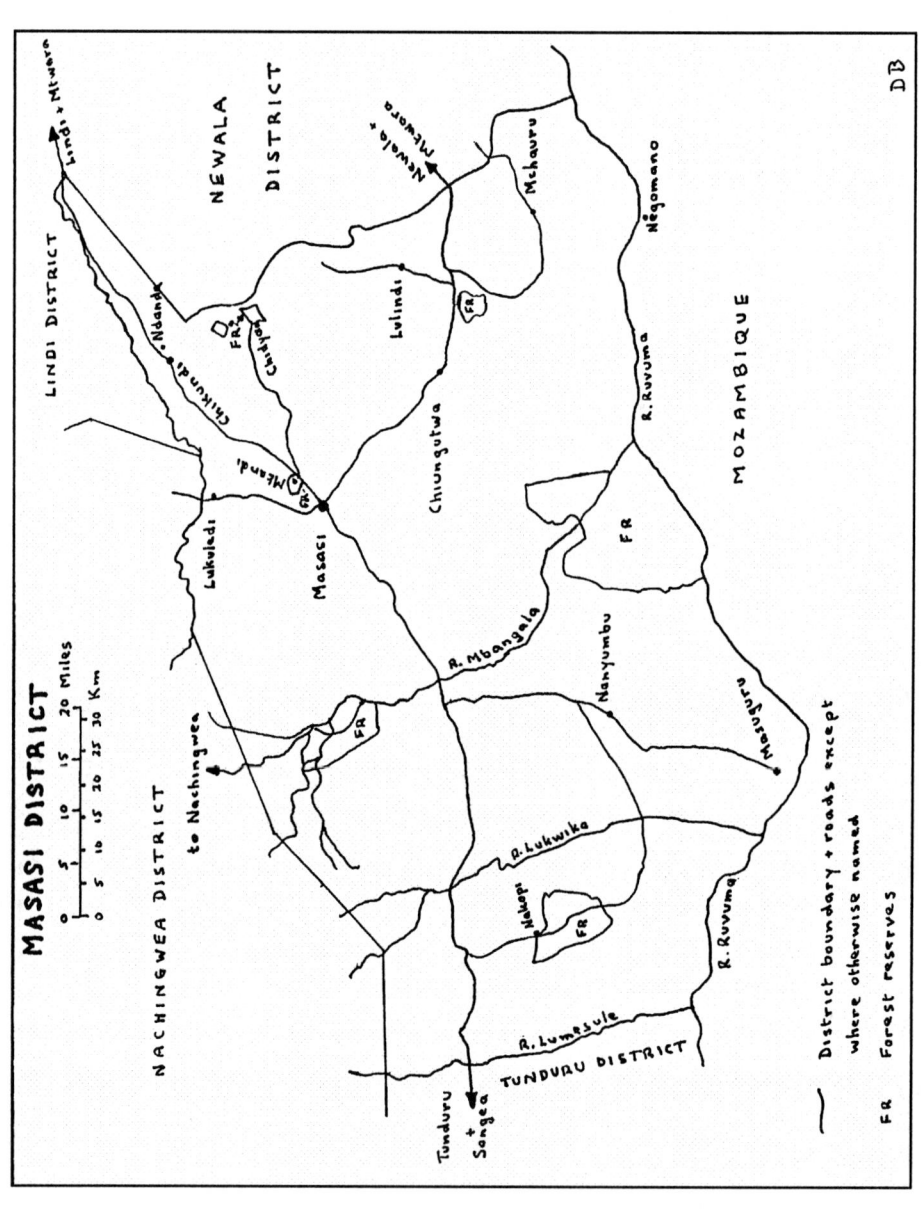

The rest of the official community was not precisely the same as in Kondoa; there was no Settlement Officer, and no need for a qualified vet as the only stock in the district were the twenty or so head of cattle at the NA farm. There was a sizeable Water Development Department depot with a number of expatriate staff engaged in bringing water down via several pipelines from the Makonde plateau in Newala district to various population centres in Masasi district. Three of them were Italians, one of whom had been taken prisoner by the Ethiopians during the war. He was one of a group awaiting their turn to have their heads lopped off when they were rescued by a British army patrol; in consequence of this terrifying experience, he had developed a pronounced facial tic.

In my second year a newly-appointed African ADO (Assistant District Officer) was posted to us; previously a Medical Assistant, Austin Shaba was a capable young man from Nyasaland, who resigned after a year or two to embark on a full-time political career. He was subsequently elected to the Legislative Council, and after independence served for a spell as Deputy Minister for Local Government, and later as Minister of Health. Other senior African staff were the Police Inspector, Head Warder at the prison, and a Head Tax Clerk who was permanently on the verge of dismissal owing to his fondness for the bottle. As was often the case, an Indian clerk ran the Government cash office. Masasi, like Kondoa, had an outposted Road Foreman who reported directly to his boss in Mtwara. A Scot married to a Belgian, the couple chose to live resolutely apart from the rest of us; I met them only twice in over two years residence.

Our domestic and social lives were much as described earlier. As in Kondoa we had a communal vegetable garden, here located below the dam which supplied Masasi township with water. The only decent cut of meat was to be had from a butcher's shop in Nachingwea, and our wives took it in turn to make the sixty-mile round trip on Saturday mornings to buy meat for the whole station. Our entertainment was enhanced by subscription to an informal cinema club, and we had a film flown down from Dar es Salaam every month or so – again to be collected from and returned to Nachingwea. The films were shown in the courtroom at the Boma, with invited Africans admitted free.

A family diversion

Settled into our new post, we had the pleasing task early in 1956 of arranging the wedding of my sister Pat, to Douglas Turner, one of my colleagues in Kondoa. They had met when Douglas visited my mother whilst on leave, and within days were engaged to be married. Pat arrived at Nachingwea airfield a week or so in advance in order to acclimatise, having come direct from the tail end of an English winter; Douglas appeared a few days later after a circuitous journey from Kondoa. The service was conducted by Canon Faussett in Masasi cathedral, and I stood in for my absent father; as we left a sizeable proportion of the local population were gathered, mostly out of curiosity since expatriate weddings were not a commonplace event. Sylvia, pregnant at the time, wrought a small miracle with the subsequent reception, catering for the whole expatriate community, including the UMCA mission. It was a personal pleasure that, wearing the Registrar of Births, Marriages, and Deaths hat, I signed my sister's marriage certificate. Afterwards, I drove the newlyweds to a rendezvous with a hired Landrover and driver; thence they had a hundred-mile journey to Mtwara where they spent a less than luxurious night in the Government Rest-house.

About a month later our son Nigel was born in Nachingwea District Hospital; it was a difficult birth and the officiating doctor advised that we should not contemplate a third child unless we were in England, or a country with comparable medical facilities. A few weeks afterwards we took a fortnight's local leave and drove up to Kondoa to visit Douglas and Pat, a four-day journey in both directions. On our return we employed an *ayah* or nursemaid for the first time, to help out during Nigel's first year, during which time Sylvia was also suffering from anaemia. Mariamu was a cheerful young woman, and thoroughly reliable; we were sorry to have to pay her off when Sylvia decided it was time to resume full-time responsibility for the children.

In Masasi we attempted to put a personal stamp on our quarters. We had brought a carpet out from England with us to liven up our next sitting room, and had some curtains made up with material purchased from Maples. We were also a little tired of cream walls, and splashed out on some cheerful emulsion paint from Lindi. Our standard issue of furniture was supplemented by a couple of pieces which I had made in my father-in-law's workshop whilst on leave, a desk and some chairs made to my design by a mission trade school, and a carpenter's bench which I installed in our car port. By this time battery-operated long-playing gramophone turntables were available; we purchased a lightweight Phillips model which thriftily utilised a 6-volt dry battery. This I incorporated in a home-made radiogram together with a new transistor radio. Our first half dozen records were ordered from England, and thereafter we topped up frugally on our occasional visits to Lindi; they were a source of much pleasure.

It was in Masasi that Oliver Cromwell breathed his last; not long afterwards, and quite fortuitously, we acquired Rack, a fully-grown black springer spaniel cross. It was some time before he grew out of his initial nervousness, but thereafter was loyally attached to Sylvia; so much so that on one occasion when we had our delightful visiting deputy PC in for dinner, Rack nipped him smartly on the ankle when, on entering, he swept Sylvia into his arms to take advantage of the Strauss waltz then issuing from our radiogram. He seemed not to hold it against me. Our new dog also contrived to put us at risk from snakebite. His favourite occupation when not sitting under Sylvia's chair or dogging her footsteps, was the pursuit of lizards. One day a lizard turned out to be a snake, and Rack crept into the house with his face swollen like a football, and laid it on the cool cement floor. I sent Issa to the NA farm to summon the manager, who had some slight veterinary knowledge, and ended up handing over our anti-snakebite serum for injection into our very forlorn dog. At least we had the satisfaction of knowing that it worked, but the serum, purchased by mail from South Africa, was not replaced. Rack, like Oliver, met an untimely end; he was inadvertently run over by a colleague who had volunteered to look after him on our next long leave.

Magisterial matters

Mick McCarthy was a Kerry man. He didn't talk much about himself, and his antecedents were, if not a closely guarded secret, obscure. He had been in Tanganyika at the time of the small-scale gold rush in the 1930's, on 'the Lupa' in Southern Highlands Province. For him as for many of the prospectors of the period who stayed on in East Africa, the bare landscape of Chunya had revealed no riches. In his mid-fifties he was settled in Masasi, where he lived in a mud-brick thatched house, a typical bachelor establishment, ramshackle, untidy, sparsely furnished, and uncurtained. Here he was looked after by one or two servants at a time, but they changed frequently, testimony to their frailty in the face of Mick's alternating moods of generosity and temper.

By way of a living, Mick built houses and schools, markets, dispensaries, and whatever the local Native Authority contracted with him to be done; he was a reliable builder who gave value for money in the very modest and Spartan specifications which district revenues ran to. As far as we could judge Mick did not eat, and the two pillars of his internal economy were whisky and beer. An innocent conversation with Mr. Sharif, our local shopkeeper, revealed that Mick's monthly drinks bill was greater than mine for food and drink, and we had four mouths to feed – though only two of them of drinking age! His grocery bill was exiguous.

Mick was a bit of a loner, but he enjoyed an occasional evening out with one of the expatriate families. On those occasions he would squeeze his ample figure into a threadbare white drill suit and honour his hosts with a tie; indeed, by going to these lengths he usually shamed me, for my more usual gesture to civilised standards was merely to substitute trousers for shorts after sundown. Invited out, and knowing that his capacity for drink could make serious inroads into our meagre household budgets, he would invariably and thoughtfully bring his own bottle of whisky. And he would, true to the general supposition that he did not actually eat, sit out dinner while the rest of us ate, and steadily lower the contents of his bottle.

As already observed, Mick McCarthy had a temper, and I once fell foul of it; in fact twice, in ironically related circumstances. One morning I was with Inspector Benedict running quickly through the list of court cases to be heard, and there was one in which Michael McCarthy had laid a criminal complaint against an African lorry driver. Brief discussion suggested that we were in for trouble.

The case was a trivial and simple one, relating to a threat of violence which had not in the event materialised – but technically common assault. The facts were straightforward and not in dispute. Mick was driving his decrepit

Bedford truck back from a building site in the bush beyond the Mbangala river, overloaded with the tools of his trade and left-over materials. On the road he met a truck going in the opposite direction and driven by the accused. In the normal course of events this would not have mattered, but there had been a severe thunderstorm. In these circumstances the only safe place for a vehicle was on the crown of the road – if there was one. Here there might be a crust of gravel, or the mud only a couple of inches deep; off the crown you were down to your axles in a heavy clinging mud before you could say knife. Now Mick was an 'old colonial' and there was no doubt in his mind as to who had right of way – himself; the African, a sturdy citizen, thought otherwise, and declined to give way. The trucks stopped, bumper to bumper, the drivers descended, and Mick let off a volley of abuse in fluent Swahili. The African did not react as a good African should; he reached under his seat and pulled out a spanner which he waved at the apoplectic Irishman, and let off an oral broadside in return.

I do not recollect what or who gave way, but in the brandishing of the spanner an offence was committed, and the complainant and accused were there in my court. Deciding that this was a typical motoring situation in which tempers had run high, I found the accused technically guilty, but gave him an absolute discharge. Whereupon Paddy threatened an attack of apoplexy at the back of the courtroom; with an audience, amour propre required an appropriate reprimand, and suppressing the beginning of what could have become a fit of uncontrollable laughter, I warned Mick of the penalties for contempt of court. He was not amused, and stormed out of the building; he did not speak to me again for three weeks.

Shortly after we had resumed normal relations I was surprised one morning to see Mick outside the Boma; his houseboy Hamisi had been charged with assault, and his employer was the principal witness for the defence. Again the facts were simple. Mick had been on safari, inspecting some of his building sites in one of the further-flung parts of the district. Before going he had carefully instructed his servant to admit no strangers to his premises and had equipped him with a whip to lend point to his stewardship. At some time during Mick's absence an innocent peasant had approached the house, bearing a basket of eggs which he was peddling. Possibly he gave some grounds for anxiety, but at all events he was chased off

119

by Hamisi, wielding a hippo-hide whip or *kiboko*. In the process the unfortunate egg seller, terrified out of his wits, had fallen down, done himself some slight injury, and smashed most of his eggs.

This time I felt that some blame attached to both the crestfallen servant and his employer, who after giving evidence sat at the back of the court expectantly awaiting Hamisi's acquital. In this he was disappointed, for I was obliged to find Hamisi guilty; knowing that the payment would in fact fall to Mick, I imposed a small fine and required payment of a few shillings compensation for the broken eggs and bruised shin. This was too much for Mick who, fuming and muttering, stormed out when a police sergeant appeared at his elbow and accompanied him to the door.

This time the cold war lasted a little longer, but a few weeks later our usual state of détente had been resumed; and the quality of his work and his probity was in no way affected by our brief personal contretemps. But the next time Mick came round to dinner he unaccountably neglected to bring his bottle of whisky; by the end of the evening mine was empty. He had made his point; thereafter the old habit prevailed and he brought his own bottle.

* * *

Not much court work afforded comparable entertainment or a great deal of interest, and some of it was downright dull. In one complete year in Masasi, two of us heard over four hundred cases, three quarters of them falling to me. Fortunately the majority of them were relatively straightforward, and the culprits entered pleas of guilty more often than not. There was one particular offence which the Native Authorities regularly referred to the district court because they felt that their own sentencing powers were too limited. This was the illegal distillation of *nipa* , prepared from the juice of cashew apples. The cashew nut grows in a singular fashion in an extremely hard shell at the end of – rather than inside – the pulpy astringent fruit commonly called the apple. The spirit distilled from the fermented juice is extremely potent, and because of the conditions in which it was made, death or blindness often followed its consumption. Hence the local wish for stiff sentencing.

Secondary school riot

It was one of those days when pressure was burdensome rather than challenging. Ron and Jill Neath were away in Dar es Salaam, summoned to attend the social and ceremonial events occasioned by the visit of Princess Margaret. In consequence I had been busier than usual, and additional unforeseen incidents also came crowding in. One of our police constables, a promising young man, had died of meningitis during the night in nearby Mkomaindo mission hospital; I had written to his parents, four hundred miles away in Tanga Province to express my condolences and promise a photograph of the grave in due course. A clerk in Chikundi had reportedly run off with his accumulated market dues, and I had sent one of the Boma messengers to track him down. The previous evening I had been out supervising the disposal of a cow which the NA farm manager suspected had died from anthrax; it was carted off well away from any habitation, partially incinerated, covered in quicklime, and buried.

I was also having to visit our small prison daily; Mkandawire, the Head Warder, appeared to have had a nervous breakdown, and I had sent him down to Mtwara with an escort for observation at the Government hospital there. These daily calls were primarily to check the rations, ensure that the cells and compound were kept clean, and that the warders were behaving themselves; they were not onerous, but took up valuable time. Normally there was a certain pleasure in visiting, for Mkandawire had encouraged the inmates to form a small band – albeit that the instruments were crude and unconventional; inspections were often carried out to a catchy musical accompaniment performed by half a dozen grinning convicts.

On this particular day, by mid-day I was feeling decidedly ragged, and lunch was preceded by a stiff pink gin, a treat usually reserved as a preliminary to Saturday curry. Lunch over, and more relaxed, I returned to the two heaps of files on my desk. Hardly had I sat down when two excited Benedictine lay brothers burst into my office. The first, a tall and handsome young German who taught at the Ndanda mission boys' secondary school, did the talking. As his tale unfolded my stomach lurched and the adrenaline began to flow. It went on for ten or fifteen minutes; after five I interrupted, summoned Inspector Benedict, and told him to be ready in a quarter of an hour with twelve policemen in safari order, armed and with minimal riot equipment – wicker shields and pick handles. There had been some sort of disorder at the school, and as I understood it school staff had been set upon and pursued by a mob of angry youngsters. They had sought refuge in the Bishop's house, and for all we knew the place was now ablaze, the Bishop himself dead. Lengthy cross-examination was not appropriate, but I guessed – correctly as it happened – that it was the young teacher's old-fashioned and offensive views on African capabilities which had provoked the outbreak, though it hardly justified the violence described, and perhaps even now continuing.

I suggested to the brothers that they went off to the house of some neighbouring Benedictines and dashed up to my own house to tell Sylvia I had to go out and might be late home. Back at the office the Bedford pickup bristled with policemen, and we were ready for off. A slight delay ensued whilst I phoned my Provincial HQ down at Mtwara; the Provincial Commissioner was out, so I left a message explaining my errand. Benedict joined me in my station-waggon, and the Bedford followed.

We were only about a mile down the road when a Citroen 2CV appeared, enveloped in a cloud of dust. It stopped and three more Benedictines struggled out, amongst them Father Joseph, whom I knew well. Yes, there *had* been trouble but our first informant had left early on in the proceedings, and if I judged a lorry-load of police to be necessary I had clearly heard an exaggerated account of events; if I took them now it would only provoke the students – an argument which has become increasingly familiar over the years. But better safe than sorry. I agreed to accompany the Fathers back to Ndanda, and asked Inspector Benedict to follow on as far as the *Liwali* of Chikundi's HQ, which was about a mile short of the mission. I told him to take it easy but keep his men together; I went on in my car to size up the situation, and would return post haste if they were needed.

It was indeed all over; tempers had cooled, and the boys stood around in scattered groups talking in low tones, and mission staff, still shaken, were recovering their composure. Signs of violence were apparent, but not marked; overturned desks in the classrooms, some doors and wooden shutters pulled off their hinges, flowers trampled down in the beds round the Bishop's house, some splintering of its front door. If any weapons had been used as alleged they had disappeared, and there were no visible wounded.

For myself this was momentarily anticlimactic. Certainly I was relieved, but also felt flat and a little cheated; it was no comfort now to have to preside over the rest of the proceedings, for it could not end there. I spent a little time with Bishop Victor and two or three of his colleagues; they were clearly concerned to play the I ncident down, partly out of regard for their own image, and partly I think because of concern for 'their boys' –the less the offence the lesser the punishment; for some form of retribution there would have to be. It was my guess that had the first brother not come rushing in to the Boma I would never have heard of the affair – or if so, only weeks later in an expurgated form.

It was also clear that I would have to *do* something; I sent a message to Inspector Benedict asking him to send his men back to Masasi, but that he should come and join me, accompanied by one constable. I said I wanted to see a representative group of boys together with the one who had by all accounts been the ringleader. I use the word boys loosely; they were fifth-formers and in the context of a school run on traditional European lines, they *were* schoolboys. But in reality they were also young adults in their late teens, some in their twenties, and less accepting of school discipline than if they had been fifteen-year-olds. As in many secondary schools, they were drawn from a number of tribes, all of which had their own social customs, so there was no one pattern of indigenous mores to which they conformed. In these circumstances alien school values prevailed, and were perhaps perceived as a quasi-colonial imposition, although they were in no way onerous. It is also fair to assume that most senior secondary school pupils at the time took a lively interest in politics. There was, then, a certain inherent tension at the upper end of the educational system, but on only a few occasions did this lead to violence; the incident at Ndanda was something of a cause célèbre

I spent the next two or three hours with a group of the disaffected youngsters. Their leader was a twenty-year old from Songea district, about two hundred miles to the west. He was an Angoni, a tribe which a little over a century earlier had been propelled northwards by the rise of Zulu militarism from a common homeland in the plateau of southern Africa. They themselves adopted Zulu organisation and tactics, and in turn became the scourge of the country through which they moved and the people amongst whom they came to rest in south-western Tanganyika. The Angoni were a proud people, and certainly they were more politically aware than many of the country's hundred-odd tribes. Young Johanes did not seem markedly militant in his demeanour – on the contrary he was somewhat subdued; now that it was over he had probably recognised the implications of his offence.

As will have been gathered, the students were restive about school discipline in general and particularly resentful of the attitudes of two or three staff members. This had all erupted when the young German teacher, in a confrontation which he had himself inspired by calling the boys monkeys, tried to discipline one of them with a cane. Fisticuffs ensued, the teacher was manhandled and fled, pursued by a number of the pupils. The uproar spread and pretty well the whole school became involved – a terrifying situation for the staff, however viewed in the cool of the evening. There *had* been a riot.

During those hours of talking not only were the facts clarified, but also attitudes, and for these I had considerable sympathy. I also tried to set the incident in perspective for the boys; politics were a matter of growing interest, and the discussion was one which in other circumstances would have been a pleasure. At dusk some lamps were brought in and we talked on; around me was a pattern of lively young faces in chiaroscuro, black skins shining in the lamplight. At the back, and a reminder that this was after all serious business, stood Inspector Benedict and his constable.

By eight-thirty or so we had talked things out, and my voice had gone anyway. The students were aware of my sympathy, but also of my position, and they realised too that arrests would have to be made, and accepted this. It was not possible to arrest the whole school, nor did I want to; Johanes and one of his friends were obvious sacrificial lambs, and they went off quietly enough with Benedict and his companion to wait in my station-waggon. I made my exit, called briefly on the Bishop to tell him what I was doing, and was back with an anxious wife shortly after ten.

At this stage it was my hope that I could follow the matter up shortly and swiftly in the District Court. But this was not to be; I might have got away with it had it not been for my message to the Provincial Commissioner. He had left an instruction in turn to the effect that I was to phone him as soon as I returned from my expedition. Thereafter the matter was out of my hands; a serious view was taken, and the Resident Magistrate (RM) in Lindi was sent up to hear the case after a further police investigation.

It was all very sad, but in the circumstances of the time when Government was still two or three years from accepting the momentum of the move towards independence, and was sensitive about civil disorder, it was perhaps inevitable. Johanes could not be dealt with as a juvenile; he was adult and had to be treated as such. He and his friend were convicted of instigating a riot, and sentenced to terms of imprisonment ranging from nine to twelve months; six of the best [28] would have met the case more equitably. The RM, Geoff Hill, was a friend, but we did not see eye to eye on this matter; I had my say and thereafter held my peace – it did not do to formally criticise the judiciary.

Eight or nine months later Johanes knocked at my office door and walked in accompanied by his father. He had lately been released from prison, the sentence reduced for good behaviour. His father, a charming grizzle-headed elder, had gone down to Mtwara to meet him, and now they were on their way home; they wanted to thank me for having given the young men a fair hearing at Ndanda following the riot, and for my unavailing attempt to ameliorate the sentence of the court. It was a nice gesture, and although by definition it could not be described as a happy reunion, it was for me a touching occasion. Johanes will now be in his sixties; I hope that he realised the potential which I thought I detected in the wake of the fracas which led to his arrest and conviction.

Introduction of cattle to Masasi

Cattle ownership is very much part of the African way of life, and yet there are rural areas in the continent where for one reason or another they are virtually unknown. The distribution of tsetse fly is often a major constraint; elsewhere their absence is simply attributable to custom and tradition. Thus, up to the 1950's the cow did not feature in the domestic economy of the more easterly districts of Tanganyika's Southern Province. True, there were commercial herds at Lindi, Nachingwea, and Mtwara, a result of European

---

[28] The then common expression for six strokes of the cane; it was a punishment which could have been awarded by the court.

initiative, and meeting largely expatriate needs for fresh milk and meat; even the Native Authority in Masasi had a small dairy herd which paid its way as a source of nourishment for the small township, and also provided manure for experimental agricultural plots. But all this was alien, and it evoked little interest and no envy or ambition amongst local farmers. However, tsetse fly were now limited to the extreme west of the district, and there was no reason why cattle should not thrive elsewhere if demand could be stimulated. One evening, whilst talking shop, Ron Neath and I discussed the possibility of generating such a demand.

Over a period of several months, through the *Liwalis,* agricultural instructors, and the District Council, we extolled the advantages of cattle ownership. Not only were they a source of food, but also of fertiliser – and goodness knows, the thin sandy soils of the district needed it. And the ox plough would be a distinct improvement on the two-foot-long digging hoe which was the sole means of cultivation at the time for all but the lucky few who were able to hire the NA Ferguson tractor and plough to till their few acres at a heavily-subsidised daily charge. The results of this campaign were sufficiently encouraging for us to enquire into the practicalities of getting cattle from the markets of overstocked Central Province to the south of the country. There followed a long correspondence with the Veterinary Department – more accurately an animal husbandry department – on ways and means.

We were to advance to them a sum of money to purchase about 150 cattle and a few donkeys. They would then send about half of them down to Dar es Salaam by rail, and thence by a former wartime landing craft to Lindi; from there they would be herded the hundred miles up to Masasi. To compare costs, the other mob were to be inoculated against trypanosomiasis and trekked across country via Mahenge, over trails little used since German times – a journey which could be expected to take many weeks. A new item appeared as a supplementary estimate in the Native Treasury accounts: Purchase and Transport of cattle. An equal sum was inserted on the revenue side for Sale of Cattle, though this apparent optimism was less a reflection of our conviction that costs would be covered than of the need to allow some slight scepticism in the Provincial Office, and to anticipate the auditor. The formalities complied with, the PC was content to give us our head. The veterinary people were helpful, and promised to lend us a Livestock Officer for as long as might be necessary to insinuate the cow into the peasant economy of Masasi district, and to attend to necessary inoculations.

The vets did us well, though six months or so elapsed before the last of the cattle arrived. The first batch came more speedily but at greater cost, and we received regular reports of their progress by telephone and telegram. There were casualties in transit, for it was an arduous journey, and adequate attention could not be guaranteed. The overland herd took longer, and their journey too had taken its toll, from sickness, exhaustion, and an occasional marauding lion; and of course the herdsmen were allowed their ration of meat.

Meanwhile we had a list of prospective customers prepared to buy at what we calculated the landed cost would be. The Livestock Officer had arrived, and made arrangements for holding and feeding the cattle, and allowing them to recover from the journey before sale. He also had the not inconsiderable task of preparing the purchasers for what was in store. They all wanted a cow and for all the right reasons, but in fact most had little more idea of how to look after and utilise a cow than would the average resident of Hammersmith or Hackney. So the Livestock Officer had all his work cut out, demonstrating how to build a cow-shed and stall, with a protective *boma*; how to milk; and later on, how to train for draught purposes. The process was not without its moments of hilarity and occasional farce.

One afternoon I accompanied Jim Parkinson, the livestock expert, on a visit to the proud owner of a new cow down near the Ruvuma river. I do not recollect the occasion in detail, but an otherwise unexciting day was enlivened by the inconclusive wrestling match with his new acquisition. In the last round he was sent flying as he grappled clumsily with an udder recently unaccustomed to human contact. Another day a customer came to collect his imported donkey from the NA farm; in the ensuing battle of wills it soon became clear that the animal had at some time been used for pack purposes, and in fact knew a great deal more about the routine of its rôle in life than its owner did. Once this had been established, the purchaser was a very happy man.

During the last years of colonial rule, the mandatory tasks of district staff seemed to grow almost daily, often in response to a rapidly-changing political situation. But there was always opportunity to make a distinctive personal mark on the local community by initiating some favourite scheme or mounting a pet hobby horse. These one-off enthusiasms did not invariably produce the desired results, and some speedily sank without trace. In most cases the longer-term outcome was unknown to us, and simply taken for granted by the local people. However, in this particular case our initiative is known to have borne fruit.

In 1994 a former deputy *Liwali* from Masasi (and later DO) visited Britain with his wife – George and Angela Naga; stalwarts of the UMCA, and now retired, they were guests of the missionary society. One day Sylvia and I joined them and the Neaths for a pub lunch near Itchenor in West Sussex. I asked George how the cattle project had worked out. It had, over the years, been a great success; cattle ownership was now the rule, but without the emphasis on numbers which is usual in traditional cattle-owning societies. He himself had four or five cows, which provided a useful supplement to diet, pension, and the fertility of his small farmstead. The original idea had been fortuitous, almost casual, the long-term outcome highly satisfactory. But few Tanzanians will now know how the Makua and Yao of Masasi District came to be cattle owners.

Not all our good intentions worked out in practice. It would hardly have been a quantum leap anyway, but we were conspicuously unsuccessful in persuading the local farmers to adopt long-handled hoes with a broad head instead of the traditional back-breaking implement with a two-foot (60cms) handle and tiny head. Nor did we induce more than a handful of our more progressive farmers to take out small agricultural loans with a view to improving their holdings and boosting their production and income. We did, however, with the invaluable help of an African Co-operative Development Officer seconded to the district for a year or so, manage to establish two moderately successful co-ops. These were concerned with the collection and marketing of the three main local cash crops, cashew nuts, groundnuts and sesame. How long the societies lasted would depend entirely on the quality of their management and service to members, and in particular the reliability of payment for produce delivered.

Appearance of a baby elephant.

I had just finished reprimanding Joseph Mrisho, our Head Tax Clerk, who had been drunk on duty again; not unpleasantly so, but his incapacity to hold drink was affecting his ability to maintain the respect of his junior clerks. It had been a bad morning altogether, and the daily thunderstorm was building up to the mid-day downpour.

Light relief presented itself in the form of Ndabisi Songwe.

Hodi – an oral knock on the door.

Karibu – approach.

We exchanged the usual catalogue of greetings, after which the purpose of his visit was revealed.

'*Bwana*, I have an elephant outside' – a very small elephant he added when I showed surprise. We left the office, and there, tethered under one of the mango trees which served as our waiting room, was a baby elephant. It stood about waist high, and looked decidedly limp and dejected.

It seemed that the young elephant's mother had been shot near Masuguru on the Ruvuma river, some seventy miles away; Ndabisi had taken charge of the orphan, and had brought it in to the Boma in the hope of reward. I say brought, but the tiny elephant had walked those seventy miles in two days, and twenty miles back along the road had forded the Mbangala river, then swollen with rain and about two hundred yards wide. In places the water had been deeper than the elephant was high, and it had crossed practically submerged, its trunk serving as a snorkel. No wonder it looked limp and dejected. I felt no great sympathy for the expectant Ndabisi, but his view of the situation was understandable, and to have withheld all recognition would have been churlish. I gave him a few shillings, (a shilling was the price of a day's labour in those days), bade him farewell, and turned my attention to the baby pachyderm.

About three hundred yards from the Boma was the Native Authority dairy farm, and here I handed over to the farm manager. The elephant was bedded down in a pile of straw, and arrangements made for bottle feeding. By evening it had perked up, and was the centre of attention for half the juvenile population of Masasi and their mothers. My own toddlers were enthralled; this was better than Christmas any day.But things did not go well; there is apparently some vital ingredient in elephants' milk which is missing from cows' milk, and after initially rallying, the patient slipped into a decline and caught pneumonia; three days later, despite the prayers and tears of his infant well-wishers, the baby elephant died. This affecting little story later found its way into the columns of the 'Tanganyika Standard' for which Sylvia was the Masasi correspondent. I usually provided the news, and she wrote the copy; it was rewarded at the rate of five shillings a column inch, and probably brought us in £5 in an eventful year.

Some weeks later a small postal package was delivered to the Boma. Inside, to my astonishment and mixed indignation and amusement, was a bronze medal, inscribed with the name of Ndabisi Songwe, and a nice little letter from the Tanganyika branch of the RSPCA. I was asked to present it to the heroic rescuer of the baby elephant. Of course the RSPCA had got it all wrong. Ndabisi and his neighbours had killed the mother elephant in the first place, for the very good reason from their point of view that it had been destroying their plots of millet. The several hundredweight of meat thereby provided would have been some compensation for this. But Ndabisi's interest in the baby elephant had been entirely mercenary, and he had already been rewarded. I wrote a polite acknowledgement to the R.S.P.C.A.; as for the medal, it lay on my desk for many months amongst the paper clips and file tabs, and eventually disappeared.

Shortly after Ndabisi's visit I was on tour in the Masuguru area. One evening, the day's chores over and the dirt scraped off, I went out after a guinea-fowl, unsuccessfully as usual. A mile or so from my tent, I rounded an outcrop of rock and was stopped in my tracks by the most awful carrion smell; it was indescribable. Twenty yards away was the rib-cage of an elephant anchored in a sun-hardened, fly-ridden, malodorous lump of putrefaction. It was here, I guessed, that our baby elephant had begun its long walk.

On my way back to Masasi I called on *Liwali* Mohamed at Nanyumbu. Coincidentally our Head Game Scout Saidi Meza was also there, looking very pleased with himself; he had every reason to be, for he had a few days earlier caught up with and despatched an elusive man-eating leopard which had killed twenty-seven people over the previous two or three years. He also told me of a man local to Nanyumbu who, whilst up a tree investigating his beehive, glanced down only to see an expectant lion awaiting his descent.

Fortunately he had a bow and a quiver of poisoned arrows slung over his shoulder; he shot the lion, which made off and shortly expired. Here was more copy for Sylvia and the 'Tanganyika Standard'.

In general, man-eating carnivores were old or ailing beasts lacking speed, agility, teeth, or all three; they were thus apt to occur anywhere. But there was a perception that there was a higher incidence of man-eaters in Southern Province, and that these were not exclusively the old, the halt, and the lame. It was a common speculation that this was attributable to the severity with which the Germans had quashed the *Maji Maji* rebellion in the south in 1905-7; a plentiful supply of fresh meat was therefore available to the local lion population, which, becoming accustomed to human flesh, developed a taste for it. Whether or not this explanation holds water zoologically I do not pretend to know.

In similar vein there is a story – allegedly true but possibly apocryphal – that a European Medical Officer visiting a rural dispensary in southwestern Tanganyika was surprised to find two lying-in patients, both of whom had mangled left arms which had been chewed by lions. It was explained that man-eaters were common, and that as a last resort the local people had developed the stratagem that if and when attacked, one arm would be thrust into the lion's mouth to engage its dentition, whilst the free fist hammered the lion's nose. Unaccustomed to the pain, and its nose put out of joint, the lion – with luck – made off. If true, one can but admire the cold-blooded courage thus exhibited.

* * *

In referring to wild life in Southern Tanganyika it is impossible not to mention the incumbent provincial Game Ranger, Constantine Ionides, affectionately known as 'Iodine'; he was one of Tanganyika's more colourful characters. An Anglo-Greek born at the turn of the century, he had packed more adventures and escapades into his life than is common. Educated at Rugby, he went on to Sandhurst, and then to join the South Wales Borderers in India. After very few years his interest shifted to Africa, and he successfully sought secondment to the King's African Rifles in Tanganyika. Three years later Africa took precedence over soldiering, and he resigned his commission to take up big-game hunting. For the next few years, and ranging over British East Africa and the Belgian Congo, he was variously ivory poacher and legitimate 'white hunter'. In 1933 'Iodine' talked his way into Tanganyika's Game Department, and in our time was a national institution and a world authority on African snakes. These creatures were a consuming passion, sometimes with some cost to his primary function, which was the protection of game, and where necessary their control.

A confirmed bachelor, 'Iodine' was also very much a loner, and not greatly interested in people; he had no time for the routines and niceties of the very informal officialdom of which he was a part. Whilst a Game Ranger he chose to live at Liwale in a remote and sparsely inhabited part of Nachingwea district, and after retirement in about 1957, moved to Newala district where he continued to collect, and extend his knowledge of snakes. 'Iodine's' predilection for solitude was largely genuine, but perhaps also partly a pose; he had a reputation to maintain. When in the vicinity of a district HQ and invited to dinner he was a companionable guest, so much so that on these occasions he could fairly be said to hold court. Well read and erudite, he would discuss philosophy, history, music and literature, and at the drop of a hat quote passages of Shakespeare or the Bible; expectations that he would regale us with tales of encounters with dangerous game were obligingly met, and in all probability he would have a snake about his person. He would invariably make scathing observations about the government which employed him, though he was not, of course, alone in this. His very particular hate was reserved for the then Establishment Officer (we managed without a personnel department), whose head he would like to have had, mounted, on the wall of his bungalow. In the late 1950's 'Iodine' increasingly lost the use of his legs, but nevertheless continued with his collecting; unable to walk any distance, he was trundled along bush paths on a sort of rudimentary cart-cum-sedan chair with a tubular metal frame and a centrally-located bicycle wheel. This preposterous contraption was easily manoeuvred with a bearer fore and aft.

Ionides belonged in a disappearing world. Essentially a nomad, he had few material possessions, and his bungalows were camps rather than homes, ready to be vacated at a moment's notice. Conservative, even reactionary, he was contemptuous of progress wherever and however manifested; he loved Africa as it had been, not as it was becoming. Like most of us he had his contradictions, and he was an impossible man to know in depth; one of his two biographers observed that he 'combined authority and courtesy, ferocity and gentleness,'[29] valuable attributes in Africa – or perhaps anywhere.

Disenchanted with some of the changes which took place in Tanganyika after independence, Ionides moved up to Kenya to continue collecting there. Later, the deep vein thrombosis which affected his legs necessitated an amputation, and the same condition in the other leg led to his death in a Nairobi hospital in 1967. He is buried on Nandanga mountain, in the vast Selous game reserve in southern Tanzania.

An attempted rape

In mid 1957 the Neaths departed on vacation leave, and a new DC was not due for another four months. It was exhilarating to be left in sole charge of the district, but also a strain; with two of us there had been more than enough to do, and working fifty or sixty hours a week there was much left undone that we would have liked to do. This tendency to overwork was in part attributable to an expanding mandatory workload, but also to the pursuit of personal initiatives and enthusiasms generated by local needs. During this interregnum, in addition to the familiar routines – court work, supervision of the Native Treasury, *shauris,* and so on, I had in quick succession to organise a district population census, and train and supervise the enumerators; attend to a visiting Director of Education; and host a brief visit by the Governor, Sir Edward Twining, his wife and personal staff.

HE was on his way to formally open the Makonde Water Scheme in neighbouring Newala district; the Government aircraft, a Percival Prince, arrived at our airstrip earlier than planned, and HE was at our front door as Sylvia hastily pulled on her clothes. 'That caught you with your pants down', he boomed as he came in; truer than he knew we thought. Sir Edward was a larger than life and genial extrovert who had done much to put Tanganyika on the map during the early and middle Fifties, and to promote its economic development. His call at Masasi was clearly intended for my benefit, as he could more conveniently have flown direct to the Newala airstrip. Apart from

---

[29] 'Life with Ionides'' by Margaret Lane: Hamish Hamilton 1963

the social chit-chat he asked a number of searching questions about the district, and was encouraging about my responses. After a light snack the party left; Sylvia and I had been invited to Newala for the main event, but I could ill afford the time, and had declined. It was a great relief that Sir Edward had planned no public speech in Masasi. He had little Swahili, and always expected the incumbent DC to interpret; but he also had the mischievous habit of slipping in the odd comment which was almost impossible to translate.

Another one-off event was a visit, spread over several days, of a King's African Rifles recruiting party led by the commanding officer of the 6th Battalion in Dar es Salaam. Some modest hospitality was both de rigueur and pleasurable, but made inroads into precious time. It was a felicitous coincidence that in the course of conversation it turned out that Col. Spanton had been my company commander whilst serving in the Manchester Regiment in Germany during my brief military career between school and university. I reminded him of his attempt to persuade me, then a sergeant, to stay on in the regiment with the inducement of a commission, and hoped that he now understood why I had declined.

With so much going on, my thirtieth birthday passed unremarked and uncelebrated. It was shortly after this that I had the dispiriting task of dealing with one of the Water Development staff who had attempted to rape the wife of a senior African colleague.

The European officials in Masasi numbered eleven adults, and we were all there, or at least in the Colonial Service, by choice – or in the case of some of the wives, reluctant acceptance. There was one exception to the general rule; Eric[30] had more or less drifted into his contract job by accident. He had come out to East Africa to work as a storekeeper for a large motor vehicle agency in Nairobi. He had liked it there and thought he liked Africa, and when he had an opportunity of improving his position by taking a similar job in the Water Development and Irrigation Department (WDID) in Tanganyika he took it. He was posted to Masasi. Alas for Eric, Masasi was not Nairobi; it was by urban standards, the back of nowhere.

Our life was parochial, but not therefore dull, and the demands of work

---

[30] Not his real name.

spilled over into our private lives to the extent that public and private often seemed indistinguishable. For relaxation we played tennis, tended our dusty gardens if so inclined, resorted to our battery-operated record players, and visited each other to talk, drink, and eat. And of course there were the children. It was into this situation that bachelor town-mouse Eric was pitched. He should never have stayed, but to his credit he did; sadly, he was unable to adapt. His noisy, bustling south London suburb yes, Nairobi yes, probably even Dar es Salaam; but not Masasi. We all did our best, but he did not respond, and across the tea-table and over drinks and dinner, conversation soon faltered. We were interested in Africa, he was not. Increasingly he spent his time alone, listening to pop music from Radio Nairobi, and alleviating his solitary state with bottles of Tusker beer. Sometimes he would go down to the trading centre and spend an evening in what passed for a bar, and having a drink with whoever might call in, and a chat if they also happened to speak English, for he spoke little Swahili.

On one such evening he fell in with our new Inspector of Police, Josephat, who had recently replaced Benedict. He was newly-promoted from Sub-Inspector and I had first met him in Kondoa two years earlier when he took over from Gurmuk Singh. He was a first-rate policeman, straight as a die, who wore authority well and trod with integrity and sensitivity the borderline between loyalty to an alien colonial government and pride in his own race and future. He had even less in common with Eric than the rest of us, but he recognised his loneliness, felt some sympathy, and invited him home to a meal.

The next morning I was woken at five o'clock by an agitated and half-dressed Boma messenger. Would I come at once? The water *Bwana* - Eric – had been found lying in the road drunk and asleep outside the quarters of the Public Works Department labourers; he was now at the police station which occupied part of the District Office block. I scrambled into my shorts and went off with the messenger, with some apprehension as to why Eric was at the police station and not sleeping it off in bed.

In the charge room, looking very sorry for himself was Eric, shirt half outside his shorts and stained an ochreous red from the road, smears of vomit down the front, hair dishevelled, glasses awry. He had, I thought, been crying. There wasn't much to be said, and he'd tell me about it later. I put my hand on his shoulder for a moment and went into the adjoining office where Josephat was waiting, discreetly apart.

A sad tale unfolded. Eric had gone home with Inspector Josephat, and had joined his host and wife in a meal of rice and curried meat. Josephat had been generous too in his provision of beer – and goodness knows how much Eric had drunk before they met in the bar. He got a little tight and silly. Some time after they had eaten, Josephat went down to the latrine at the bottom of his compound. Whilst he was away Eric had forced himself on Josephat's wife and attempted to rape her – a breach not only of the law but perhaps worse, of the couple's hospitality. My heart sank; what a mess, what a bloody, half-baked stupid thing to do!

I sent Eric home to clean himself up, and told him he must consider himself under house arrest and stay there; he was not going to run away – there was nowhere to run to. I would see him later. I took a statement from Josephat, commiserated, and went to see Eric, now clean and spruce but pale and subdued. He denied none of it. I said I'd decide what was to be done as quickly as I could, and at least end the uncertainty. I did not loiter, for circumstances had created unease between us; I had knowledge of what he wished he hadn't done, and I was no longer a neighbour but the DC and, Inspector Josephat notwithstanding, also Officer in Charge of Police.

I went home, washed and shaved, told Sylvia about it, lapsed into silence and fortified myself with a half-hearted breakfast. Then down to the Boma where I closed the door on myself, ostensibly to think what best to do, though the answer was obvious. Ironically, African customary law did not invariably regard attempted rape or even rape itself as a criminal offence; matters could sometimes be satisfactorily resolved by the payment of compensation. But Eric was not an African, and his offence was subject to the Penal Code; moreover, the reputation of government and the law itself was at stake. Eric would have to be charged; there could be no attempt to play it down, only a degree of compassion when the whole sorry business was over.

In the circumstances I could not hear the case myself, nor of course did I wish to. I reported over the phone to my Provincial Commissioner; he would send a Resident Magistrate up from Mtwara or Lindi. I had another chat with Eric, and arranged for him to stay with a neighbour until the trial was over. I had him formally charged, let him out on bail, and agreed with his senior,

Roger Buckingham, that he carry on working to keep him occupied. The RM came up two days later and convicted Eric on his own plea of guilty; he was sentenced to twelve months imprisonment and ordered to pay compensation. We offered what comfort we could, but it was no comfort at all, for although Josephat and his wife had perhaps forgiven, Eric could not forgive himself. He left us under escort for Mtwara, and was of course dismissed from Government service. He was released after nine months, and returned to Nairobi or to the England he should perhaps never have left. Eric was at bottom a nice lad, and there was no malice in him; had he not been drunk he would never have behaved as he did. But because he was in the wrong place at the wrong time he became one of Africa's numberless little casualties; they were not exclusively black.

The previous year Eric's predecessor had been caught selling Government stores to some Indian traders; on that occasion too I had the duty of remanding him on bail pending trial by a visiting RM. These two events were not of course any reflection on the WD & ID in particular; they were an unfortunate coincidence. By way of contrast there was 'Ches' Kolosowski, a warm-hearted Pole who had flown in a Polish Coastal Command squadron during the war, and whose sauerkraut and pork was a welcome gastronomic diversion. He was instrumental in helping a local carpenter, Norbert Johanes, set up a mechanised workshop. Norbert made a good deal of furniture for the NA, for shops, and for the upwardly mobile; he wanted to expand, and had some months earlier asked me to get hold of a catalogue of woodworking machinery. He also enquired about a Government loan, but after doing his sums decided to accumulate a bit more capital and avoid borrowing. This done, I helped him choose a bandsaw, drill, circular saw, and planer. 'Ches' designed the workshop layout, specified what was required in the way of drive shafts, bearings, belting and so on, and selected a suitable diesel engine. I then placed an order for the whole lot with an import-export firm in Dar es Salaam, and weeks later it all arrived by road transport. 'Ches' then supervised its installation, all without any payment of course. Norbert organised an opening ceremony and party to which 'Ches' and I were invited. Later, his business flourishing, he paid for the construction of a modest building for use as a youth club.

Visit to Portuguese East Africa

The Ruvuma river bounded Masasi district to the south; it was also the international boundary between Portuguese East Africa or Mozambique, and Tanganyika. Rivers make convenient and clearly defined boundaries, but unless particularly turbulent also tend to unite rather than separate the people living on either bank. Thus many nominal Tanganyikans in the south of the district had friends and relations across the river, and vice versa; and over the years there had been a steady trickle of population from Mozambique into the border districts of Tanganyika. There was traffic to and fro for practical as well as social reasons; to get a better price for one's cotton or carvings, to seek better medical treatment, to smuggle cheap brandy from south to north, or to escape the law, and in particular the unpleasant form of corporal punishment involving the beating of palms of the hand or soles of the feet which was commonplace south of the river.

Naturally we were curious as to how the Portuguese ran their colony, but we had no contact with officials across the border, and there was no good reason to visit. However, after three months of holding the fort and the arrival of a new DC imminent, I succumbed to curiosity, and sent a letter by messenger to my opposite number at Negomano just over the border. This resulted in an invitation to visit and stay overnight. A week or so later I set off with Mzee, and en route picked up the *Liwali* of Mchauru, who wished to join us. We hired a dugout canoe to ferry us across the river, and half an hour later I was enjoying a cup of coffee with the Portuguese official in charge of the district, and his agricultural colleague. As far as I could judge these were the only expatriate officials in Negomano. Conversation was convoluted, and conducted in a mixture of English, Portuguese, French and Swahili; but we managed.

I learned that Portuguese colonial administrators were selected at about age 18, and then went direct to a college devoted exclusively to their training; this for two (or possibly three) years. In this respect their preparation was more thorough than was ours; however its purpose was simply to enable officers in the field to carry out the policies and instructions emanating from Lisbon; even Governors had little discretion in the Portuguese colonies. Nor were there any new-fangled notions about preparing the colonies for independence; their sole function was to meet the requirements of metropolitan Portugal and to resettle unemployed rural Portuguese. In Negomano district the main rôle of the two expatriate officers was to ensure that the local farmers met their quota of cotton production as determined by more senior bureaucrats in the capital, Lourenço Marques (now Maputo). They were also, of course, responsible for maintaining law and order; one component of this was a good road to provincial headquarters to facilitate the rapid movement of troops, with the bush cleared a hundred metres on either side to inhibit ambushes.

My reaction to the lack of any obvious development intended to improve the lot of the African population was one of sadness tempered by the reflection that despite international criticism and the onset of local national politics, perhaps we weren't doing too badly. In Negomano only one school, in Masasi approaching a hundred; in Negomano one small hospital, in Masasi three hospitals, two leprosaria, and upwards of twenty rural dispensaries. In Negomano all marketable crops were sold to government at prices marked down *by* government; in Masasi upwards of a dozen markets in which farmers sold their cash crops and surplus grain to traders at prices which were generally thought realistic. None of this conferred any very profound insights into the hows, whys, and wherefores of Portuguese colonial administration, but I was very grateful that I lived and worked north of the Ruvuma, a view subsequently endorsed by my two travelling companions.

On a purely personal level, my opposite number was a friendly and generous host. He lived in a modest bungalow somewhat smaller than my own, shared with an African woman housekeeper whom I took, rightly or wrongly, to also be his mistress. Adjacent to the house was a flourishing vegetable plot, almost a smallholding, such as might be seen almost anywhere in rural southern Europe, complete with chickens and a couple of goats.

After dinner, a little puzzlingly, I was asked if I'd like to indulge in a little hunting; not wishing to appear ungracious, I feigned enthusiasm, was provided with a shotgun, and off we went in the DO's Jeep. This was equipped with a spotlight, with which the agricultural officer swept the surrounding bush. After a few miles of seemingly aimless driving around he picked out a hare which made off with frequent changes of direction. We followed as best we could, my companions whooping with excitement, and blasting away unavailingly. The proceedings left me unmoved, and I later returned the shotgun – a little apologetically – without a shot fired.

Next day the DO accompanied us down to the river, where a canoe was waiting. As we made our way back to Luatala and Masasi, the *Liwali* and Mzee seemed just about as smug as I did; the *Liwali* was particularly glad that, unlike the sub-chief at Negomano, he had a great deal more to do than simply follow instructions and meet cotton production targets.

* * *

Shortly after this visit, my new DC arrived in Masasi; this was Geoff Thirtle, whom Sylvia and I had both met in our brief Manyoni days. The remaining six months of my tour could have been difficult; Geoff was only a year senior to me, and after two years in Masasi I was familiar with the district, whilst he was not. Fortunately he responded to this situation with tact, often seeking my advice and normally accepting it. More potentially serious for the district was the contrast between Ron Neath's style and his own. As remarked earlier, Ron was of the more liberal and forward-looking tendency; Geoff, though several years younger, was distinctly authoritarian, with conservative and paternalistic views more appropriate to the 1940's than the mid-1950's. He had unfortunately been much influenced by his previous DC, a notorious dinosaur. My own attitudes were very close to Ron Neath's, though I also recognised Geoff's honesty, and the sincerity of his belief that the greatest good of the greatest number was best and most swiftly secured by firmness and direction. Here again Geoff did not make an issue of our differences and we got on perfectly amicably. He respected my views, in recognition of which I gave him my support, although this was not invariably unqualified. When I thought he was wrong I said so, and he never took this amiss. We became good friends, and it was a pleasure to meet him from time to time during our next tour, at which time he was posted to my new Provincial Commissioner's office. He later married the Bishop of Masasi's secretary, and we kept in touch until his untimely death from chronic asthma twenty-odd years later.

A bogus witch-doctor

The least enthralling aspect of New Year's Day was that it was followed by two weeks or more of hard slog on the Native Authority's Final Financial Statement. Its preparation was not a difficult task, but its completion was an occasion for satisfaction as well as profound relief; the chore was invariably delegated to a DO. Many of the items in our expenditure and revenue columns would strike a chord in the heart of local government officials in this country – staff salaries, maintenance of public buildings and of roads, revenue from local rates[31] and so on; others were less familiar – court fees and fines, rewards for vermin destroyed, sub-chiefs' salaries, and revenue from beer and game licences, marriage and divorce fees, and the sale of coffee seedlings and livestock.

In the January of 1958, Thomas Mwegama, the very capable NA Treasurer, had assembled all the unpaid bills, and drafted the Statement. There ensued a day or two of juggling with various sub-heads of expenditure and revenue, and a final attribution of debits and credits to ensure a result approximating to our approved estimates. At the end of it we issued nearly a hundred cheques, all dated 31st December. We were now ready for the last lap. At the end of it there was a repeated inexplicable error of fifty cents in the balance – two and a half pence! The fact that it was so small was a credit to the Treasurer's book-keeping, for he had something like sixty or seventy sub-heads of expenditure and revenue, and a total budget of something over £100,000[32]. This derisory discrepancy should not have mattered, and of course did not in any real sense, but in those days there was no formal device for entering a corrective entry 'unexplained error'. I spent several evenings literally burning the midnight oil, and completely baffled, resorted to a bogus entry. This had the effect of putting the discrepancy on the other side. I was obvious losing my grip and a severe bout of conjunctivitis was not helped by my nocturnal toil.

Relief came in the form of reported witchcraft a few miles from Lukuledi,

---

[31] These had been permitted by legislation since the mid-1950; they tended to range between 40p and 60p a year for adult males.

[32] £2 million equivalent in 2004.

twenty minutes drive from Masasi along the road to Nachingwea ; I was deputed to go and see what it was all about. The official view of witchcraft was embodied in the Witchcraft Ordinance; I do not recollect whether it was the law itself or the practical interpretation thereof which was curiously ambiguous and liberal, but it was one or the other. White magic or *uganga,* in effect traditional medicine employing herbal remedies and psychology, tended to be beneficial and therapeutic even though accompanied by a great deal of mumbo-jumbo and theatre, and was acceptable. It was reputed that when ill, John Young, DC of Utete district for many years, called on the expertise of one Nguvumali, a famous local practitioner, in preference to the incumbent Medical Officer. And the police in Dar es Salaam once retained the services of the same *mganga* to help them with their investigations because of his skill as a seer; that is until the Chief Secretary got wind of it and ordered that the practice be discontinued as being un-British and inconsistent with twentieth-century police methods. Witchcraft or *uchawi* however was another matter, and anyone who purported to practice it or who maliciously accused others of doing so, was liable to severe penalties in addition to almost certain banishment to a remote part of the country; such was the strength of superstition – or belief.

The present incident was reported in a handwritten note sent by messenger from Father Odio, who ran a little trade school at Lukuledi; their main activity was carpentry and they turned out some excellent furniture, and also more delicate items including – a little strangely – guitars. I set off to Lukuledi in my station waggon, with a Boma messenger in the event of an arrest being necessary. It was a dull, drizzly sort of day, and overnight rain had turned the top inch or so of the road into mud. Progress was slow, for the road had recently been graded and was steeply cambered. Several times I lost the centre and slid down into the verge; and once found myself edgeways on, the car straddling the crown, wheels spinning, and resolutely failing to respond to steering or accelerator.

We arrived at Father Odio's pretty thoroughly plastered with mud from knees downwards; after cleaning up, exchanging gossip, and sharing a pot of coffee, we were ready to go on. The Father provided us with a guide and pointed us in the direction of Nambawara, five miles away in the bush to the west. Our guide stepped out more briskly than I would have wished, and the crepe rubber soles of my desert boots – admirable in the dry season – were no aid to progress. I slipped and slithered along whilst the guide forged ahead, bare toes giving him a foothold. It was a totally forgettable walk, with nondescript bush pressing close on either side. After an hour or so the trees and scrub receded and gave way to a patchwork of little fields, overgrown but rapidly being cleared for the new year's sowing of maize and millet.

We reached the headman's hut, rectangular daub and wattle walls, a shaggy thatched roof, and a small door from which a drift of smoke filtered. To the rear was a small dried mud grain store, raised from the ground, and also thatched. A few chickens scratched listlessly in the dust under the eaves, and a grimy child sat there too, scarcely more active, temporarily abandoned by mother, aunt, or elder sister. The headman was a slightly built, wizened man in his fifties, with legs like a sparrow, and somewhat bowed. He wore a black cotton wrap round his waist, reaching roughly to mid-calf; and over it a dingy white calico shirt. On his head, clean shaven, was the little round white *kofia* which was a common badge of Islam.

Almost needless to say, our bird had flown – as well he might. The headman, looking thoroughly sheepish, told us what had happened. This *mganga* – loosely, a healer – had arrived the previous evening, strung around with his bags of bones, little gourds, and feathers. With his urbane manner he had won the confidence of the villagers who drifted in to scrutinise the visitor. He had then gone into a trance or thrown a fit, and generally run through his repertoire of histrionics. As a finale he underwent assault from evil spirits which lurked in the neighbourhood. He would be only too glad to get rid of them – for a fee.

By this time something in the order of fifty people were gathered, and they were suitably impressed, and agitated. They would be grateful, and happy to pay, if the *mganga* would cleanse the village. A sum of one shilling a head (5p) was demanded for the exorcism The self-styled witch doctor then went through his routine, casting the bones, and drawing signs in the dust; all very impressive no doubt, by firelight. He declared the village safe – well, almost, but there was a slight snag. Some of the more malignant spirits were unexpectedly tenacious and hadn't responded to the first round of spells and incantations. It was no surprise to hear that those spirits were particularly attached to a handful of those assembled, the lame, the blind the deformed, and the old. For a small additional sum he would winkle them out; that was another ten shillings. Another ritual was performed, and the *mganga* was satisfied that the legions of the damned had departed; he collected his fee and followed suit. Not bad; sixty shillings for a couple of hours work, as much as a labourer earned in two months at the time. In the cold grey light of dawn, the headman realised that his village had been not so much cleansed as taken to the cleaners. And as is so often the lot of those in authority, it was all *his* fault, and the villagers were scornful of his gullibility. Hence the message to Father Odio, and subsequently to the Boma. He wanted retribution. The immediate trail was cold, and I returned to Masasi with the messenger empty-handed. But word went out, and some days later our counterfeit *mganga* was apprehended. Geoff Thirtle and I decided, that he should be charged not under the Witchcraft Ordinance, but under the Penal Code for obtaining money by false pretences; this was less contentious, and less likely to attract the curiosity of the High Court when our fortnightly court returns were scrutinised. He pleaded guilty and I sentenced him to several weeks' extra-mural labour; the money found about his person was forfeited and returned to the villagers of Nambawara by way of compensation. As for the Final Financial Statement, the short break followed by a weekend did the trick. Inspiration flowed, and this time a new fictitious amendment worked; the accounts were impeccable.

This account of a relatively trivial case of purported witchcraft should not lull the reader into dismissing the whole notion of witchcraft and sorcery out of hand. Not all Africans believed in it of course, but where local communities and individuals accepted its existence as a fact of life, the nastier variety could be a baleful and disruptive influence. In extreme cases it could take the form of psychological pressure leading to deteriorating health or death, or the administration of herbal poisons. And of course for most victims there was also a client paying for the desired outcome. The extent to which malevolent forms of witchcraft were practised could not be known; it was certainly not a common occurrence in every district, but that it existed at all was justification for the Witchcraft Ordinance. Robin Lamburn, a long-serving UMCA missionary in Masasi assured me that he knew of an instance of a human sacrifice having taken place a few years earlier in neighbouring Tunduru district at the behest of a visiting *mchawi*, allegedly the aforementioned Nguvumali. This had been reported to him by a local African pastor, and Robin in turn had passed it on to the then DC Tunduru. The matter was investigated, but unsurprisingly no evidence could be found; and of course, if true, there would be no witnesses as the whole village must have been complicit in the murder.

Leave

In February Sylvia and the children preceded me on leave, this time travelling by sea. I saw them off to Dar from Nachingwea on an East African Airways DC3, and was reminded of a recent accident at the Kilwa airfield, their first stop; a propeller had come adrift and ploughed into the cockpit, killing the pilot. The existence of an airfield at Kilwa was reputed to be entirely due to the initiative of the local DC some years earlier. Provided with funds for famine relief work on district roads, he had diverted some of them into the construction of an all-weather airstrip. Subsequently the Official Gazette published a listing of airfields designated as currently suitable for commercial use. Kilwa did not of course feature, and the DC wrote off to have the omission remedied. An astonished civil aviation authority found the Kilwa runway up to standard, and thereafter it was included in the regular Southern Province air service. No doubt the DC was given a formal ticking off, his enterprise tacitly approved.

A few weeks later, having done a little over three years in Southern Province with only a fortnight's break, I too departed on leave; it had been a tiring tour, and I looked forward to a rest. There was a tinge of melancholy too; most of my colleagues, expatriates and Africans, were also friends, and I knew that I would meet very few of them again in the future. This was particularly so in the case of Eben Pienaar, our Afrikaner agricultural Field Officer, who in very few years would retire to South Africa. He was conscientious and effective in his work, and a good friend; he could always be relied on to put things right when my own car maintenance failed to produce the desired result. He and his English wife Gladys were a delightful couple; childless, they would have made excellent parents. I had not expected to see them again after Masasi, but in 1974 a duty visit took me to Botswana, Lesotho and Swaziland, and three days leave allowed a detour to their small farm in the Transvaal, to which they had retired in the early Sixties. Here they had initially lived in a corrugated iron shack whilst he built a small and very basic bungalow with his own hands, and put down a borehole. When I visited, Eben ran his farm solo, with the part-time assistance of an African schoolboy;

there were no domestic staff. They lived very frugally, and had little to show for their twenty-odd years in Tanganyika; not all white South Africans lived in luxury.

There were also some admirable missionary personalities with whom I had more tenuous friendships, and whom I would also be sorry to consign to the past. In the UMCA, there was Dr Frances Taylor who had reputedly rebuilt much of Mkomaindo hospital with a legacy; her colleague Dr. Marion Robinson who later married the Bishop, Mark Way, who was succeeded by Trevor Huddleston a couple of years later; Ronald Heald, the ballet dancer manqué, who had put on weight and now, employed by the Leprosy Relief Association and terrified of catching leprosy, ran a leprosy clinic adjacent to the UMCA hospital in Lulindi; and there was the austere but kindly Kathleen Beresford-Knox, head of a girls' secondary school at Ndwika. Most formidable of my UMCA contacts was the diminutive but indefatigable Canon Robin Lamburn, diocesan Education Secretary, and in this context the recipient of government capitation grants after I had scrutinised and approved his claims; in retirement he went on to run a leprosy settlement in Utete district, and was later awarded the Albert Schweitzer Prize.

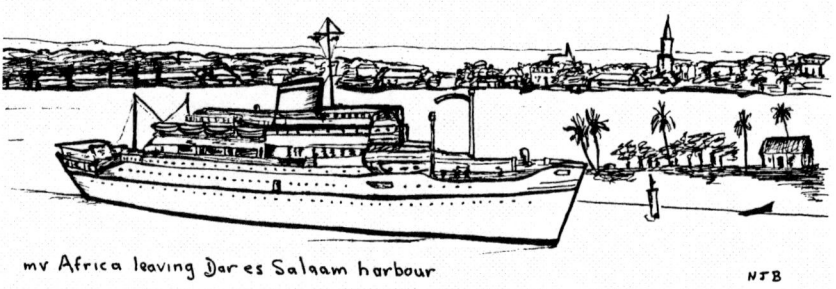

mv Africa leaving Dar es Salaam harbour   NJB

In the rival camp of the Benedictines were Sister Thecla, who had been at Ndanda hospital since German times; and Sister Lia, who, recruited to teach English, found herself put in charge of a sizeable leprosarium. And there was Father Odio, the friendly and generous head of the Lukuledi trade school; always helpful, he arranged for a lay brother in Rome to give me a conducted tour of the city whilst staying over for a few days on my way home. Preceded by a few balmy spring days in Athens, Rome came as a shock; the weather was not as hospitable as the Benedictines, and the temperature remained resolutely below freezing for the duration of my stay.

Norbert Johanes' workshop, Masasi

Nanyumbu Native Court in session

Crossing the Ruvuma to Mozambique

Piped water, Masasi district

En route from Dar es Salaam
to Mwanza

Village celebration, Masasi district

Approaching Nansio pier, Ukerewe

Sir Richard Turnbull presenting medals

Coffee seedlings for distribution

Homestead, mainland Ukerewe

View from Kurwirwi Hills

Rugezi ferry

Recreational weekend safari, Ukerewe

Ngorongoro crater

Author with District Councillors at Moshi

Sylvia with Nicola and Nigel

Dam nearing completion

Sylvia and other voters, 1960 General Election

Family afloat in Baumann gulf

Nicola & Nigel with a clutch
of ostrich eggs, Serengeti

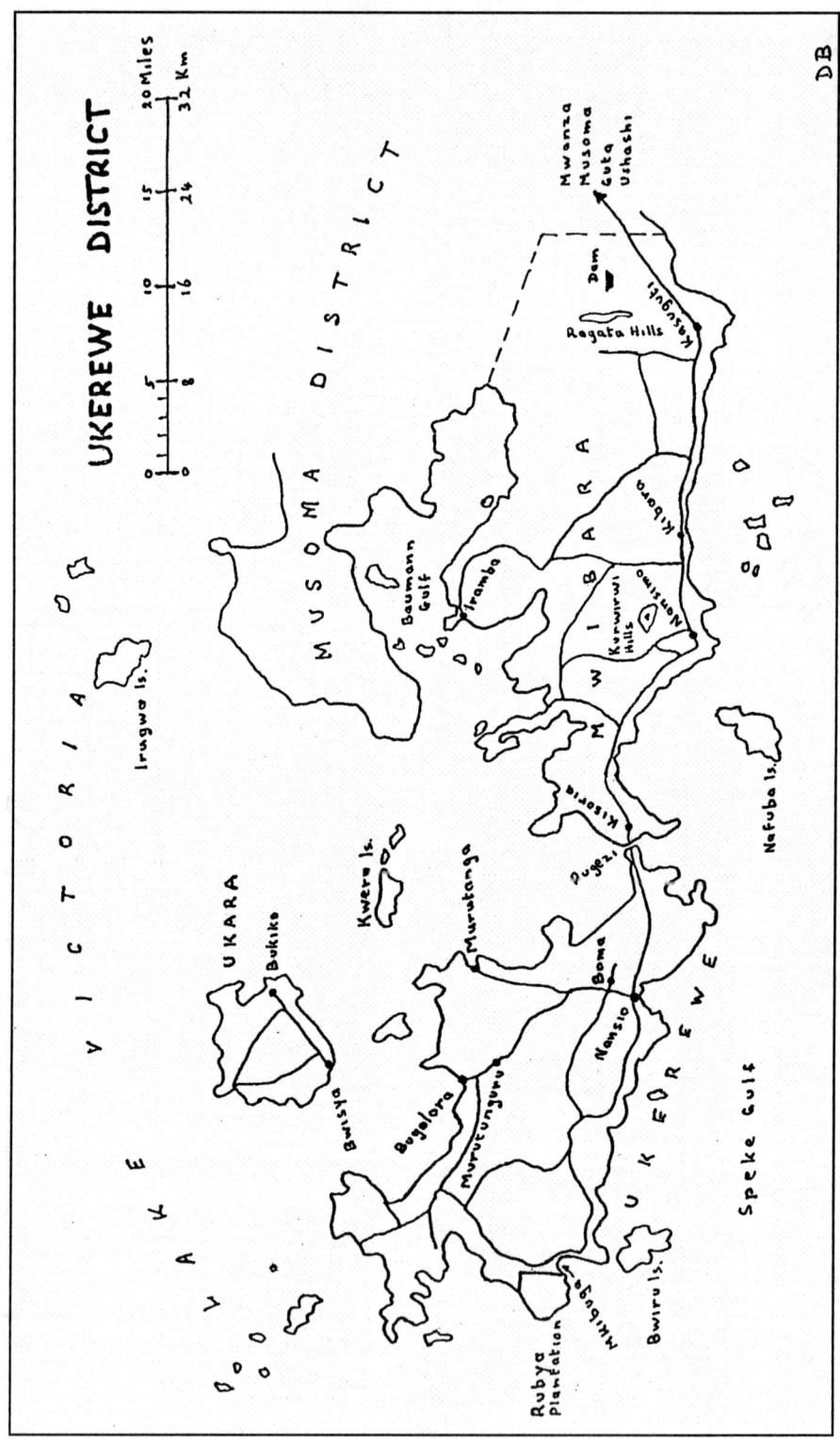

CHAPTER FIVE

Ukerewe

Arrival

R eunited with the family, and living out of suitcases whilst enjoying the hospitality of parents and relations, time soon began to drag. I was anxious to get back to work, the more so since the arrival of a letter announcing that I was to take over Ukerewe district on Lake Victoria. This time we made our own travel arrangements, starting with a rail journey to Venice, where we paused for sightseeing, and to meet an old college friend and his wife who were fortuitously holidaying there. Then a restful week on the beach in Caorle before boarding the Lloyd-Triestino mv *Africa* for the swift ten day voyage to Dar-es-Salaam. As before, Issa and Mzee were there to meet us and accompany us to our new post.

At the Secretariat I was briefed by Basil Stubbings, the current head of the Provincial Administration; he described Ukerewe as a lively and difficult district, the local people politically aware and not reticent about showing it. I left him with some apprehension. As on my first tour, we took the night train up-country, this time bound for Mwanza, situated in the south-east corner of the lake. On the platform seeing off a colleague was an old army chum with whom I had shared a barrack-room in 1947; he was now wearing the white cassock of a UMCA missionary. The next morning we halted briefly at Manyoni, where I had begun my career six years earlier, and the following day arrived at Mwanza, 'capital' of Lake Province.

Here I had a more detailed briefing from my new Provincial Commissioner, Stanley Walden, affectionately known as 'Fanny', and his deputy 'Jimmy' Riddell. At seven the next morning we drove down to the pier where the mv *Alestes* was due to leave for Nansio, Ukerewe's little port and commercial centre. Once aboard, the children were soon adopted by the captain, a large and cheerful Luo from Kenya, and Hassani, the shy but

157

friendly engineer. We got to know them both well during the next two years, after which the *Alestes* was replaced by the elderly *Tilapia* with a different crew.

I anxiously watched our station waggon being winched aboard by muscle power, and shortly afterwards we were off, with a cargo of supplies for the Ukerewe shops and cotton ginnery, and a colourful throng of passengers with their bundles and boxes, baskets of fruit, dried fish, chickens and the varied basic adjuncts of rural African life. Out of the harbour we headed north across Speke Gulf and an hour or so later passed a cluster of rocks and their resident cormorants. As long again, and Ukerewe island came into sight, and three hours after leaving Mwanza we tied up at Nansio pier; the journey by road would have taken twice as long. My predecessor had already left, and we were met by an outgoing DO who had unaccountably transferred his allegiance to Marks and Spencer, and a newly-arrived cadet, Christopher Child.

Waiting for the Ukerewe ferry   NTB

Our heavy baggage had arrived from Masasi, a dozen or more trunks and packing cases. Sylvia, Mzee, and Issa set about putting the house in order; it was of the same design as our previous quarter except that it had a guest wing and a corrugated iron roof. I retreated to the Boma. There followed an intensive period of familiarisation, inevitably a little daunting – 'However am

I going to get on top of this?' – but knowing from experience that I would. Over the next few weeks everything fell into place, relationships were established with colleagues, traders and other businessmen, missionaries, and the Native Authorities. We expatriate officials were a mixed bunch. Christopher and I were the only Englishmen, although a third, Guy Hart Dyke, turned up later in the shape of a forester; the agricultural Field Officer, David Mowat, was a Scot; the District Foreman, Eddie Murat was from Mauritius; the Medical Officer, Dr. Tiagi, was an Indian, and with his Nepalese wife, our next-door neighbours; and the nursing sister, Martha Dalton, was Irish, later to leave and not be replaced. She and Sylvia were the only European women on the station. Towards the end of our second year the Tiagis were replaced by the Swedish Count Mörner and his Norwegian wife. To add to the variety, the District Advisory Council employed a married Seychellois mechanic, Reg Rouillon, and a Greek Cypriot building supervisor, Mr. Vassiliou, whose contract was shortly to expire. He spoke no English and execrable Swahili, always at the top of his voice; this earned him the apt nickname of *Bwana Kelele* – the Bwana who makes a lot of noise. The senior African staff comprised the police Inspector, an Assistant Veterinary Officer, Cuthbert Hatibu, and the Head Tax Clerk; the busy cash office was run by a pair of able and reliable young men from Nyasaland (Malawi). My own Head Clerk, Festus Ganzile, turned out to be as efficient and productive as any clerk I have come across before or since.

In the wider non-African community there were probably two or three hundred Indians, mainly of Gujarati descent, and a handful of Omani Arabs; most of these were traders. Also scattered around the district were a number of missionaries; the White Fathers numbered a French Canadian, the memorable Father Vachon, who spoke after the manner of Maurice Chevalier, a brace of Dutchmen, an Alsatian, a Dutch lay doctor on contract and several teaching and medical nuns from various European countries. The African Inland Mission was in the charge of a gentle German couple; their resident teenage daughter must have been very lonely. At Murutunguru was a cotton ginnery managed by a Devon man, Jack Leach, with the assistance of a South African engineer, Ian Summerset; and at the other end of the district , at Kibara, another ginnery was run by an Indian, always spoken to and of as GB. There was also a rice mill and one which extracted oil from cotton seed, both owned and managed by Indians.

Ukerewe was the smallest rural district in the country with 500 square miles[33]; but it also had the densest rural population, averaging 250 to the square mile, and varying from over 600 in Ukara to less than 50 in the extreme east. By way of contrast it was one-twentieth the size of Manyoni district, my first posting, but had more than double the population. The district comprised a number of inhabited islands, the largest being Ukerewe and Ukara, together with a sizeable piece of adjacent peninsular mainland to the east, locally called Mwibara. The largest ethnic group were the Kerewe, who inhabited the main island and Mwibara, where there were also numbers of Jita, who had moved in over the years from neighbouring Musoma district. Ukerewe chiefdom was unusual, though not unique, in having a system of land tenure which included a form of occupancy approximating to freehold. The Kerewe, closely related to the Haya on the western shore of Lake Victoria, had a traditional chief, here known as the *Omukama*, and the tribal historian could rattle off his lineage back to the time of Henry VIII with barely a pause for breath. The then chief, Michael Lukumbuzya, was a man of about my own age, a thoughtful and congenial product of Makerere University College in Uganda.

Over on Ukara, the local administration was in the hands of the elderly and moribund Chief Mataba, whose people claimed descent from a wandering group of Galla, whose homeland is in the Horn of Africa. His incumbency was characterised more by indolence than any obvious misrule, though his fellow Kara seemed less concerned about this than I later became. All the same, the more adventurous of them left home and settled on Ukerewe island and, increasingly, in Mwibara. By Tanganyika standards Ukerewe was fairly prosperous, and although farmsteads were small, they were well-tended; cotton flourished and generated useful cash incomes, and the lake teemed with fish. Almost everyone, it seemed, had a bicycle. There was also a strong tradition of self-help, with community projects organised by the Native Authorities and undertaken with good grace, and without pressure from Government.

The immediate problems about which I had been warned resolved themselves. An unwillingness on the part of one of the Kerewe sub-chiefs to

---

[33] About the size of Hampshire plus the Isle of Wight

allocate land for the construction of a small rest-house became irrelevant when I decided we didn't need one anyway; I would order a lightweight tent which I could sling into the back of my station waggon and set up unaided wherever I chose to spend a night. Resistance to the establishment of a forest reserve and plantation took longer to overcome, but painstaking and often tedious discussion eventually bore fruit, and work on demarcation, clearing and planting began. It would be an exaggeration to say that the next two and a half years was a period of unalloyed bliss – but it came close.

* * *

We arrived in Ukerewe in September, and by the end of the year we were well settled in. A few days before Christmas, and shortly after sunset, we were just starting our evening meal en famille when there was a sudden sound which began as a whisper and seemed to herald an imminent rush of wind; within seconds it had evolved into the rising note and volume of a choir in action. The headmaster of the nearby middle school at Bukongo had quietly assembled his boys just below our dining room window, and was treating us to a surprise carol concert. It was a delightful gesture and we were completely bowled over; unfortunately, since it *was* a surprise, we were not equipped to dispense hospitality on an adequate scale, but we did our best. Thereafter the head and I developed a warm relationship and I was a regular visitor to his school.

Here is it worth mentioning the *kichekesho*[34] or school concert. It was very common for the senior school in the vicinity of the Boma to invite expatriate officials to the annual concert. At these there would invariably be a sketch taking off government at large or the DC in particular; these were usually amusing and often quite witty. Other turns tended to result in one or more of us paying a forfeit by performing in some way. It was all good clean fun, probably as good for us as it was for our hosts. It was not long before, in this context, I was required to pay for our carol concert by making a fool of myself at the middle school's next concert.

---

[34] Literally 'a little something to laugh at'.

Visit by the Governor

Some months after our arrival in Ukerewe, a visit by the new Governor, Sir Richard Turnbull, was announced. We were not overjoyed, nor did the prospect fill us with alarm, but we were curious to meet this newcomer who had until recently served in Kenya. He was viewed with suspicion by the African nationalists because of his association with the suppression of Mau Mau; on the other hand he had established a good personal relationship with Julius Nyerere, who was clearly destined to be our first African Prime Minister. HE (His Excellency) was to speak to my District Team, address the District Council, and present medals – one to our slothful Chief Mataba of Ukara, the other to the very capable Local Courts Adviser, Alypius Munyaga. The preparations were not complex, and consisted amongst other things of dissuading Eddie, the District Foreman, from rushing around whitewashing everything in sight; HE would see us as we really were, warts and all. In pursuit of the same objective, I had the sub-chief of Kasuguti undo some recent cosmetic road repairs undertaken by the PWD along the road leading into the district from the east. I knew perfectly well that the PWD were not spending the requisite amount maintaining that road, the only one in the district for which we were not responsible; and for a second class trunk road it was in a deplorable condition. I judged that they would hastily patch up the worst of it shortly before the Governor passed along, and that after the next shower it would be as bad as ever. On the eve of his arrival two or three gangs of labourers restored part of the road to its previous defective state. It was customary for a DC to meet the visiting Governor at the district boundary, in this case a good two hours drive away; but HE was a thoughtful man, and arranged for us to meet at the Rugezi ferry, only twenty minutes down the road.

There Chris and I awaited the party from Government House. The meeting and greeting was relaxed and I climbed into HE's Daimler to accompany him to our house at Kabingo. I enquired how he had found the road from Guta into the district; he had not been impressed. I agreed that it was a bad bit of road, and needed closer attention than the PWD was able to give; we could, I said, do it better and more cheaply than they. As indeed proved to be the case when funds were subsequently sub-allocated to us for this purpose.

162

Contrary to popular belief, life in the Colonial Service – at least in post-war Tanganyika – was remarkably free of pomp and ceremony. There was one custom however, which was positively feudal; when the Governor visited a district the DC and his family were required to move out of their house whilst the gubernatorial party moved in. My knowledge of medieval English history is limited, but I doubt if Henry IV would have expected it of his baronial hosts when he progressed round the country, though he may have outstayed his welcome and eaten them out of castle and home. However, it made sense, and so it was that after tea and an exchange of social amenities, we left our house and moved in with Eddie, reappearing later in the day as guests in our own house when HE held a reception for the great and not so great in Ukerewe. When it was over and the guests had departed, HE's Private Secretary[35] and I settled down until the small hours writing the Governor's speech for the morrow. He provided the main content, I the local slant, and we differed from time to time over the finer points of Swahili syntax.

It was a short night, for HE had a predilection for early morning walks in the bush, preferably up hillsides. Ukerewe island was thickly peopled and there was no bush; and the nearest hill of any size was twenty miles away on the mainland. So, starting shortly after five, we drove round the island in the Daimler instead; that we were able to do so without damage or embarrassment was a tribute to the standard of Eddie's road maintenance. It was an enjoyable hour, the Governor interested in local developments, concerned to provide support if it was possible to do so, and to reassure – for at this time we sometimes felt somewhat neglected by a remote Secretariat preoccupied with national politics. At one point I complained about the excessive number of telegrams emanating from Dar es Salaam in code, the deciphering of which all too frequently had to be done in the evenings or at weekends. Rarely was the message so urgent that it could not have been dispatched by sealed letter. I singled out one particular telegram which had run to a scribbled side and a half of foolscap in which we were advised on the line to take if tackled by local politicians about the recent independence of British Somaliland – soon alas to be swallowed up by the former Italian Somaliland more ruthless in the practice of realpolitik. I had spent two or three hours one Saturday afternoon

---

[35] A DO on attachment to Government House.

getting it into plain English by thumbing through the massive Government Telegraph Code, and couldn't conceive why the exercise had been undertaken in the first place; and I said so. The Governor smiled, sympathised, and then after a short pause added. 'As a matter of fact I instructed it to be sent out myself'. There followed a somewhat longer pause.

Sir Richard did not share the exuberant bonhomie of his predecessor. Tall, slim, and athletic, he was more cerebral and austere, and not given to exchanging inconsequential chit chat. I was reassured by our conversation whilst touring the island, and looked forward to further discussions when he came to the Boma after breakfast. There he met our local staff and then joined me and the rest of the District Team in my office. Here we briefed him on developments in the district, and HE then brought us up to date on the national political situation, and Government's relations with TANU; there was marked tension over the rate of progress to internal self-government, and some concern over national security. This last was never far from our thoughts, for although we had a nice tidy emergency plan for the district, it would have been unrealistic to assume that our resources were equal to the demands which might be placed upon them. It was a matter of profound relief that it was never put to the test.

It was then time to break up, shower, and change for the presentation of medals and the meeting with the District Council. I had by this stage in my career acquired a ceremonial white drill uniform, but had so far managed to avoid wearing it. On this occasion I had a narrow escape, by persuading the Governor's PS that the Kerewe were relatively sophisticated, and wouldn't be much impressed by the uniforms, egret plumes, and gilt-handled swords tucked under armpits. On the other hand they *would* be eager to hear what HE had to say. So we wore lightweight tropical lounge suits for the occasion. In retrospect I have regretted my persuasiveness; it would have been appropriate to have worn it just once before consigning it permanently to a trunk in an English attic.

The District Council headquarters at this time comprised a semi-derelict mud-brick building about forty feet square, which provided inadequate accommodation for the Treasurer and Secretary and their staff. A new HQ had been approved, and the contract awarded to a firm of Italian builders. Meanwhile the council had no debating chamber, and the District Court, set four-square in the centre of the imperialist Boma, also served to nurture local political and developmental aspirations when it doubled as the council chamber. The Governor's speech was well received; in it he gave some indication of future political and constitutional trends, and of course referred to the increasing democratisation of local government. At this time I was the ex-officio executive chairman of an exclusively nominated District Advisory Council, whose purpose was to advise me, and whose views, ideas, and support I in turn sought; less than two years later I became adviser to a largely elected council which chose its own chairman , and went on to make its own decisions.

After the speech came the presentation of medals. Inspector Jackson Ntenga [36] had his police contingent drawn up on parade – khaki shorts and tunics with nickel plated buttons, navy blue tarbooshes and puttees, with lanyards at the shoulders, leather belts and superannuated Lee-Enfield rifles; these were the foundations of our local security, and there would have been a dreadful pull of conflicting loyalties had there ever been serious political unrest. But now they were on parade, their main duty to look smart and businesslike. The routine evolutions were performed, and HE stepped forward, with his ADC carrying the medals; I stood to one side and watched. The Queen's Medal for Chiefs sometimes tended to be no more than recognition for long service and longevity, and these were Chief Mataba's main qualifications. Dressed in a blue serge jacket over a white *kanzu* or gown, and topped off with a red fez, he leaned heavily on a walking stick as the medal was hung round his neck and the citation read. Alypius Munyaga, repository of Kerewe history and law, had done more to earn his award; the following year, after our reorganisation of the local court system, he became largely responsible for the training and guidance of four or five local stipendiary magistrates who would take over the judicial function hitherto carried out by Chiefs and Sub-chiefs.

The modest ceremonial completed, we departed for lunch and to change back into shirts and shorts. In the afternoon we were joined by our PC, 'Fanny' Walden, who had come over from Mwanza in his motor launch *Speke* to meet and confer with our visitors, and accompany them back to Mwanza the following morning. In the evening we took a stroll, for HE liked to keep in touch with the people he governed; in Dar es Salaam he regularly made an

---

[36] A fictitious name, for reasons which will later be apparent.

early morning bicycle tour of the town, accompanied by the rather less enthusiastic African mayor.

On our return we parted company, HE to have a quiet evening with his wife, whilst I went back to join Sylvia in Eddie's house. 'Fanny' Walden was staying in the rest-house, but was to dine with Chris and his mother, who had recently come out to Tanganyika on a visit. Her brief stay was not unadventurous. Chris had gone over to Mwanza to pick up a new Landrover, a gift from his mother, and coincidentially to meet her at the airfield. On the way back it had broken down, and mother and son had stayed the night in the premises of an Indian trader somewhere along the road between Mwanza and Guta. A few days later Chris took her over to Ukara island by *mashua*, a local sailing boat. A broken rope had caused spar and sail to fall overboard and the pair had spent an anxious half hour speculating on the likelihood of their reaching the nearest rock if obliged to swim for it. On the present occasion Chris was to create a good impression by giving 'Fanny' a decent evening meal, prepared by his mother. Now it was one of 'Fanny's' more eccentric and endearing social habits to fall asleep almost immediately after dinner. In company this was always politely ignored, and the pretence maintained that he hadn't really been to sleep at all; this evening he got it all wrong, and fell asleep *before* dinner. Waking after his habitual twenty minutes he got to his feet, thanked Mrs. Child for an *excellent* meal and retired to the rest-house. Unfortunately we had already eaten when Chris sent round for assistance with the surplus food.

The following morning our visitors took their leave, Lady Turnbull having helped prepare sandwiches for the journey. The departure at Nansio pier produced a final comic incident. Chris had found a small wooden box which, covered with maroon cloth, was to provide an additional step to overcome the rather long vertical gap between the landing stage and the *Speke's* deck; HE leaped down without difficulty, ignoring the box. His lady, more amply proportioned, stepped onto it, whereupon it collapsed. With this minor mishap laughed aside the *Speke* drew away and our visitors departed. Sylvia resumed control of our domestic arrangements, and I spent the rest of the morning preparing for my first session with the District Advisory Council.

There was an initial slight awkwardness as we silently speculated how we would get on together, and later a prolonged contretemps when a number of councillors tried to initiate a debate on an area of policy reserved to central government. This was not a good start, and in mid-afternoon, after sending a warning note to Sylvia, I invited the councillors home for refreshments. In the ensuing informal gathering any remaining frostiness disappeared; there would be disagreements in the future, but there were never any further doubts that my concerns, like theirs, were for the district.

We resumed our deliberations until sundown, when I sent for lamps. For the rest of the evening we dispersed into committees, and I attached myself to the one dealing with natural resources, with David Mowat co-opted to discuss a paper which he and I had been working on. In this we proposed a programme of modest agricultural development over a period of several years, and which could be sustained entirely from local resources and revenues; it was a pleasure to find the committee so receptive. At ten o'clock I called a halt. It had been a good day. We resumed at nine the following morning. When the light faded in the early evening I again sent for some lamps. At this, our only overtly nationalistic sub-chief[37] jumped to his feet protesting that he was tired; his sentiments were echoed around the court room. I chided the members for their lack of stamina, observing that it was just a normal working day; *I* was at it *every* day. *'Ndiyo Bwana, lakini umezoea'* – yes, but *you* are accustomed to it. A vote was taken, and we adjourned until the morrow; I cannot say that I was altogether sorry.

Family affairs

Shortly after HE's visit one of my mother's weekly letters announced that my father, plagued with bronchitis since being gassed in the 1914-18 war, was seriously ill with emphysema. I wrote to him at once suggesting a few months recuperation in sunny Ukerewe; he died before receiving it, and my mother's subsequent telegram asked me to break the news to my sister Pat, whose husband Douglas was now Provincial Tsetse Officer in Mwanza. I alerted the crew of my official motor launch, and we chugged across to Mwanza that

---

[37] In fact the one who had objected to the construction of a rest-house the previous year.

afternoon, four hours hard labour for the elderly Perkins diesel. I didn't look forward to the meeting with Pat; she had been closer to our father than I, and in the event took his death badly. I offered what comfort I could, stayed overnight, and returned to Ukerewe in the morning. Largely because of his prolonged absences from the family home, I had never known my father well, and had looked forward to remedying this after his retirement – which was to have been the following year.

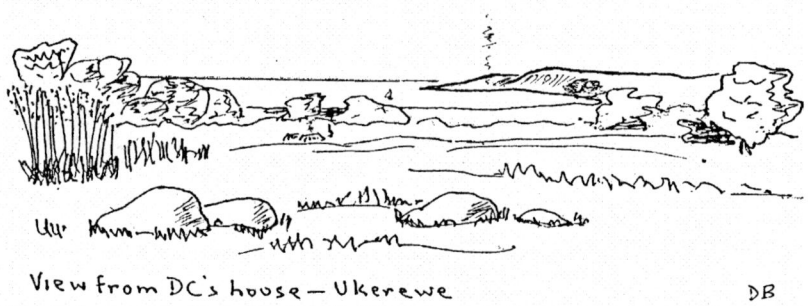

View from DC's house – Ukerewe   DB

Domestic and social life in Ukerewe was not significantly different from that in Masasi and Kondoa. On the culinary front there was an abundance of lake fish, and a range of local vegetables which made it unnecessary to grow our own. As the senior government official I had to do a good deal more entertaining, and we had a small guest wing for overnight visitors. Sylvia was an exemplary hostess, and in particular kept a motherly eye on my bachelor colleagues, Chris, David, Guy, and Eddie. We were also fortunate in still having Issa and Mzee with us; they were very much part of the family, familiar with our ways, and we with theirs.

Our children, Nicola and Nigel, were the only expatriate youngsters on the station. Their everyday playmates were Rashidi and Saidi, Issa's two children; in consequence they were both bilingual. They also got on well together, and were good at entertaining themselves with few toys, and imaginative use of minimal props – in particular a playpen, a few cardboard boxes, and an old army blanket. There was also a weekly get-together with the ginnery expatriates at Murutunguru where there were four South African children. On our occasional visits to Mwanza our offspring came into contact with other expatriate children at the Club, and discovered how unkind small children can be to outsiders.

In 1959 Nicola had her fifth birthday and so became eligible for formal education. In the absence of a suitable school, we availed ourselves of the excellent correspondence course run by two admirable ladies in the Education Department in Dar es Salaam. This was designed for the benefit of officials in rural areas; with the aid of teaching notes and textbooks provided, mother took on the teaching – essentially the three R's and 'art' – submitting work to Dar for marking and comment. Sylvia embarked on this task conscientiously, but with some trepidation; thereafter she had little time on her hands. It was a credit to her and the correspondence course that on return to Britain, Nicola slotted into her new class without any problems.

The vacancy for a dog left by the demise of Rack whilst we were on leave was filled by a golden Cocker spaniel, Kim. Ordered surreptitiously from a breeder in Nairobi, he was my Christmas present to Sylvia three months after our arrival in Ukerewe. It was a stroke of luck that a Kenya Police Air Wing pilot was able to deliver him to our airstrip whilst en route to Mwanza only a week or so before the 25th; he was then kept, out of sight, by a neighbour until Christmas morning. When we later went on leave we left him with the Rouillons, and they were delighted to keep him when we opted not to return to Tanganyika. When their contract expired they took Kim with them to the Seychelles, where he sired a new range of floppy-eared dogs.

The landscape of Ukerewe district was attractive, with the varied juxtaposition of land and water; and at a height of 3720 feet (1134m) the climate was equable. Picnics were a favourite diversion, for which we sometimes made use of the launch. Then there were day trips to the grassy plains over on Mwibara to watch the game; more rarely we stayed for a weekend under canvas, perhaps as many as twelve of us in three or four tents. These were occasions of sheer pleasure, enjoyed by adults and children alike. At night there was relaxed talk round the campfire, and later an enveloping silence broken only by the occasional yap of jackal, whoop of hyena, and two or three miles away – roar of lion in the Ragata Hills.

On my last recreational day out on the Mwibara plains I received my comeuppance as a marksman. Hitherto usually reliable with a rifle when hunting for the pot, I shot but failed to kill a Thomson's gazelle. I hit and shattered its shoulder; it ran off swiftly on three legs and I followed, and as I got in range it scampered off again. This process was repeated again and again over a distance of a couple of miles until finally a second shot finished it off. We and our neighbours had some succulent Tommy for the fridge, and Mzee and Issa had their share; but I never shot anything again.

Development of a Forest Plantation

On the western tip of Ukerewe island, at Rubya, were the remains of a few square miles of rain forest, and Forestry Department botanists had judged that it would be a suitable area in which to establish a 'production reserve'; more usually reserves were designated to conserve and manage valuable indigenous hardwoods, inhibit soil erosion, and protect the water table. My predecessor had secured the acceptance of Chief Lukumbuzya and his chiefdom council for setting up the reserve, but the Kerewe living in Rubya were less than enthusiastic. Initially there was vigorous opposition to the idea, and the project was seized on by local TANU supporters as a rod for Government's back – in practice my own. After a series of tiresome but necessary public meetings and talks with the TANU Chairman and Secretary, opposition was withdrawn.

Guy Hart Dyke was posted to us as Assistant Conservator of Forests with the express brief of setting up trial plots of fast-growing softwood, and to establish a plantation which would eventually run to about four thousand acres. Quite by chance I had at the time a small sum of money with which to build a new rest-house near the Boma, the existing one having been earmarked for adaptation as the police station; news of Guy's arrival provided the incentive to get the job done. It was up in less than a month, and Guy arrived just in time to select his own colour scheme, Wedgwood blue and white. Here he lived for the next few months whilst supervising the building of his own house at Rubya, and getting the trial plots started.

Guy was a competent forester but an indifferent architect, and his house when complete resembled a child's drawing. It was well sited however, about a hundred yards from the lake shore, and Guy cleared an arc of bush and thicket to give an unrestricted view from the house. However, the land being level and the water-table high, the septic tank could not be dug to the proper depth, and its upper part had to be built above ground level; it was not an object of beauty. Furthermore the WC had to be even higher, and was in fact installed on a plinth some three feet high, approached by a number of steps. The window was adjusted accordingly, where, as an estate agent's puff might have enthused, it 'afforded extensive views over the lake'. The rather bizarre sanitary arrangements encouraged an element of vulgar ribaldry at the house-warming party, though more indelible memories were left by the legions of tiny sandfly which infested the shore, and which brought the more tender skins up in agonising bumps.

Meanwhile several plots of seedlings had been planted, and records set up. There was one more problem to be solved; we did not have funds to pay labour to keep the plantation weeded during its first two or three years. Patiently, over a period of several weeks, Guy recruited a number of local squatters; the arrangement was that they would grow their own annual crops in the tree plantation, concurrently tending their maize and millet whilst at the same time controlling the weeds which would otherwise have over-run the tree seedlings. There were occasional minor disputes, but on the whole the scheme worked remarkably well.

Guy left Ukerewe shortly before I did, and was replaced by a young New Zealander. Unlike Guy he was married, and his wife took an instant dislike to Rubya and the remoteness of her new home; it was twenty miles from district headquarters. Her reaction was not surprising, and for every wife who took to the lonely life of up-country Tanganyika there were probably two or three who didn't. I recollect squalls over Rubya and I'm not sure that there wasn't a nervous breakdown, or what could have been attempted suicide. I did what I could and urged an early replacement, but events just then became tangled with my imminent departure, and the young forester and his wife became my successor's problem.

A few years later I was working in Nigeria for the British Council when I ran into Guy, newly-arrived to grow trees for the Government of Northern Nigeria, and based in Ilorin. I told him of a recent article I had read in one of the national English-language dailies. A staff reporter had been to Tanzania to write a series of feature articles about the other side of Africa. One of these had been devoted entirely to the forest reserve at Rubya which Guy had started and nursed through infancy, and over which we had both sweated blood in the preliminary stages. The reserve had flourished, but the facts of its genesis had been stood completely on their head. With astonishment I read that its establishment had been a triumph of local and nationalist persistence

171

and far-sightedness in the face of determined opposition by 'the colonialists'. The Kerewe, I read, had insisted upon the reserve, and had planted it up despite the efforts of the colonial administration to prevent it; the Forestry Officer had been particularly active in trying to frustrate the Kerewe in their ardent desire to plant and develop a timber reserve – a strange rôle indeed for a forester. We laughed, and refreshed memories with a bottle of Star beer.

Five years later I was back in Ukerewe at the tenth anniversary of independence. One of the high spots of this brief visit was a run out to Rubya. The nursery had grown, and the Tanzanian Conservator and his staff operated from a substantial office block, outside which a green, gold and black flag hung limply from a flagpole. The view from a nearby rocky knoll was impressive and a sea of conifers twenty and thirty feet high marched to the skyline. Towards the lake a swathe had been systematically cut through the forest, and a lighter, half loaded with logs, lay alongside a timber jetty. It was all very impressive and I said so. I then narrated the content of the Nigerian newspaper article and my companions dissolved in paroxysms of laughter.

Guy's house, now occupied by the Conservator and his substantial family, was little changed; the present incumbent thought no more of its location or his fortune in being stuck at Rubya than Guy's antipodean successor and his wife had done ten years earlier.

* * *

Ukerewe provided another example of the local folk memory being at variance with fact. Ukerewe island was separated from mainland Mwibara by some 150 yards of water, and a chain ferry connected the opposite banks; the road provided the only access to the island by land. The pontoon was powered by four or five labourers who, when not engaged in hauling the ferry across, sat in a thatched shelter chatting and playing cards or *bao*, a board game found pretty well everywhere south of the Sahara. The pontoon could take a truck or bus and a car at a time, and numbers of cyclists and pedestrians; at busy times there could be a considerable queue of vehicles on both sides.

A year or so after arriving in the district I thought it would be advantageous if the ferry could be replaced by a causeway, with a small pontoon in the centre which could be easily moved aside to allow the occasional passage of fishermen's canoes. To this end I sought the support of the District Council, and appointed a small working party of councillors to take soundings across the channel; amongst them were the local Chairman and Secretary of TANU, Hussein Bituro and Godfried, who seemed delighted to be involved in a practical undertaking. We then calculated the volume of spoil which would be needed to form the causeway; the cost of shifting this would later determine whether the proposal would go ahead.

I put the case to 'Fanny' Walden, and some time later funds were allocated and the construction put in hand by the Public Works Department (PWD). The clincher was that the causeway would facilitate trade in general, and speed up the movement of the annual cotton crop out of the island. Work proceeded slowly, and for months a solitary mechanical excavator scooped sludge from the lake and deposited it along the line of the causeway; as it dried out it was levelled, compacted, and topped with hardcore and gravel. It was just about complete at the time I left the district.

Two or three years later, after independence, unprecedentedly heavy rains combined with a new control régime at the Owen Falls dam in Uganda, permanently raised the level of the lake; the causeway was submerged, together with much of the adjacent low-lying shoreline. The gap between island and mainland widened to about two miles, and an antiquated diesel car ferry was put into service. As for the causeway, this has been forgotten – but not the construction work; local tradition now has it that we outgoing British had been mining gold and making off with it whilst the going was good. Oral history as related by old men is not invariably reliable.

Conspiracy to murder

Nations, like people, have a capacity for self-deception, and something of the national character is apparent in the pattern of such delusion. It is a peculiarly British tendency to assume that national institutions for which we have a high regard or attachment are 'the envy of the world'. One such fond assumption – particularly strong amongst Parliamentarians and lawyers – concerns the judicial system. Certainly it has features which inspire respect both at home and abroad. But if the law is frequently an ass in its country of origin, it could appear even more asinine in an Africa which had but one foot

173

in the twentieth century, the other rooted in a variety of traditional tribal cultures. And its application was a constant source of not unfriendly friction between the two factions who administered it – the professional judiciary which answered ultimately to the Chief Justice and the lay magistracy of District Officers which was answerable to the Governor. In general 'we' thought 'them' too much concerned with law and too little with truth and justice, and they thought of us as amateurs – well meaning no doubt, but amateurs nevertheless.

Ukerewe Boma   DB

In Ukerewe there were about eight or nine murders a year; after each, a Preliminary Inquiry or PI was held, and if the evidence warranted it, the accused was committed for trial by the High Court. Somehow the murderers were always found guilty only of manslaughter, with a sentence of rarely more than two years. It was common knowledge locally that if you wanted to do away with someone, all you had to do was get drunk, pick a quarrel with your victim and beat him to death with a hoe or club; you then pleaded that you were so drunk that you didn't know what you were doing, said you were sorry and wouldn't do it again, and found yourself back home a year or two later.

At the time murder was a capital offence, and this perhaps was the trouble. A judge had no jury to share his burden, and although he was assisted by two African assessors, the onerous duty of conviction was essentially a solitary and lonely one. It was hardly surprising that judges were disinclined to convict for murder. However, the prevailing alternative was scarcely calculated to encourage respect for British judicial processes, and these derisory sentences were the subject for representations by the District

Council, by the Chief of Ukerewe, and by myself – all equally unavailing.

It was against this background that we had our most spectacular and bizarre murder. I was playing host at the Queen's Birthday party in June 1959 when Inspector Jackson Ntenga took me aside; one of his constables had just reported the murder of an Indian shopkeeper at Kisoria. Could he be excused? Thereafter, the party palled; the threat of civil unrest which had built up over the previous few months pending a decision by the British Government on progress towards independence had not yet receded, and the murder of a non-African could have had a political motive. I had asked Inspector Jackson to let me know as soon as he had anything definite to report, and he returned late in the afternoon. Yes, the Indian, had clearly been murdered, his throat cut, and the body found near the lake; it seemed likely that he had been killed during the course of a burglary, and dragged away. In the normal course of events I would have left the investigation to the Inspector, but sensing a possible political content, I got on to Provincial Police Headquarters with the police radio telephone. Jackson was a little taken aback, for I had not previously used it, preferring the advantages of poor communications and minimal contact with higher authority.

Hardly two hours later I went down to the airstrip to meet a Cessna aircraft, from which stepped Detective-Inspector Nayar and an African Detective-Sergeant. Inspector Nayar was a slightly built and diminutive Madrasi who exuded an air of confidence and efficiency which in the event proved to be wholly justified. Within thirty-six hours he had got the whole case buttoned up. The briskness of his investigation was equalled only by the ingenuity of the scenario which he unfolded.

The murder had been planned and executed by three Africans, Nelson Lutenga, a district councillor, James Bwiru[38], a local beer retailer, and no less a master-mind than Inspector Jackson. As to the motives, Nelson had wanted to borrow money for business purposes, with nothing but his dignity for security – and had been refused; James had debts for the supply of beer, and these he wanted cancelling; whilst Jackson, a married man, was inspired by jealousy. His mistress at Kisoria had been generous with her favours, and had extended them to, amongst others, the Indian shopkeeper; Jackson was – not entirely reasonably – aggrieved.

---

[38] Not their real names.

It had all been carried out very thoughtfully. The Indian was known to all three conspirators. Also, by chance, he was a keen hunter, and the trio invited him out to shoot duck on the lake. On the appointed day they met at a pre-arranged rendezvous on the lake shore about dawn, the murderers having made their way there in the dark and therefore unobserved, or so they supposed. The Indian was allowed to shoot the first duck; whether it was flighting or sitting is immaterial, but it was dead and some yards from the shore. The Indian took off his outer garments and plunged into the lake. There he was shot in the neck with the Inspector's Webley revolver; they finished him off by cutting his throat, and at the same time carving out evidence of the gunshot wound. One round was later found to be missing from the police armoury.

The killing took place in the water, so there were no bloodstains on the ground or clothing; the corpse was later dressed. The Inspector and his friends may or may not have intended to carry the body back to the shop, but by then the sun was up and the risk too great; they left it. Later, perhaps during the investigation, goods in the shop were pulled off the shelves and a door splintered, to give the impression of a break-in and theft. The Indian had lived alone.

So far so good. It had been intended that Inspector Jackson would go through the motions of conducting an investigation; he would arrest someone on suspicion, and subsequently, with my permission, release him for lack of sufficient evidence, and close the case undetected. It would have worked perfectly had I not in total innocence radioed Police HQ; Inspector Nayar did the rest.

Almost the perfect crime, and certainly a perfect investigation. But at this point things began to go wrong. None of the witnesses who had emerged to give oral evidence – much of it circumstantial, but conclusive – were prepared to make formal statements and testify to their veracity in court. For the Inspector, in the short period of freedom left to him before he and his partners in crime were arrested, let it be known that on his release, he would have his revenge. He would exercise his power as a policeman to pay them back, or as a Nyasa – and Nyasas were notorious in these matters – he would turn himself into a crocodile and have the witnesses for his larder. It worked, and thereafter Inspector Nayar met with a wall of silence. Persuasion, threats, cajolery, all were of no avail; he had to drop the case, and after as protracted an interval as was reasonably possible, withdraw the charge and release the culprits.

This was extremely mortifying. It was bad enough seeing Nelson Lutenga and James Bwiru from time to time, prudently silent but insufferably smug. But the prospect of continuing to work with Inspector Jackson was quite intolerable. I was able to arrange his early transfer to Provincial Headquarters, partly from self-interest, partly in the hope that with him out of the way, the villagers of Kisoria might relent and come forward again as witnesses.

After some weeks it was clear that this was not going to happen, and with some reluctance I decided that the application of counter pressures would be justified. I told the headman of Kisoria that I would turn a blind eye to any measures that he might take, short of violence, to persuade the witnesses to speak up again. He shared my own view of the situation and needed no further bidding. Two weeks later Inspector Nayar returned to take a number of sworn statements, the case was re-opened, and the murderers arrested once again. At the close of the Preliminary Inquiry, this time by a Resident Magistrate from Mwanza, the accused were sent for trial. The case seemed cast-iron, so much so that I began to reflect that after conviction I would be required to compile what was familiarly known as a Death Report; in this context, a DC was asked to investigate locally and to advise the Governor whether there were or – as in this case – were not, any extenuating circumstances which might lead to the exercise of clemency.

I need not have worried. A British judge found the trio not guilty. This was almost entirely my own fault. When contacting the headman of Kisoria, pressure of work had prevented my going to see him, and I had sent a handwritten note asking him to come and see me, but also giving an idea of what I had in mind. This note had subsequently found its way into the hands of the defence lawyer by hand of the brother of the woman in the case, who was one of the key witnesses. He, ironically, was a police inspector, based in Mwanza, but also one whose family loyalty transcended public duty; he did not want his sister's amorous exploits aired in court. 'What exactly did you *mean'*, the defence advocate asked me as I stood in the witness box, 'when you wrote 'I know I can trust you not to go too far....'?' I told him exactly what I had meant. At the end it was beyond the judge's comprehension that a police officer in a district remote from central authority could so effectively intimidate witnesses or that the witnesses could be so spineless as to succumb to his threats and to withdraw their evidence. As for the trick of turning himself into a crocodile – nonsense! On the other hand, my permitted counter-threats had, by implication, been only too effective, and the evidence thereby secured unreliable – notwithstanding that it tallied precisely with the evidence voluntarily given in the first place. At least the judge had the good grace not to be openly critical in court of the conduct of the DC from Ukerewe.

Our three worthies were acquitted; two of them returned to the island, and Jackson Ntenga was transferred away from the province altogether. There was nothing I could do about the other pair except grin and bear it; they were even more smug than they had been before.

Some months later the same High Court – it may not have been the same judge – called for one of my own case files for the purpose of reviewing it[39]. I had convicted one of the islanders of 'conversion not amounting to theft'; in fact he had taken a bicycle without permission, and subsequently dumped it at the other end of the district. I gave him a good talking to and a week or two of extra-mural labour, and ordered him to pay a few shillings compensation to the owner. The High Court increased his sentence to 12 months imprisonment on the grounds that bicycle theft had become far too common – which might have been the case in Mwanza, but was not so in Ukerewe; in any case, the bicycle had not been stolen. I wrote and protested and was politely told to mind my own business.

It was all very galling, but with independence little more than two and a half years ahead, perhaps it didn't matter a great deal in practice, and our successors could order affairs as they saw fit, and perhaps more effectively in some respects.

A dam planned and completed

Ukerewe island was, by rural African standards, closely settled and densely populated, averaging about four hundred people to the square mile. There was no 'bush' as such, and the only land which was not utilised in some way was that comprising the rocky outcrops which were scattered over the

---

[39] All proceedings in district courts were heard in Swahili and recorded in English by the magistrate; the High Court could send for any case file for scrutiny and possible revision.

island. Each village area had its small forest reserve for firewood, and overgrown fallow land alternated with patches of cultivation. The island had some of the visual characteristics of a European landscape which had been formed by settled peasant farmers over many generations. Compared with much of Africa it was tidy and well cared for, small plots of food crops and cotton covering the cultivated area, and tree-lined roads, firewood plantations and fruit trees giving the island a well wooded appearance, as do England's hedgerows and coppices.

The part of the district which lay to the eastwards, on the mainland or Mwibara, was different. Here, a broad wedge-shaped peninsula thrust towards the island, with Speke Gulf to the south and Baumann Gulf to the north. At its centre a small massif, the Kurwirwi hills, rose steeply for two thousand feet, and was both game and forest reserve, home to a few surviving sable antelope. Elsewhere a few small hills relieved the generally flat or undulating terrain, and east of the Ragata Hills almost level and treeless plains extended another twenty miles towards Guta in Musoma district, and beyond again through a broad belt of sparsely settled bush, to the Serengeti plains and national park. Depending on the time of year, a sizeable population of plains game ebbed and flowed and circulated in this easterly part of Ukerewe district; Thomson's gazelle, wildebeest, zebra, giraffe, a few topi, and bushbuck. These in turn sustained a handful of lion and leopard in the Ragata Hills, a rather larger number of wild dogs, hyena, and jackals, and an unknown number of poachers. The activities of these last were curbed, but their existence, combined with the slow spread of settlement and agriculture from the west, meant that by the late Fifties, the end of our stock of game was in sight.

Sad, perhaps, but inevitable, and it would be unrealistic to expect the African peasant farmer to subordinate his own interests to those of foreign tourists and pressure groups. The important thing was, and still is, to ensure the proper protection and management of game within designated reserves, and the protection of endangered species elsewhere. As for the rest, the most one could aim for was the reasonable protection of people and their crops from animal depredations and the protection of game from the large-scale poacher. The farmer who shot an occasional gazelle to feed his family was one thing; the poacher who shot or snared meat by the lorry-load or to secure tourist trophies was something quite different.

At all events the game which roamed the 150 or so square miles at the eastern edge of the district was increasingly under pressure. The peninsula was gradually filling up with local Jita and their brethren from the north in Musoma district, by Kerewe from the west and even by settlers from Ukara island. Much of the soil was excellent for cultivation, deep and black, and the sparse scrub was easily cleared. Over a period of two or three years a handful of relatively wealthy absentee entrepreneurs, some of them not even resident in the district, had sent tractor drivers in to plough a hundred or more acres apiece, and put the land down to cotton. This was not illegal, and it conformed with the usual pattern of the customary right to use land not already being used by someone else; though a sweetener for the sub-chief probably helped on these occasions.

It was the tractor that upset tradition; there was no provision for controlling this kind of exploitation, and with independence glimmering on the horizon there was little prospect of persuading the District Council to make a regulatory bye-law. But they might, I thought, take an interest in controlled settlement of the area, based on the provision of water supplies, and complemented later by a school, market, dispensary, and trading centre. Plots of land could be properly surveyed and laid out, hunting of game regulated in order to provide a continuing source of meat, an agricultural co-operative perhaps set up, and so on. By guiding and indeed accelerating a development which was going to take place anyway, at least the get-rich-quick absentee farmer could be kept in check and the small-time farmer assisted within a balanced social and economic framework not entirely divorced from tradition.

The peg on which to hang and develop this idea had to be a source of water where at present there was none, and to plan a pilot settlement round it. David Mowat, our excellent agricultural Field Officer, was as enthusiastic as a reticent Scottish nature permitted, and on my verandah one evening we worked things out over a bottle of Tusker beer.

The following week we set off to look for a dam site in Mwibara. David liked open air driving, and his short-wheelbase Landrover was laid bare; canvas tilt left in the garage, windscreen down, and windows removed. We loaded our safari gear after an early breakfast, and set off with Ibrahim his cook, and Johanes, a Boma messenger, nestling amongst the baggage behind.

At the Rugezi ferry the crew hauled on the chain with their customary coordinated lethargy, leaving breath for the rhythmic chant which punctuated their labour and cheered the leisurely traveller – and we were in no hurry. At Kibara, we stopped at the police station and quarters. Sergeant Yakubu had a thankless task; he and his two constables would all rather have been at district headquarters, for Kibara was very much a one-horse settlement. But it also had something of the character of the frontier about it; authority was not highly regarded, and it was a haven for petty criminals from both Ukerewe and neighbouring districts; hence the police detachment. Determining that something would have to be done about their poor housing, and scribbling an entry in my notebook, I returned to the Landrover; David was fidgeting, anxious to get on to the plains, and we accelerated out of the police compound to the accompaniment of squawking chickens and cheering children.

From Kibara onwards the road was notoriously bad, dried and rutted black cotton soil broken here and there by stretches of rock where stones thudded up under the wheel arches. Fortunately a brisk wind coming off Speke Gulf blew all our dust away from us.

Nine or ten miles further on, just beyond the low but distinctive Ragata Hills, we turned north off the road and across country, intending to make camp a mile or so east of the hills, and to carry out our search from there. Up and over a small rise the plains were laid out before us; ahead they stretched to the silver strip of Baumann Gulf, beyond which was the blue mass of the Majita plateau, whilst eastwards they shimmered into the distance and disappeared into the haze and heat of unseen burning grass. A mile or so to the north east was a herd of wildebeest, dark against the hay-coloured grass, and a few patches of light brown – small groups of Thomson's gazelle. A few zebra were dotted about, and I counted over twenty giraffe before giving up. Down the slope, and half a mile ahead, a line of bush ran away at an angle, indicating an otherwise imperceptible drainage channel where water flowed in the rains. We would camp down there, for there would be firewood and some shade. We bumped along to the watercourse, disturbing a leopard and a couple of dozing jackals on the way, selected a site, and unloaded. As ever, a figure emerged from nowhere, and came forward to offer help and satisfy curiosity. And perhaps to satisfy hunger too; it would be surprising if the *Mabwana* were unarmed and would not want something for the pot. If he surmised thus, he was correct; David was a compulsive hunter. No sooner had

181

we emptied the Landrover than he unslung his rifle and went off to get a Tommy for our evening meal, accompanied by the newcomer who would say a short prayer and cut its throat before it died, as prescribed by the Koran. I put my feet up under a tree, and waited for the kettle to boil, a cup of tea being as much a ritual in the bush as in an English drawing room. As the tea brewed I heard a shot, and a few minutes later David was back with dinner; Ibrahim took over and began skinning and disembowelling it a hundred yards or so from camp – there would be flies, and scavengers would appear in the night.

After a quick sandwich lunch we began traversing the area in broad sweeps, trying to identify a sizeable catchment area which would justify our serious attention. By dusk we thought we had found one. We also found a poacher. As we drove along another little line of bush I spotted a movement. We headed towards it, and a man broke cover, making for what we later saw was a bicycle. He mounted it and pedalled off furiously, but of course he hadn't a chance. After a short chase we came up with him, took him and his bicycle on board and bumped back to where we had first seen him. Whilst I kept an eye on the prisoner, David went off to investigate, and came back with perhaps seventy yards of grass rope arranged in a series of nooses. This had been pegged down at intervals, the loops coinciding with gaps in the undergrowth, and placed at various heights. Our passenger, looking decidedly anxious, agreed that they were his.

This posed a problem. Recollection of our recently shot Tommy caused a momentary twinge of unease, but brief reflection and enquiry revealed an essential difference. David had a game licence and had simply wanted something for the pot; the poacher reluctantly admitted that his purpose was to sell the animal carcasses to butchers just across the district boundary in Guta; they in turn supplied meat as far away as Musoma. The extent of this indiscriminate killing of game at the time concerned and angered me a good deal, and on a later occasion, accompanied by a Boma messenger in the office Landrover, I chased and caught a trio of the people from Guta who had a lorry half full of dead animals, ruthlessly shot from a moving vehicle. Such was respect for authority at the time that their rifles were handed over without a murmur, and bringing up the rear I escorted them to the Boma to be charged and tried. This time our captive had more modest ambitions, but they were illegal all the same. He also should have been charged and tried; but the nearest sub-chiefdom court was miles away, the District Court four hours drive from our camp. Whichever way you looked at it, our prisoner was an embarrassment; we had either to let him go or keep him tied up for perhaps another twenty-four hours. I thought a little and then set out the alternatives. He could come back to the Boma with us and be tried, in which case he would undoubtedly be convicted and fined or sent to prison – or both. Or, he could surrender his bicycle and we would call it a day. He was in no two minds, and having made his choice, climbed out, backed away making his *salaams,* and fled.

By late afternoon of the following day we had identified a likely dam site, and by way of a makeweight, another spot to the west of the hills where the configuration of the land was suitable for the construction of a *hafir*. This is simply an earth bank in the shape of a crescent or open box, facing up a gentle slope to catch and retain rainwater. But all this was in the future. The first stage of our enterprise was complete, and we set off back to the island – tired, sweaty, dirty, sunburned and well content with the *safari* that had so felicitously combined utilitarian purpose with pleasure. The next morning I arranged to have the bicycle painted bright red with the letters GT (Government Transport) on the crossbar. We had long needed an extra bicycle at the Boma but I had never got round to ordering one; our windfall filled the gap admirably.

It was some time before we had anything to show for our initial reconnaissance. Satisfied that the project had merit, we consulted the District Council; although we could not hope to meet capital expenditure from local revenues, future costs incurred in maintaining the dam and providing modest amenities for new settlers would fall to them. Fortunately the members were keen, and urged me to press ahead

At about this time David went off on vacation leave, to be succeeded by a Field Officer who was brazenly and intolerably idle. I wrote to 'Fanny' Walden asking him to have a word with 'Paddy' Drennan, the Provincial Agricultural Officer, and if possible have David posted back to Ukerewe on his return from leave, provided that he was agreeable. He was, and so was able to see the dam completed.

Meanwhile, I had put the proposal to my PC for consideration at provincial level; it was approved, and funding provided by the Lint and Seed Marketing Board, perhaps attracted by the prospect of increased cotton production a few years hence. A soil scientist came to satisfy himself that any water collected would not simply seep away into the subsoil. Then came the surveyors, and later an engineer to supervise construction; after completion a land surveyor would return to lay out our agricultural plots. Before going on it would be as well to dispel any misapprehension which might be nurtured as to the kind of dam which was envisaged. This was to be no Hoover Dam; it would be made of earth, some 250 yards long and twelve or fifteen feet high. Of no great depth, the wall would be straight, rhomboid in section with a broad path along the top, and widening to about sixty feet at the base. It would catch and retain rainwater running off three or four square miles of country, and with luck would meet the needs of a few thousand people and their domestic stock. Its capacity was estimated at thirty million gallons.

The bulldozers and graders came in to do the heavy work, and the dam was finished off by hand labour, its top levelled and the upstream slope covered with chunks of stone to prevent damage. On the other side we would plant grass when the rains began, to bind the soil together. The job was finished remarkably quickly, and shortly before they went home on leave, I took the family out for a Saturday picnic just as the path along the top of the dam was being finished off; young Nigel, whose ambition at the time was to be an engineer so that he could have dirty hands without being harassed, was most impressed.

For David and myself it was all very satisfying. There at one end of the dam was a small house and office which would be occupied by its custodian and – later – regulator of the water supply. At the other end was the spillway to take off surplus water; below it would be a plantation of eucalyptus and cassia siamea for building poles and firewood. Buried in the dam wall was a pipe, and at the downstream end were domestic water points and cattle troughs. My thoughts ran on ahead, visualising a patchwork of farmsteads and houses, cattle paths defined by barriers of sisal, a protective hedge to keep stock away from the dam and to prevent pollution. But this daydream was not – alas – to materialize, at least not in my time; with independence round the corner, the attention of government and public turned increasingly to constitutional and political matters, and local practicalities often went by default. Our surveyor did not return and any future settlement would probably be unplanned.

A few weeks after Sylvia and the children went off on leave the rains began. Resisting the temptation to dash out to the dam, I waited two or three weeks and then went out for a farewell visit. The water level was well up the dam wall, the spillway damp, the cattle troughs full of water, and work had begun on planting a thorn hedge round and just above he water's edge. On the lower side of the dam the grass had taken and was spreading. The little house was occupied and I had a short chat with the caretaker. As I walked away a pair of ducks came flighting in, and I stopped to watch them splash down. It was a little under two years since David and I had first visited the site.

As I prepared to leave, a figure appeared in the middle distance, arms waving and an old army greatcoat flapping about his person; the impression was that of an overgrown and demented crow. He came panting up, face glistening with sweat, a broad grin disclosing a less than full complement of teeth. He thrust out his hands, took one of mine, and shook it vigorously. Then, expectantly, 'Do you not remember me *Bwana?*' I confessed that I did not. 'But surely you must remember…' 'Where, then did we meet, father?' He was in fact little older than I, but the courtesy was appreciated. 'We met in your court last year *Bwana;* you sent me to prison for nine months'. And then I remembered – I had been obliged to convict him for a rather nasty assault on his elderly father. Where else would one come across such uncontrived magnanimity?

On the way home I met a familiar acquaintance. Beyond Kibara the road passed close to the lake shore at a point where one of our best middle schools stood on a low bluff overlooking Speke Gulf. The headmaster, an old friend, sat on the roadside; he was waiting for a lift to Kibara, so I could not help. I remembered my first visit to his school, when I had been impressed by the way in which it was run, and by the standard of discipline. This had its comic aspect; a large notice board on the verandah outside the headmaster's office bore the legend 'School Rules'; these were –

1. Minor offences such as untidiness, fighting, smoking etc, may be dealt with by prefects.
2. More serious matters such as assault, arson, and theft must be reported to a teacher.
3. In case of murder, rape and similar offences, the headmaster must be informed immediately..

I do not recollect any murderers from the school finding their way into the District Court; perhaps they got no further than the headmaster.

Not all projects went as smoothly as the dam. My predecessor had proposed a scheme at Mkibuga on the south west side of Ukerewe island, which was to combine both drainage and irrigation in a small area adjoining the lake; this was to extend rice cultivation, already a valuable local food and cash crop. I was no less enthusiastic about this than about my dam, but for one reason or another it never seemed possible to assemble the appropriate specialists to carry out a feasibility study and survey; they were probably engaged on larger schemes elsewhere. Then, during 1960, a colony of tsetse fly, carriers of sleeping sickness, was found to inhabit this very limited area. Douglas Turner, my brother-in-law, came over from Mwanza with some of his 'fly boys' to investigate; he thought that because tsetse were confined to Mkibuga, it would be possible to eradicate them, and initiated a programme of spraying. This was in progress at the time I left, but I doubt if the project ever came to fruition.

Towards a local magistracy

It was usual for Native Authorities (NAs), whether traditional chiefs or appointees, to combine administrative and judicial functions. In the second of these rôles they could deal with a number of offences which were common to the penal code and to customary law – theft and common assault being obvious examples; and they could also adjudicate on infringements of local bye-laws. But their main function was to sit on cases involving African customary law which had no place in the law books. The volume of appeals to the DC was generally a fair indication of the standards of justice meted out. In Ukerewe such appeals averaged about one percent of the three thousand or so cases heard annually, but in some districts they proliferated, especially where litigation was a form of local sport or entertainment.

In a few of the more populous, prosperous, and sophisticated districts, the chief's administrative and judicial functions had been separated, and an indigenous magistracy installed. In one particular Ukerewe exemplified this model at the time I was posted there, and in Bukerebe chiefdom judicial appeals from lower courts were heard almost exclusively by the deputy chief, acting in effect as a magistrate. A year or so later, with the agreement of Chief Lukumbuzya and the chiefdom council, I set about extending the model downwards, with local magistrates taking over the judicial rôle of the five sub-chiefs in Ukerewe. In doing this I was concerned less with the principle of separation of function than with the need to improve the performance the sub-chiefs in their local government rôle; for this they needed more time and training, and the opportunity to take on additional financial and administrative responsibilities.

However, before taking the plunge I arranged for a party of us to visit Moshi, to study and observe the system there, where the Chagga had operated a separate magistracy for years. Our group comprised Chief Lukumbuzya, a couple of sub-chiefs, two or three district councillors, and Alypius Munyaga, our local expert on customary law. Together they filled the ambulance –our only suitable means of transport; I travelled by car, accompanied by Sylvia and the children. The ambulance took the long way round, northeast into Kenya, and then looping southwards, back into Tanganyika via Nairobi to Arusha and Moshi; we took a short cut across the Serengeti. The trip was more adventurous than I expected.

We set off a day behind the rest of the party, after an overnight stay at Ushashi in Musoma district; an early start the next morning should then have ensured arrival in Moshi by evening. To guide us along the way I had bought a Mobil road map, which clearly indicated our route across the Serengeti, up and around the side of Ngorongoro crater, and on to Arusha and Moshi. The night at Ushashi was an uncomfortable one; with Sylvia succumbing to bouts of nausea, departure in the morning was delayed until the arrival of the young African in charge of the nearby NA dispensary, who supplied some medication.

Heading south-eastwards for sixty miles or so, we entered the Serengeti national park at Banagi, and pressed on to Seronera, then simply a group of thatched rondavels providing basic accommodation for the few visiting tourists and officials, and the Game Department staff who lived there. We had no time to loiter, and the opportunity to watch game in the Serengeti was postponed for a year or more. Beyond Seronera the road – more accurately a track – was less well-defined than it had been; an hour later the single track gave way to half a dozen sets of wheel marks made by vehicles choosing their own paths. This was all very disconcerting; where was the road shown on the map? We carried on in what I took to be the right general direction, and after some time were cheered by the sight of a signpost. Relief was short-lived; the single arm pointed left, directing anyone who was interested 'To the Dunes'. It was no help to us. By this time we must have been very close to Olduvai Gorge, where the Leakeys were digging and scraping in their search for the remains of early man; on our map the gorge was situated on the non-existent road. We carried on past the signpost towards an upward thrust of high land which I judged was the rim of Ngorongoro crater, and perhaps twenty miles distant.

After a short time the grass thinned out and the car's engine suddenly began to labour for no obvious reason, and stalled before I had time to change down. Trying to start again, the wheels spun, and dug us down to the axle in seconds. This was a new experience. I got out, and all became clear, what I had confidently assumed to be the usual inch or two of dust on top of more solid soil or sand, in fact concealed dust and more dust. It was volcanic ash from the long-extinct volcano, and we were as effectively bogged down in dust as if it had been mud. But this was the middle of the dry season, and we were not equipped to extricate ourselves from mud; we simply had no traction. It seemed a good time to have a belated picnic lunch whilst we pondered the options.

We could sit it out, though it might be days before another vehicle appeared, and our supply of water was limited; Seronera was a good two days walk away. Ahead, I could probably reach one of the habitations near the southern rim of Ngorongoro in a day, and I might chance upon a Masai herdsman along the way. This seemed the best option, though without a firearm for protection, I wasn't thrilled at the prospect. I would set off early in the morning. After our snack and with time on my hands I decided to have a rather forlorn attempt to get the car moving. In the back of the station wagon was a short plank. I scooped away enough dust below the rear bumper to insert the plank and on it my jack; and was able to lift the axle clear of the ground and raise the rear wheels enough to give a little clearance. There followed the chore of packing dust under the wheels and creating a gentle slope forward. We then set about collecting as much dry grass as we could to pack under and ahead of the wheels, but this seemed a poor substitute for the sacking and panels of expanded metal which I carried during the rains. No sacking; but we had a couple of old army blankets in our luggage. These were laid out, folded, and stuffed under the wheels, and forwards for another three or four feet. I lowered the jack; wheels dropped onto the blanket, and the rear axle was clear. I would still need to push, and once the car was moving – assuming that it did – it mustn't stop again or be allowed to stall.

Sylvia took the steering wheel; I told her to start with plenty of power when I shouted, and to keep moving however much the engine protested, and not to change gear. I opened the passenger door, moved to the rear and shouted, and began to shove; the car moved, and gained momentum. I was able to snatch up one of the blankets before tearing off in pursuit and hurling myself clumsily into the passenger seat. A half mile or so in low gear, and we were on firmer ground; we stopped to let the engine cool down. Further along, the outline of Ngorogoro crater became clearer, and we began to climb into the undulating grassland characteristic of much of Masailand This had something of the morphology of Pennine moorland and the South Downs, but on a grander scale, with no trees – just miles and miles of grass; and fewer people. We met a solitary Masai standing elegantly on one leg and leaning on his spear; I stopped, and after exchanging greetings he confirmed that we were more or less where I had hoped we were.

By the time we reached the crater edge it was nearly sunset, but we still had about 150 miles to go and so we had to be content with the briefest of stops to take in the view across and into the crater; it was breathtaking. The setting sun bathed most of the landscape with a golden glow, but shadow picked out and moulded the contours, revealing curves, hillocks, and little valleys which would otherwise have been invisible. On the crater floor were herds of game or cattle – they were too far away to be sure. North-westwards, whence we had come, the rolling downland descended gradually to the tawny Serengeti. A DO lived somewhere in the vicinity, on detachment from his District Office; what a gem of a posting. Somewhere along the road south-eastwards, across a narrow valley, we saw a small group of elephants, highlighted by the last of the sun. In no time it was dark, and it was nearly 11 o'clock before we reached our hosts in Moshi; they were friends, John and Gela Inman, who had been our neighbours in Lindi four years earlier.

The next day and for the rest of the week I joined the rest of the party from Ukerewe. We were impressed with Chagga judicial arrangements, and with their hospitality. For good measure, and by pre-arrangement, we also had the opportunity to see something of their extensive and largely successful community development programme; this inspired a certain envy, and in Ukerewe we certainly didn't have the resources to initiate comparable activities –not in my time at any rate. But we could manage the five new local magistrates. I later reported favourably to 'Fanny' Walden and to the District Council, supported by other members of the visiting party. The necessary budgetary adjustments were made, the magistrates selected and trained; by the time I left Ukerewe eighteen months later they were firmly established, and the continued low incidence of appeals confirmed their acceptance by the public. Most important from my own point of view, I was able to concentrate the attention of sub-chiefs on their rôle in local administration. In the event this came to nought, and within two years after independence the new government had swept aside all traditional and statutory local authorities, replacing them with party apparatchiks.

For the journey back to Ukerewe we decided on discretion, and returned through Kenya by way of Nairobi, Nakuru and Kisii. The first part of the drive to Nairobi was a pleasure, along one of the few stretches of tarmacadam road in the country; this ended at the Kenya border, after which we had five punctures, four of which I had to repair at the roadside whilst passing trucks and buses enveloped me in clouds of red dust. Back home, the blanket which had saved our bacon in the Serengeti was washed many times, but always seemed to retain a whiff of volcanic dust. As for the road which disappeared, I wrote to the Director of Public Works about it; in reply he assured me that there was no public road across the Serengeti, so the question of its maintenance did not therefore arise. I didn't bother to write to Mobil.

Political development and security

Notwithstanding the Mau Mau rising in Kenya and the received left-wing political wisdom that colonialism invites – indeed requires – armed insurrection to ensure its eventual demise, there was only a brief period during my nine years in Tanganyika when security seemed in any way threatened. There were never any imperial troops stationed in the country, and the

Tanganyika battalion of the King's African Rifles was never in fact called out in support or protection of the 'civil power'. In each of the eight provinces there was a mobile para-military police General Service Unit; these were rarely needed or used in the capacity for which they existed. Typically, in an up-country district, law and order was maintained by a small police contingent headed by an African or Indian Inspector or Sub-Inspector, who was answerable to the DC as well as to a more distant Provincial Commissioner of Police. In Ukerewe our police strength worked out at one constable to about nine thousand inhabitants – not a ratio suggestive of a police state, and far lower than in Britain. Apart from the police, each Native Authority had a few messengers, answerable to chief or sub-chief; these were also a combination of village policeman and court orderly.

The Africans of Tanganyika have an innate sense of what constitutes good behaviour, and this is reflected in ritual courtesies and mutual hospitality. They also have a great capacity for laughter, and can derive pleasure from the most unpromising circumstances. I always found them, with few exceptions, to be good-natured and law-abiding; this was just as well in view of the exiguous resources available for policing. Of course there was a certain amount of crime, but it was usually spontaneous rather than systematic, simple and straightforward, not planned or devious except in cases of murder; and, as in country areas the world over, there was no criminal class as such. In a rural district it was not usually thought necessary to lock one's door at night, and on *safari* it was possible to leave things lying around in camp all day without fear of anything disappearing. Crime was certainly on the increase, but it was largely petty crime, committed for purely personal motives and was in no sense a threat to national security.

However, opposition to colonial rule, largely conducted by TANU (Tanganyika African National Union) under Julius Nyerere, became such a threat, albeit relatively briefly. Until the mid-1950's there was little significant popular opposition; a conservative peasantry comprising some ninety percent of the population tended to be unresponsive to the idea of rapid political change. They had yet to be wooed by the new political class. This is not to say that rural people were passive; they could, and did, object to measures which were introduced heavy-handedly or with insufficient regard for local sensibilities. But this almost invariably reflected objection to the local impact of a specific policy rather than to the colonial government as such. Thus, from time to time some well-intended local measure would arouse resentment – compulsory inoculation or dipping of livestock for example – which in turn could sometimes lead to a campaign of non-cooperation, and the arrest and conviction of known ringleaders. But usually such disputes would be settled in exhausting public meetings at which DOs and specialist staff explained the issues and discussed them with hundreds of people in the areas affected. Generally, though not always, the measure would eventually be accepted, with or without modification. Sometimes, when the results were seen to have been beneficial the local folk-memory had it that the original action had been wrung from an unwilling government.

At the national level the substantive dispute between TANU and Government was over the pace of progress towards independence, over 'when' rather than 'if'. TANU sought a swift end to the British Trusteeship despite the chronic shortage of indigenous educated, skilled, and experienced manpower in both the public and private sectors[40]; conversely, Government saw these deficiencies as good reason for a more measured movement towards independence. Julius Nyerere was faced not only with a conscientiously conservative government but with a conservative peasantry which had to be won over. This was well under way by 1958, although to persuasion had been added downright misrepresentation and propaganda intended to undermine Government, and the authority which it exercised. Sadly these tactics also had the effect of souring relations between local politicians and officials who in many respects were not unsympathetic; it also sowed discord between the traditional Native Authorities and their people, and ensured a degree of friction in matters of local government and development at a time when co-operation and goodwill were needed if an independent Tanganyika was to get off to the best possible start.

By late 1958 Julius Nyerere felt sufficiently confident to press Government for an early advance to internal self-government, a demand later accompanied by the threat of widespread civil disorder. Thus it was that for several consecutive months in 1959 there was an increased concern for

---

[40] At the time of independence there were fewer than 100 African graduates and only 1 medical doctor.

internal security, accompanied by a degree of personal anxiety as to what lay ahead. It was difficult to imagine the people with whom I debated in the council chamber, or engaged in serious or lighthearted conversation in street or farmstead, taking up arms. And yet the signs and portents were ominous; threatening noises by leading TANU politicians, secret meetings addressed by their provincial henchmen, intimidation by party activists of people who refused to join TANU or contribute to its funds; and with almost every post there were sealed envelopes reporting the current security situation in some detail, and announcing measures to be taken in the capital, ports, and major provincial centres to contain violence if it erupted. In one sense this was reassuring and inspired some confidence that our seniors in the steamy corridors of power knew what they were about. It also made those of us in the remoter up-country stations feel rather lonely and exposed. Not for our benefit would the limited national forces be deployed, but for the protection of the larger centres of population, ports, airports, power installations, water supplies and so on – and quite rightly so. But it did drive it home to those of us in remoter areas how naked we were.

Meanwhile the daily routine went on much as before, but with differences. I found myself approving more political meetings; there seemed no point in not doing so, and if approved I knew where they were and could find out what went on. Unapproved, they would have been secret and illegal. I pursued several reported cases of intimidation and boycotting, and convicted an overenthusiastic TANU member for barring access to the village well of a farmer who was not disposed to join the party – but who was as much entitled to the water as the next man. Following a brief visit to Provincial Headquarters in Mwanza, I brought back with me a sackful of tear-gas grenades, and on my return instituted a twice-weekly session of riot training for my thirteen policemen; for this they were equipped with steel helmets, wicker shields, and pick-handles, with pre-war .303 Lee Enfields slung across the back in reserve. The rifles, easily represented by critics as a symbol of oppression, were in fact a measure of weakness – a substitute for more policemen. The more heavily a policeman is outnumbered by a hostile crowd the more ruthless and violent he has to be to compensate for lack of numbers; in the last resort it becomes a matter of 'them or me'. Fortunately, in Ukerewe as in most districts, this philosophy never had to be demonstrated.

For my own part I rehearsed in simple and unambiguous Swahili my own version of the Riot Act in the event of it having to be read to some mob intent on mayhem and destruction. To this end I had been supplied with a battery-operated loudhailer. In common with fifty-odd other DCs I consulted my colleagues and revised our district security scheme. In retrospect it seemed ludicrously optimistic, but perhaps not entirely so, for the habit of deference to authority was still there, which gave an advantage to whoever retained the initiative. It did not at the time appear entirely improbable that we could achieve the limited but substantial objective we set ourselves – of getting the whole expatriate population[41] of the district in to Nansio and if necessary, away to Mwanza by commandeered ferry. My main worry was whether, given the emotional stress to which they would be subjected, and the pull of conflicting loyalties, it would be realistic to assume that our small police contingent could be relied upon – or whether I should take personal control of the armoury and issue firearms to colleagues and trusted expatriates. A sad thought ….. Sergeant Mohamed, nearing retirement, was a splendid man, epitomising now devalued clichés – but he *was* the salt of the earth. Surely *he* couldn't be doubted; and yet survival might depend upon doubting. In the event neither he nor his Inspector nor any of their men were put to the test, and when the political temperature began to drop, their own relief was manifested in an epidemic of horseplay and laughter in the police lines. *They* had had their worries too.

However, there were still some weeks of tension, in which I frequently wished for some demonstration that although we in fact still just about ruled with the consent of the governed, we also had teeth; a pass or two along the lake shore by a flight of jet fighter aircraft from Kenya, the appearance of a (non-existent) gunboat to awe the fractious, even a show of force by the riot police from Mwanza; or, less bellicose – and probably more effective – a stately progress through Nansio by the band of the Grenadier Guards. The nearest I came to this was a borrowed LP record of the same band playing a selection of regimental marches, which I unexpectedly found to be a great boost to my fluctuating morale. One lunchtime, Sylvia and the children having gone over to Mwanza for a week to stay with Pat and Douglas, I found

---

[41] Including Asians.

194

myself pacing up and down my verandah to the cheering thump and swing of 'Sussex by the Sea' at full blast. At that moment I could have quelled any mob with a glance – and perhaps a word or two; and yet, on reflection, even this prop was an illusion, for our military music is too light of heart and full of fun for fighting; it is music for country fairs and deckchairs on the sea-front, and for self-congratulation when the fight is over and won. It is not designed to intimidate.

It is difficult to convey the mood – or succession of moods – which then affected the small community of foreigners in the situation described. There was no immediate danger of the kind which has since become commonplace in so many parts of the world; indeed it was the novelty of the threat as much as a fear of its obvious personal consequences which lay at the root of our several anxieties. In the case of Tanganyika nearly forty years of British rule had been remarkably peaceful, the relationship between governor and governed essentially good-natured; this characteristic, which we had hitherto taken for granted – and upon which our presence depended – was at risk of being destroyed. It was not that Juma Bende down in the town suddenly became an enemy or thought any the less of me, or that I thought any the less of him; but the rules were changing, and before they were redefined he might be asked to break them in the name of race and dimly perceived nationhood. And it might be difficult for him to resist the call.

Meanwhile, the flag was hoisted outside the Boma every morning and lowered just before sunset; and life went on as usual but perhaps a little more deliberately and self-consciously than hitherto, anxieties studiously concealed. In the township we responded with irony, unconcern or jest when informed that our houses and cars had been prematurely allocated to some over-optimistic local citizen, and had an appropriate selection of replies to the popular political greeting of the day, '*Uhuru*' – Freedom. To this we would cheerfully add the rider '*na kazi*' – and work; or, more subtly '*Marahaba*' – the traditional acknowledgement by a person of standing when greeted by a social inferior. The point of this was that the equally traditional greeting which evoked this response was '*Shikamu*' – 'I clasp your feet'. The implicit juxtaposition of the humble *Shikamu* for *Uhuru* was more usually received by laughter than chagrin; the laughter – on these and other occasions – was perhaps our greatest reassurance that the worst would not happen.

In Ukerewe there was another intangible reassurance. The islanders had a characteristic which they shared with islanders everywhere – a touch of xenophobia. They were an independent lot, as I had discovered; and it was a quality for which I was known to have some sympathy and respect. They were not easily swayed by the fire-eating rhetoric of visiting politicians, whilst to some extent I, a foreigner, had been assimilated into the island community and was known to be on their side and to have represented their interests when I judged it right to do so. So, despite our physical isolation – indeed, partly because of it – we expatriates in Ukerewe perhaps had less cause for anxiety than if we had been in Mwanza or Dar es Salaam; it is, after all, the urban mob which typically constitutes the threat to governments. All the same, it was an uneasy and dispiriting few months, and it generated too much adrenaline for comfort.

It was at night that confidence was at its lowest ebb. With doors and windows wide open, a familiar range of sounds penetrated to our oversensitive ears. Was that rustling in the elephant grass caused by wind or a dozen pairs of feet? That clamour down in the town, a mile away, was probably a wedding celebration – but could it be the beginning of a riot? For several months we slept with pick-handles under our beds, with looped thongs to wrap round the wrist to prevent them being snatched away; a sharp crack across the shins of any intruder would, we thought, meet most circumstances. For the exceptional case I had an automatic pistol and box of ammunition in the left hand drawer of our tallboy. This was quite improper, for so paternal was the colonial ethos that we were not allowed to own hand-guns for self-defence, and there was no point in seeking permission to have one – it would have been refused by the Provincial Police Commissioner. However, I had inherited from my predecessor a confiscated 7mm automatic of Italian manufacture which had hitherto remained locked in my office safe – and was soon to be returned there.

Eventually it all blew over, our most dramatic incident some conspiratorial muttering outside Christopher's window one dark night, followed by a shower of stones on the corrugated iron roof; and even that might have been mere mischief. Despite the various concerns enumerated here, and in fairness to the people amongst whom we lived and worked, I have to say that at no time was I ever at the receiving end of any abuse, threat, hostility, or unpleasantness; I would judge that this went for most of us. That some expatriates were subjected to hostile behaviour is also true, though this was perhaps more common in the heady days immediately after independence, when ill-disciplined party officials and newly-installed functionaries occasionally abused their authority by embarrassing and humiliating Europeans and Asians – and in some cases engineering their deportation. Ironically, the most serious outbreak of violence before independence was directed at fellow Africans, when a mob in Dar-es-Salaam attacked six policemen and hacked them to death. The incident prompted universal revulsion.

Details of a new constitutional advance were agreed late in 1959, and a date fixed for a general election and internal self-government in 1960. Julius Nyerere, future Prime Minister and President, visited Ukerewe during a subsequent tour of the Province. In Nansio township he addressed a crowd of thousands, made the obligatory ritual swipe at the colonial government – and then came to tea on our verandah. This in itself would have been anathema to some of the more conservative DCs who had begun their service before the war, but even we newer recruits to the imperial rearguard, who sought only to temper the winds of change, often had ambivalent feelings towards him. We could accept, and indeed admire, most of his principles, but not the methods frequently employed by party activists to implement them. It was perhaps this contrast between Nyerere's high principle on one hand and the often irresponsible and sometimes ruthless conduct of his party hacks in the field which tended to stick in one's gullet at the time.

Later affectionately designated *Mwalimu* (Teacher), Julius Nyerere had an attractive personality, with an easy informal manner, a ready wit, a nice sense of humour, and uncontrived charm. In thinking that his model of African socialism and self-help could exempt Tanganyika from the harsher realities of world economic conditions he was mistaken, but it is a tribute to his long leadership that it has so far avoided revolution, coup, and bloodletting; and is still one of the few countries in Africa where government policy is determined more by regard for the public interest than by greed, opportunism, and cupidity.

It was shortly after Julius Nyerere's visit that Sylvia revealed some of her hitherto-concealed earlier fears, and her own private survival plans in the event of our security scheme coming unstuck. The most imaginative of these was that she would blacken the children's skin and her own, dress African fashion, get down to the lake and paddle across to Mwanza – a mere thirty miles or so – in our inflatable plastic paddling pool. That was optimism for you!

Early in 1961, with independence barely a year ahead, two large brown paper parcels arrived from the Central Office of Information in London. When opened I was surprised and nonplussed to find a couple of hundred copies of the latest portrait of the Queen and Duke of Edinburgh. The timing of this offering seemed staggeringly inept, and I left the parcels, contents partly visible, in a corner of my office. Some days later a police constable who had been sent to see me spotted them and enquired what the pictures were; I told him. His face lit up and he asked if he could have one. I invited him to help himself, warmed by this display of continuing loyalty to a distant monarch. By the end of the day the entire police contingent had trooped in and taken one; the news got around, and within a week they had all gone. On purely objective grounds the COI initiative was misguided, but the local response in our little corner of Africa was heartening. What would our critics have made of that?

Surreptitious replacement of a house

About the end of my first year in Ukerewe, Christopher was replaced by another cadet; he went on to serve under the anachronistic DC who had earlier been a bad influence on Geoff Thirtle. Chris had proved an excellent colleague; he was capable, and had a cheerful informal manner towards African staff and public alike. This may in part have been attributable to his having done National Service in Kenya with the Uganda battalion of the KAR (King's African Rifles), in which he also gained a head start in his fluency in Swahili, and made the acquaintance of a certain Sergeant Idi Amin – later the notorious dictator of Uganda. His capacity for putting people at ease was well illustrated when, one morning, I entered his office and found him in conversation with an old man; both were sitting cross-legged on the floor. I withdrew, and when I quizzed Chris about it later, he explained that he had invited his visitor to sit on a chair, but he had instead sat on the floor. It had seemed only polite to join him there; a trifling incident, but an illuminating one. In lighter vein, it was Chris who, more abreast of musical fashion than the rest of us, introduced the European community to 'rock and roll' by way of Bill Haley and the Comets.

I was sorry to see Chris go, but was, in the event well-pleased with his successor cadet, Tom Collingridge; he also had done his stint of National Service, in his case with the Somerset Light Infantry in Malaya countering the Chinese communist insurgency. Tom was accompanied by his wife Anne, daughter of missionary parents; they had an infant son, and a golden retriever which was soon in a state of intermittent warfare with one of David's two dogs. They took over the house vacated by Christopher.

New house — Ukerewe

D.B.

The Boma and Government quarters were situated on a low ridge at Kabingo, a good two miles north of Nansio. The houses occupied by the DO and District Foreman had been built at derisory cost about fifteen years earlier; the walls were of mud brick, on crumbling stone and cement foundations. The one vacated by Chris, and now occupied by Tom and family, was in particularly poor condition; the best that could be said of it was that the corrugated iron roof kept the rain out. But nothing kept the termites out. They came up through the cracks in the cement floor and chewed the grass mats, and the walls and window and door frames were riddled with their tunnels; every morning dried mud was scraped off the walls and woodwork, the termites concealed therein swept up and thrown to the chickens. Because the building had been 'temporary' in the first instance, little had been spent on it, and its general condition was such as would have had Labour MP's asking awkward questions in the House had it been occupied by – or even offered to – one of their constituents. It was a poor home for a bachelor, but barely tolerable for a family.

Something had to be done. At this time the Public Works Department were quoting about £4,000 for building a two-bedroom house, but with independence only two years ahead, it was unlikely that Government would spend so much on a new staff house. So it proved, and the request to my PC was turned down. However experience, training, and the nature of the job itself all combined to reinforce the philosophy that 'no' was rarely an absolute, and more commonly only a more or less temporary obstacle requiring the exercise of a certain amount of patience, persistence, and ingenuity in varying degrees.

A persuasive but essentially transparent plea that the DO's house needed a guest room adding to it produced an unexpected allocation of £800. By raiding my own vote for the maintenance of public buildings I found another £400. With this £1,200 and free extra-mural prison labour, Eddie the District Foreman reckoned that he could just about build a two-bedroom house to the modest plan that I had sketched out. So we went ahead, the new house going up in the garden of the old one. Quite fortuitously there was a very competent mason amongst our convicts at the time, and with the prospect of remission he went to his new task with a will; in any case it was more congenial work than cutting grass or chopping wood, which would otherwise have been his lot. Eddie was no slouch, and within two months Tom and family were installed in their new home. Demolition of the old house was begun, but this inspired little zeal, and it was a slow business carting the debris away.

It was just then that my new PC, Peter Bell, decided to pay a visit. He was installed in our guest wing and at the end of the first day we decided on a game of tennis. I tried to take him the long way round but he had been to Ukerewe years before, and knew the short cut. This took us past the half-demolished house and Tom's new one. He was curious, and he was not stupid; I am sure that even as he asked he knew what had been going on. I judged it best to come clean, and confessed. He withheld judgment and we went on to the tennis court. I did not consciously play badly, but I was certainly not at my best, and lost narrowly. During an interval in a whispered aside to Tom, I suggested he invite us round for a drink afterwards.

Later Peter inspected the house, admired the stone fireplace, and grunted in approval when I told him how little it had all cost. We drank our beer on the verandah looking out over the lake; straight ahead was Kweru island and half right the Majita massif. Housing was now the least of our worries, and we talked of this and that until dusk. As we walked back to my house Peter nodded towards the ruin of Tom's old house; 'Well done', he said, 'let's forget it', and turned to other things. 'Fanny' Walden had recently left on retirement, and it was a relief to find that his successor was no less supportive, and even more tolerant.

By way of contrast I had greater difficulty explaining my dereliction away to my successor when I left the following year. The handing-over process required him to assume responsibility for the total stock of Government buildings in Ukerewe, identified not only by description but by year of construction. The DO's house was reputed to have been built in 1945; Tom's was clearly much more recent. The new man was not wholly convinced that he was safe in signing the housing inventory, and did so only when he realised that he had little choice in the matter. I was leaving two or three days later, and had signed as having handed over; reluctantly he added his own signature.

Eleven years later, on the tenth anniversary of independence, I visited Ukerewe again as a guest of the Tanzanian Government. My former home, apart from the garish internal colour scheme, was much as it had been a decade earlier, and I enjoyed an hour or so reminiscing with the Area Secretary[42]. The little house once occupied by the Collingridges had been carefully maintained, and it could scarcely be a matter for complaint that what had been a lawn was now a vegetable patch.

A fictitious disturbance

In Ukerewe we had a total police establishment of sixteen, including three at Kibara on the mainland. A steady incremental growth in the crime rate was the obverse of the growth and change that was taking place in other respects – improved agriculture, increased prosperity, greater politicisation. On these grounds we qualified for promotion to a bigger league, and early in 1960 our African Inspector was supplemented by Asistant Superintendent (ASP) Daudi

---

[42] The designation DC was changed soon after independence, but reintroduced in the 1990's.

Amri, newly appointed to the rank. He was a small man with a large moustache, and he bustled with energy and efficiency; his swagger stick always seemed just a little too big.

Early one morning, just as I was sitting down to prepare some notes for the District Council, ASP Daudi knocked on the door and stepped inside, exuding an air of excitement. There had, he said, been some sort of disturbance over on Ukara island; a man had run amok, and should he assemble a squad of constables to go over and sort it out. Firm details were scanty, and it was impossible to distinguish fact from fantasy in his informant's tale, but he had the story and was sticking to it. I was sceptical, and also sensed in Daudi an ambition to distinguish himself. This had within it the prospect of over-reaction. 'Right, be here with four constables in fifteen minutes; but I'll come with you'.

I dashed home to tell Sylvia I'd be out for the day, grabbed a sandwich, and went back to the Boma. Daudi's men were already in the back of the Landrover pickup, business-like in their safari dress; khaki shorts, navy sweaters, and khaki pill-box caps resembling those worn in the British army in Victorian times, but without a chinstrap. My motor launch moored off Nansio pier was not going to be any use for the outward trip; it was on the wrong side of the island. But it would be a reliable means of getting back, so I arranged for it to be taken round to Ukara for the return journey later in the day.

We drove to Bugolora, the focus of which was an oil mill and its attendant jetty. Here were half a dozen *mashua*, miniature undecked dhows with lateen rig and sails. They were twenty to thirty feet long, rough but sturdy in construction, with much-mended sails and rigging which did little to inspire confidence, but which would no doubt suffice until next time a sail ripped, rope broke, or spar split. From this point of view there was nothing to choose between them, and after minimal haggling with the owner, we chartered the craft nearest the end of the pier.

Ukara lay about five miles to the north, and we headed towards Bwisya at the southern end, close to where the trouble was. But what trouble? On a day like this? The sky was blue, the few clouds white, and a wind from the starboard beam pushed us briskly over the lake. This too was clear and blue, and spray blew off the waves into our faces. I chatted light-heartedly with the constables, but Daudi remained somewhat aloof; if there had been a quarter deck – or indeed any sort of deck – he would have been pacing it, swagger stick under arm. If he was exhilarated, as I was, it had little to do with our onward rush, with water gurgling at our stern, sail bellying, and wind in the rigging.

We arrived, and were met by a guide who was to take us to the scene of the incident. This was only ten minutes walk away, and I listened in vain for sounds of uproar, however diminished. All was peaceful. Insisting that the constables stay behind, I set off with Daudi, and we shortly reached the village headman's hut. He greeted us a little sheepishly, as did his captive, a wiry middle-aged man whose ankles were bound, but whose demeanour gave no hint of any desire to flee.

So *this* was the disturbance and here was its instigator. Well, there *had* been a disagreement and a bit of a scuffle, and during the next half hour or so I heard all about it as the headman and prisoner gave their respective versions. There had been a small village meeting, and a minor dispute had arisen between the headman and this particular individual. The headman, feeling his authority threatened, had laid hands on the man who had been so imprudent as to challenge it. In the ensuing struggle the man's portable radio had been damaged and he had lost his temper. Transistors were a new invention and hitherto the radio, although not a novelty, had been a cumbersome affair run on a large dry battery weighing three or four pounds. But our delinquent had a new transistor radio which he not only treasured for its own sake, but which was also a social asset, attracting an audience every evening to the small clearing outside his hut. No wonder that he was upset and eventually had to be forcibly restrained. But that was hours ago; tempers had cooled and everyone had gone home. All was contrition and the headman obviously wished he'd kept quiet about it; our arrival was an embarrassment. For myself I felt momentarily a little cheated, but on the whole relieved that this had been a non-event. Only Daudi seemed disappointed, but he soon regained his good humour. I sent him back to rejoin his constables and return to Kabingo with a message to my long-suffering wife that I would be away for another day.

It seemed a pity to be in Ukara and not make a little more of it. By this time a small crowd had assembled round the headman's hut, so I stayed and chatted, outlining our district development plans and where Ukara fitted into them. Ukara's biggest problems were overpopulation, some limited but severe soil erosion, and proportionately fewer schools than the rest of the district – though contrary to received wisdom, this last evoked little concern. We talked of the rain and crop prospects and, delicately, of local dynastic matters. Old Chief Mataba could not live much longer; there were two contenders for the succession, a layabout drunkard of an elder son who was heir apparent, and a bright, energetic, and public-spirited younger son, Joseph. So it was important to know what people were thinking.

Later, fortified by my sandwich, I set off to walk across the island to the 'capital', Bukiko; here was the local administrative centre, the court, a dispensary and the Chief's house. On the way there were anti-erosion ditches to be examined, some land reclamation work to be evaluated, and a Middle School to visit. On arrival I called on the court clerk; he had to be rousted out of his house, and he smelled strongly of millet beer. I then learned that there was to be a chiefdom meeting the following day, so decided to attend. There was no point in calling on Chief Mataba at this time of day; it was late afternoon and he would have been in a state of torpor, combined effects of old age and alcohol. On this occasion I was not bearing my usual half-bottle of whisky.

I headed down to the lake shore along a switchback path weaving between boulders and rock outcrops and little pockets of sandy soil scooped into saucer-like depressions. These holes in the ground represented an indigenous and very effective form of soil and water conservation. They were of such a size and depth that they never filled and so there was no run-off, and all water which fell into them eventually went downwards into the soil. Additionally, and depending on temperatures and humidity, dew formed within them to provide a little extra moisture. Another traditional conservation measure was the stall-feeding of cattle. Given a balance between population and available land, these techniques could not be bettered, and soil erosion elsewhere on the island was the result of overpopulation and abandonment of traditional practice.

Ten minutes' downhill walk brought me to the lake shore. At the little jetty was the *Mukama,* and under an adjacent mango tree were the crew, asleep. It seemed a good idea, but I was not tired; I climbed a rock and sat and contemplated the lake. Ahead a small rocky islet was populated by cormorants; and around to the right was a little headland near which, not so long ago, a witch doctor lived who – I was assured – had the facility of turning himself into a crocodile at will.

Rested, and after a cup of tea, I strolled back towards Bukiko on the off-chance of seeing a bull fight. Some distance short of the Chief's house was a level area of ground where these events were held, and sporadic shouting from that direction confirmed that my short walk was not wasted. I arrived between bouts and some lively betting was going on in anticipation of the next confrontation. A circle of perhaps fifteen yards diameter had been marked on the level ground, and into this ring two proud owners now led their bulls on rope halters, for on Ukara these contests were between bull and bull. The two animals were walked round each other, and then at a signal from the referee the halters were removed. There was no sudden thunder of hooves or flurry of dust. The bulls regarded each other solemnly rather than aggressively, and walked round a little, one perhaps with slightly more curiosity and confidence than the other. Meanwhile there was serious debate taking place at the ringside, and though I did not know the Kara language, a bystander explained in Swahili that the finer points of the contest were being discussed. To me it all seemed as stately as a minuet, and somewhat less lively. Eventually, the preliminaries over, the bulls placed their heads together and pushed….withdrew a little and pushed again. And so on. In a very few minutes the nerve of one of the bulls gave, and he broke and ran for it out of the ring, closely followed by the victor, and both in turn briskly pursued by their owners, intent on retrieving them before damage was done. It was all very gentle and good natured, notes and coin changed hands, and the owner of the losing animal came in for a certain amount of chaff. I talked a while with my Swahili-speaking informant, and as preparations were made for the next bout, bade him goodbye and returned to the *Mukama*.

Dusk fell and the mosquitoes swarmed; I gave up any idea of sleeping, netless, on the floor of the little bamboo rest house, and moved into the cabin of the motor boat; this was mosquito proof, but stifling. Later I chatted for a while with the boat's crew, who shared with me their evening meal – a plateful of cold rice and a banana. I missed my bottle of IPA, but slept well notwithstanding, the boat moving gently, and bumping the stone jetty from time to time.

Breakfast consisted of another banana, but the main preoccupation was getting my whiskers off with the mechanic's razor and a sliver of kitchen soap from the galley. Africans' facial hair is generally neither thick nor strong, and razor blades last a long time. This particular razor blade must have been in use for a very long time indeed, and shaving was painful and bloody. However, I was able to turn up at the chiefdom meeting looking more or less respectable, though necessarily a little crumpled.

We started off going through the minutes of the previous meeting, and I picked up various points for action and comment as we went along. But we had hardly got started on the new business when there was a commotion and shouting outside the courthouse. There a man was laid out on the ground, unconscious; dried blood covered his face, and had discoloured and stiffened the dingy calico cloth which was knotted over his shoulder. Blood still oozed from a nasty dent in his head, and it was clear that his skull was broken. His breathing was very shallow. The Rural Medical Aid from the dispensary hard by was already in attendance, cleaning the wound; he then spread some ointment over it and bandaged it.

A few yards away was the attacker, in the custody of one of the Chief's messengers; he had found the victim talking to his wife, and without further enquiry had beaten him over the head with a digging hoe. I did not fancy the injured man's chances, but speed was clearly of the essence. We got him into the chiefdom Landrover as best we could, with the culprit and his escort in attendance. The track down to Bwisya was frightful at the best of times, and now it seemed ten times worse as I tried to strike a balance between speed and minimum discomfort. Unfortunately, I had already sent the launch round to Bwisya to pick me up there, so it was road or nothing.

When we arrived, there being no jetty, the launch was anchored offshore. Somehow our casualty had to be got aboard. I had a door unscrewed from the nearby dispensary, and the still unconscious figure laid onto it and then roped down. Then we placed the door across the gunwales of the dinghy, rowed across to the launch and with some difficulty manhandled the door and its attachment on board and in turn lashed it to the cabin top. Also with us were the assailant and his escort. Off we went, flat out at about ten knots. At Bugolora I borrowed a Peugeot pickup from the oil mill, and twenty minutes later we were at the hospital a hundred yards or so from the Boma. Here Dr. Tiagi took over.

In the evening he came round for a drink. It was about nine o'clock and he had just finished operating; the patient was 'comfortable'. Next morning he was dead, and we had another murder case on our hands. An hour later the quick-tempered husband was brought in; he wished to make a statement, in practice a confession, and the wheels of justice began to turn. This was always a melancholy business on the human level, though the edge was taken off it by the necessarily somewhat clinical enquiry which the processes of law required. In this particular case the husband who confessed to the killing would not hang, and would in the event probably be convicted of manslaughter on a plea of guilty. I finished writing, read the statement over to the accused, who agreed that it was correct and applied his right thumb print. The constable saluted and took him away. Next month there would be another….and then another…

Safari by water

It was said that in the 1930s a DC might expect to spend twenty days or more a month touring his district. It may or may not have been strictly necessary, but it kept him in touch with a scattered rural population and allowed a way of life which was not possible twenty years later. At the end of my first year in Ukerewe the volume of statistically measurable work had almost doubled during the preceding two years, with no increase in either expatriate or African staff. Concurrently with this, the increasingly rapid democratisation of local government made insistent demands on that most precious commodity, time; this tended to retard the pace of development at a time when we no less than our critics were anxious to accelerate it.

In these circumstances I counted myself lucky to be able to get out on tour for a week every month and then usually only for a day or two at a time; fortunately it was a compact district. These excursions were undoubtedly useful, although not always cost-effective in terms of achievement to time spent; they were also invariably therapeutic, and it was always a relief to escape the unremitting pressure of the Boma – the papers to prepare for Council meetings, estimates for some new proposal to work out, coded telegrams to decipher, the never-ending *shauris,* and an increasing incidence of court cases to be heard.

207

In Ukerewe the official provision of transport was one Landrover and a motor-launch, the *Mukama;* the last was grossly under-utilised. It was built of timber, and was decked from stem to stern; forward of the wheelhouse was a hatch leading down to the fo'c'sle, which provided cramped accommodation for the crew of three – a coxswain, mechanic and deck-hand. Aft of the wheelhouse the deck and cabin roof were shaded with a substantial aluminium canopy, whilst below there was a cabin with two bunks, and the usual cramped toilet arrangements. In practice I usually slept on the cabin roof, retreating into the stuffy interior only if assailed by 'lake fly'; these little brutes, appearing in dense clouds over the lake from time to time, could penetrate an ordinary mosquito net, but not the fine copper mesh which screened the cabin. Assembled en masse over the water, they could suffocate the unwary or inebriated fisherman.

The district, apart from Ukerewe island itself, and the adjacent mainland, consisted of about a dozen inhabited islands, most of them with only a few families. Ukara was the largest after Ukerewe itself, with an area of some thirty square miles and a population of around twenty thousand. There was Irugwa, away out of sight to the north east, off the coast of Musoma district. And just to the north was Kweru, a long narrow island, running four miles east to west. I saw it daily from my office window, and after we had been in Ukerewe for a little over a year I thought it was about time to make a visit. There were also things to be done in the northern part of Mwibara, the mainland peninsula, so it seemed a good idea to make a family expedition of it. Sylvia needed a change of scenery, and the children were thrilled to bits at the prospect. Nicola was then four and Nigel two.

Transport was generally fairly capacious, and we were not subject to the constraints which are the lot of the traveller by train or aircraft. On the appointed morning we piled our impedimenta into the Landrover and set off to Murutanga with Sylvester at the wheel. The *Mukama* had set off two or three hours earlier round the eastern end of the island, to await us. When we reached the wooden jetty, the launch was tossing rather briskly at its moorings, for a fresh wind was blowing from the north and the dark blue waves were frothed with white. We took our precautionary sea-sickness pills – unavailingly in Nigel's case – and went aboard. At the stern a miniature red ensign blew out, enlivened by the addition of our national emblem, a giraffe's head. Our boxes and bundles were manhandled over the rail; the black tin trunk, originally grained with brown paint, and purchased for five shillings in an English junk shop some years before, and on tour destined always to contain the bedding; the green canvas-covered mattresses wrapped round the folding stand for the canvas wash-basin; the safari chairs; the plywood box full of pots and pans; and the various cardboard boxes containing food and drink. We were only being away for two days, but if it had been a fortnight it would not have made much difference.

Fishing boats, L. Victoria   N J B

Mzee, our cook, took up his position at the prow, sitting on the bundle of his own personal belongings, tied up as ever in a striped and coloured woven grass prayer mat. The crew, wearing faded blue drill shorts and tunics, went to their tasks; wiry little Salim disappeared below to start the engine – an elderly and temperamental Perkins diesel; Mohamed, large, overweight, and slow-moving, took the wheel; and Victor concurrently cast off and held us away from the jetty with a boat hook.

It took only about twenty minutes of butting against the wind and waves to reach the western end of Kweru. I scrambled damply ashore via the dinghy, and then walked to the school near the centre of the island, accompanied by the headman and two or three elders, and a small procession of fishermen, farmers, children, and the idle and curious. The family stayed aboard and I was to meet them a couple of hours later at the other end of the island. The *baraza* or public meeting was relaxed and straightforward. The islanders had few complaints; they lived there by choice, and accepted the lack of amenities as a quid pro quo of their otherwise untroubled lives. I had little to offer them, but promised to send materials to repair the school if they would provide the labour. I also thought we might run to an additional classroom and teacher. Attendance was good, and fees, five shillings (25p) a year, had been promptly paid. I checked what drugs were needed in the dispensary, and cast an eye over the diary of cases treated – mostly malaria, hookworm and minor injuries, and the occasional extraction, without anaesthetic, of a bad tooth.

An hour later I rejoined the *Mukama*, tugging gently at its moorings behind the shelter of a small sand-spit covered in eight-foot high reeds. A number of fishing canoes were variously drawn up on the beach or floating in a few inches of water, depending on whether the owners were coming or going. Sylvia had bought some freshly caught tilapia, and Nigel, having earlier parted company from his breakfast, had regained his composure and humour, and was chattering away in Swahili with the fishermen. We made our farewells and chugged away, turning the spit and heading eastwards into Baumann Gulf.

The next half hour was distinctly unpleasant, the *Mukama* corkscrewing along broadside on to waves and wind. Once in the gulf it calmed down. On the north shore the Majita plateau rose steeply for over a thousand feet straight from the lake shore. Our own shoreline, to the south, was less spectacular, with low lightly-wooded hills running down to a narrow plain where cultivation alternated with grass and scrub. We anchored a little offshore in a sheltered bay and settled down to a belated lunch; Mzee excelled himself with the tilapia.

It was not particularly hot by African standards, and the wind, despite the shelter of Majita, still blew cool across the gulf. There was no excuse *not* to do anything in the afternoon, but this voyage had an element of holiday about it and the next hour or two was spent lazily en famille. After tea, the sun being a little lower, habit reasserted itself. I went ashore, striking off south-eastwards with the intention of taking a rough arc through south and west, returning from the southwest. An hour or so later, several wayside conversations behind me, and half a page of cryptic scribble pencilled in my notebook, I found myself traversing a hillside and walking westwards. Ahead, Ukerewe island was a dusty gold with the sun lying low behind it, the lake a mirror of pewter. To the right Majita seemed a little less impressive from my modest two or three hundred feet above lake level. Below, a couple of miles away, a miniature *Mukama* was embedded in the indigo of the gulf. It was time to return.

I headed diagonally down the slope towards a plume of smoke that was rising vertically in the cooling air, the wind having dropped. Fifteen minutes or so later I approached a homestead through a patch of dry maize stalks. To the right was the owner's house, mud-walled and well-thatched, with an ostrich shell skewered on the ridge as a fertility talisman.. Opposite was a smaller dwelling which probably housed one or more of the womenfolk; a few chickens scratched and pecked desultorily, and a dog - evidently not retained for reasons of security – slept under a small lime tree. The householder and his son sat on wooden stools near a fire on the bare earth clearing between the huts, and nibbled at roasted maize cobs. There followed the usual prolonged exchange of greetings.

A minute or two later, the ritual completed, I was invited to sit, and lowered myself onto a narrow log instead of the proffered stool. My host's wife appeared from the kitchen, and carved out some lumps of *ugali*, a stiff porridge, for her family. I declined, gladly making do with a charred head of maize in default. Half an hour later, the sun already sunk below a spur of the hill, I stood up to leave. It had been a relaxed and rewarding interlude. With independence approaching it was natural that conversation should turn to politics. He of course wanted *uhuru* (freedom) sooner rather than later, whilst also having a lively awareness of all that might go wrong. Like myself he had a high regard for Julius Nyerere and some of the party elders, but very little for his organisers in the provinces, many of them opportunist ne'er-do-wells. Not long before, the Provincial Secretary of TANU had put it about that everyone who did not join the party would, after independence, have nails knocked into their heads or be expelled from Tanganyika. And more direct and immediate intimidation was rife; not quite the vision that the idealists had in mind, either locally or in Hampstead and Islington.

I told my host where I lived in Kabingo, and asked him to call when next he visited Nansio; he said he would, and I set off down the hill towards the *Mukama*. Soon I was on board and sluicing myself down with water from an enamel bowl; ridiculous with all the lake outside but the lake also had bilharzia, and the bowl was liberally laced with Dettol. The canvas washbasin referred to earlier now held two submerged bottles of Tusker, evaporation of water from the canvas ensuring that the beer was somewhat cooler then tepid. By now there was little light left and the mosquitoes were troublesome. I had Salim start the engine and take us a quarter of a mile offshore; here we dropped anchor, and were unmolested until next morning.

Not that the night was altogether restful, and in the small hours there was released over and round us a thunderstorm which lake and sun had generated slowly during the previous day. It was typical of a summer storm towards the end of the dry season; not a great deal of rain, but almost continuous thunder and lightning for half an hour or more.

We woke a little blearily to a cool and laundered morning, and after breakfast went ashore, Sylvia and the children to pass the time as best they might, myself bound for a *baraza* a couple of miles inland. The headman and a companion were there to show me the way. I was a little puzzled that they had difficulty in keeping up, and then the penny dropped. In Kondoa and Masasi I had been accustomed to walking twenty or twenty five miles a day, the locals twice that. But Ukerewe was small, and distances short, and the Kerewe, relatively prosperous, had embraced the bicycle with enthusiasm. With the cycle and canoe the chief means of transport, they had, it seemed, become unaccustomed to walking any distance.

This last point had some bearing on the main item on the agenda, whether we should build a primary school in the area, and if so where. It was axiomatic that to justify the cost of building and running a school there had to be reasonable certainty that it would fill up. And with a sparse and scattered population here on the mainland there was some doubt of this – especially with the local disinclination to walk very far. At the end of our discussion I reluctantly concluded that wherever we built next year's two new primary schools, neither of them could be here.

The second most important matter was less contentious. The inhabitants of several adjoining village areas wished to hire a group of itinerant hunters from Majita to clear the area of vermin, and had voluntarily raised the fee of £25 which was demanded. Might they be allowed to go ahead? This I was able to agree to, though not with enthusiasm; it was a death sentence for numbers of baboon, monkeys, porcupine and wild pig. But together they could destroy a third of a man's crop between planting and harvest. It was a scale of depredation which would not be tolerated in Europe, so why in Africa?

After another hour or so of question and answer, and with the sun by now high and hot, we broke up. Out of consideration for the headman I said I would make my own way back to the lake; besides, I had a detour in mind. I wanted to look at a *charco*, a miniature reservoir some twenty yards square, to see if a hand pump with a filter might be fitted to extract more or less clean water for domestic purposes; in the event it did not look very promising.

As I was leaving, my eye fell on a small piece of stone with a dull metallic sheen; it looked interesting and I put it in my pocket for subsequent despatch to the Geological Survey. It was late in the afternoon when I got back to the *Mukama*. As I climbed aboard, the engine was already running and the anchor being hauled up. We immediately headed westwards, making for the Rugezi channel where two hundred yards of water separated Ukerewe island from the mainland. Here Sylvester was to pick us up in the Landrover.

The sun had already set by the time we reached Rugezi, the western sky improbably colourful, the intervening land-mass half in darkness, the unbroken surface of the channel reflecting what little light leapfrogged over the island from the departed sun. It was perfectly still, and the burble of our exhaust was a vulgar intrusion. A wading bird called from the reeds, and we passed a heron, poised immobile until we were well out of the way. Then we heard singing; the language was Kerewe and I did not understand it, but the sound was rhythmic and melodious. The silhouette of two canoes appeared further along the channel, the fishermen paddling slowly but strongly towards us in time with their song. We passed, and they shortly turned westwards out of sight. By now we were at the ferry. We exchanged shouted greetings with the team of men whose job it was to haul the pontoon to and fro along its cable. They were resting on the eastern shore, and brewing up by the look of it. The engine idling, we slowly approached the opposite bank, disembarked, and clambered into the waiting Landrover. Twenty minutes later we were home, with the bath running, and the children at their supper.

The piece of rock turned out to be galena or lead ore, and the geologists were quite excited. But although I visited the *charco* again I was never able to find another sample of galena; and neither was the geologist who later came to have a more professional look. It was all very strange and a little disappointing. Some months later when I returned home from the Boma I found a man and his wife sitting by the kitchen door chatting to Issa. It was the couple whom I had met on the hillside overlooking Baumann Gulf. I chided them on not announcing their arrival to my wife, and took them round to the front verandah from where they could see a prospect of the lake from *my* house. We took tea, talked for a while, parted, and never met again. Our brief acquaintance was one of many recollected with pleasure and gratitude that they happened at all, and regret that – with the march of history – they ceased.

* * *

I wondered then and have wondered since how the Africans amongst whom we lived and worked saw us. There was ample evidence that on an individual basis we were judged on our personal characteristics, attitudes, and conduct. But collectively? Here were these pink foreigners, often well-educated, who appeared out of nowhere to run their country, and live in places which most literate Africans aspired to get away from. *Why* were they there? What was in it for them? Were they there by choice, and if so, why? Might it be as punishment for past errors or sins that they had been sent away from their homelands?

I do not imagine that the African peasant was greatly exercised by these considerations, but it would be surprising if there was not at least a passing curiosity. Certainly few Africans would have appreciated the possibility of job satisfaction. So what was it? We did not live in great style, and we shared some of their deprivations. Were we perhaps rewarded with unimaginable riches paid into distant bank accounts? What did the man think who had welcomed me to his homestead in Mwibara, and who had in turn visited me at Kabingo? Did he think anything at all, or was I at the time simply an inexplicable fact of life, to be taken for granted and not speculated about?

The perceptions of educated Africans could be more readily imagined. Probably most saw us as performing a useful function, and a good many – especially those in the civil service – identified with our motives and concerns, whilst also seeing us as an obstacle to their own employment and promotion prospects. To those fired by political considerations we were presumably regarded primarily as an affront, usurpers of power which for various reasons, good and bad, they wished to exercise themselves. But what of the unsophisticated rural population who were our major preoccupation? I would still like to know what they made of us, not as individuals, but as a collective phenomenon. One characteristic which I believe most were aware of and appreciated was our objectivity and detachment from local influences; sometimes our judgments and decisions were mistaken, but this could never be attributed to favouritism, nepotism, family or tribal loyalties, or bribery.

General Election

The concept of statutory multi-racial government had run its course by the late Fifties. Its introduction had been a bold or reactionary step, depending on your point of view, the idea being that legislative power should be shared equally by the three main races. It could have worked, and indeed did work, but only very briefly; but with this even division of representation when the population numbered nine million Africans, a hundred thousand Asians and perhaps ten thousand European residents, it was politically doomed as the all-black government of Kwame Nkrumah replaced colonial rule in the Gold Coast in 1957.

In 1960 we had a new constitution, and arrangements were in train for the holding of a general election later in the year. The positive aspect of multi-racialism was expanded to become non-racialism, whilst TANU opened its doors to non-African membership. Several Europeans and Asians were invited to stand for Legislative Council on the TANU ticket, and a number did so.

Most districts in the country comprised a single constituency, and in each the District Commissioner was the Electoral Officer, Returning Officer, and general factotum. Legislation was drafted and approved and preparations made. The franchise had qualitative limitations, and voters were required to be literate and have an income of £75 a year. In practice this meant that the new government would probably be elected by only about twenty to thirty per cent of the adult population, who would nevertheless be representative of the public at large. For most of them it would be a new experience; in African society the exercise of democracy was personal and had existed only at the village or tribal level, and even the district was often too large and impersonal

215

to comprehend or stimulate loyalty and interest. The nation state was something else again, the dream and goal of a handful of thoughtful politicians, an assumed source of wealth and power for others less scrupulous.

Up-country the greater part of the population had little idea of what it was all about, except for a general recognition that this election was the passport to independence. If the mechanics of the process were imperfectly understood, there was pardonable excitement about the consequences, and by now an eagerness to be in on the act. Tom Collingridge and I held numerous meetings around the district, under trees and in court-houses at sub-chiefdom headquarters; these buildings were open-sided, and a gathering of a hundred inside would be tripled by those assembled outside. We talked ourselves hoarse and distributed leaflets, and with the additional if subjective support of the local party hierarchy – for there was only one – we were satisfied after a couple of months that our public relations work had been comprehensively done.

One of my last explanatory meetings was at Nansimo, about twenty miles away on the mainland part of the district. It was a wet Saturday morning, and cold by tropical standards – it was probably about 70F (21C), at any rate chilly enough to make a sweater comfortable, though not sufficient stimulus to exchange the comfort of shorts for the restriction of trousers. At breakfast I asked Nigel, then aged four, if he would like to come; he would and he did.

We set off in my station waggon, and drove eight miles eastwards to the Rugezi ferry, where the causeway was progressing well. The chain ferry was manned by the usual cheerful stalwarts, staunch TANU supporters to a man, who usually entertained or provoked passengers with political songs as they hauled on the chain. On this day they were a little subdued, spirits dampened by the light but steady rain; at nearly four thousand feet rain was not the warm rain of the coast, but chilly as well as merely wet.

A few miles further on we came to a little river, normally a dry gully. It was only a few yards wide, but was now running two or three feet deep; too much for my car to negotiate even with the fan belt removed to prevent spray flying about under the bonnet. In the back of the station waggon amongst my essential travel accessories was an old rain cape. I took it out, and after removing my boots and slinging them round my neck, hoisted Nigel onto my shoulders where he draped the cape over us both. A pity there was no-one there with a camera as we waded across. Not far away on the other side was a hut, and under the eaves a bicycle was propped against the wall. The owner came out in response to my '*Hodi*', wreathed in clouds of smoke – or perhaps steam. Was he using his bicycle this morning and if not, could I borrow it for a couple of hours? He seemed pleased enough to oblige and no doubt reflected on the extravagant ways of this European who would pay two shillings for brief use of a bicycle.

The road was sandy rather than muddy, but damp sand is not the easiest of surfaces to ride on, and Nigel's added weight was no help. He sat on the carrier, invisible under my cape save for his legs; we must have looked a very strange animal indeed. It took about twenty minutes of hard pedalling to get to the sub-Chief's HQ at Nansimo. By this time the rain had stopped and the sun was trying to break through; I was sweating furiously and glad to remove the cape. And so we rode up the avenue of trees leading to the open courthouse. The crowd of about two hundred was clearly appreciative of my egalitarian mode of transport, and delighted with my passenger. He turned out to be an excellent if unpremeditated warm-up act, for he could chatter with them in Swahili; and his fair hair, bleached almost white by a short life spent under the equatorial sun, seemed to excite as much interest as the forthcoming election. The rest of the morning was a great success, and Nigel chortled away at the rear as we free-wheeled away down the avenue after taking our leave, trailing behind us the audible goodwill of the local electorate-to-be.

Then came the registration of voters. Advice on the income qualifications was scanty, perhaps deliberately so. Where houses were built and occupied by the owner, and never rented, what was their value expressed as income? What was the value of half a dozen patches of land totalling two or three acres and growing a combination of cotton, maize, millet and pumpkins – especially when they were neither owned nor rented, but simply *used?* This election was to be a training exercise, a formality; the result would be a foregone conclusion. There seemed little point in quibbling about the income qualification; as far as I was concerned pretty well anyone who was of age and could fill in the registration form was eligible. We ended up with an electoral roll of some fifteen thousand out of a total estimated adult population of about seventy thousand. Sylvia knew all about it, for she had the task of typing the rolls, the names being allocated under the planned polling stations.

217

The next stage was publicising the polling procedures. Another round of public meetings, and endless hours of talking. On one such occasion I was sitting with a small group of thirty or forty people at an indeterminate spot under a clump of mango trees. It was towards the western end of Ukerewe island, the lake invitingly blue and sparkling; it was an invitation we never accepted, for there was bilharzia, and for two and a half years we resisted the temptation to bathe or swim. At this time it seemed more alluring than another hour or two of talking and another sore throat. But the audience was appreciative; the Kerewe had a reputation for political liveliness, and what is now called full and frank discussion ensued. It was all very good humoured, except for one man, a sour and cynical wiseacre. He knew it all, and whilst an amiable dialogue was sustained with the rest of the group, this individual was determined to make the most of his opportunity. It was not every day that the *Bwana* DC was available to sharpen his wits on; the interruptions and barracking became more frequent. At each intervention I gritted my teeth and rolled my eyes upwards; and each time the sympathy of the others shifted in favour of their visitor. After all, he had taken the trouble to come out here and talk to us man to man, and here was old so-and-so letting the side down. It was inhospitable. At length old so-and-so pushed it too far, 'Why is it' he said, 'that I shall have to walk a mile to the nearest polling booth?' – he would probably have walked five to the nearest beer shop – 'Why cannot it be built closer?' Twenty or so heads turned towards him and told him to shut up. He didn't. The audience switched from Swahili into Kerewe, and my baiter took to his heels amid a shower of clods and mango stones, pursued by a nondescript dog which was roused from its afternoon slumber and anxious to enter into the spirit of the occasion. The rest of the meeting went well, and at the end of it I bought a chicken and was presented with a few tilapia, most delectable of freshwater fish.

The election when it came had a distinctly Gilbertian quality, but at least we had one. In all but a few of the seventy-one constituencies, the TANU candidate was returned unopposed. Ukerewe was one of the few, and an intrepid local man, Joseph Mafuru, ran as an independent against the TANU nominee, relying heavily on the support of the Jita residents of Mwibara. Not only that, but he found the requisite number of supporters who were prepared to put their signatures on his nomination papers.

218

Thereafter, the plot thickened. First one, then two, then others amongst the signatories denied having put their names down. If this was true then Joseph Mafuru had forged their signatures. A complaint was laid by TANU, and the independent candidate was charged with falsifying his nomination papers. It was a case which I could normally have heard as the local magistrate, but doubling as Returning Officer it would have been improper to do so. As it was outside the formal competence of Tom Collingridge, I asked for the Resident Magistrate in Mwanza to come over, which he did a few days later. The hearing was brief, and Joseph Mafuru was convicted and sentenced to three months in prison. I had my doubts, and was pretty certain that the signatories had been intimidated by local TANU members. However, the evidence was solid, and Joseph had no witnesses of his own – how could he have had?

At this point, sheer farce set in. Whether by accident or design our electoral legislation had not envisaged this situation. There was no means of halting the election, and although Joseph had been convicted and his nomination was void, the election had to go ahead. If elected he would have been disqualified, and perhaps rioting would have ensued. But the poll had to take place regardless of these considerations. Polling stations were set up at the appointed locations, supervised by expatriate officials drafted in from neighbouring districts; the turnout approached a hundred per cent, the ballot boxes were brought in, and I presided over the count. The total of votes cast was fourteen thousand odd, of which over eight thousand were for Nicas Buhatwa the TANU candidate and something over five thousand for Joseph Mafuru. A close-run result and testimony to the sturdy free-thinking of the Kerewe, Kara, and Jita electors.

At the time of my arrival in Ukerewe, Nicas had been storekeeper for the District Council; he had subsequently been tempted away by the Bukerebe Cotton Union, a co-operative society which had offered him greater responsibility and a bigger salary. He was a good man who would, I thought, make a good Member of the Legislative Council[43], and he had already shown himself to be a responsible district councillor. I was well-satisfied with the outcome of the election, and thankful that it had gone off smoothly. Not so the local TANU officials or the defeated Joseph in the immediate aftermath. The

---

[43] Later the National Assembly.

TANU Secretary accused me of having rigged the voting because Nicas had not won by a bigger margin; as for Joseph, he was convinced that had I not fixed the result, *he* would have won!

The reader may be curious as to why Joseph Mafuru was still around following his conviction. It was obviously not expedient to lock him up before or during the election. In the metaphorically cold grey light of the dawn which followed the celebration of Nicas Buhatwa's victory, Joseph Mafuru went off to prison for three months. It was hard, and probably unjust, but he seemed remarkably composed and philosophical about it. I was glad that I was still around when he came out of the *'hoteli Kingi Jorji'* some weeks later. I suppose *'Kingi Jorji'* trips more easily off the tongue than *'Kwini Elizabeti'*, but the old Swahili euphemism for prison persisted despite the coronation seven years earlier. Joseph Mafuru was perhaps a shade subdued and he had lost a pound or two, which he could well afford; but he appeared to have no hard feelings. More important, the TANU people seemed to harbour no animosity – after all, they had won.

Meanwhile, during Joseph's absence, things had moved on apace. The Governor remained, but Julius Nyerere was Chief Minister, his government responsible for all matters excluding security and foreign affairs. My new Minister for Local Government was Rashidi Kawawa, a former leading trade unionist and accustomed to opposing Government. On a subsequent visit to Ukerewe he seemed a little uncertain whether he was a part of Government or still in opposition.

Excitement over a cow

The equator passes through Lake Victoria, but at nearly 4000 feet (1219m) in the middle of the wet season it can be decidedly dank and chilly, though perhaps not quite chilly enough for a fire which we were sometimes lured into lighting. On these occasions we were soon driven into the corners of the room furthest from the fireplace, whilst sweaters were hastily discarded and handkerchiefs dabbed at perspiring foreheads.

The lake produced some spectacular thunderstorms at all seasons, but during the rains these were just punctuation marks in the general daily downpour. Towards the end of the wet season early in 1960 we had two days of particularly heavy rain and one exceptionally noisy thunderstorm. It is inscribed in the family memory because Sylvia got a nasty electric shock as she washed her hands at the kitchen sink, the consequence of lightning hitting the water tower two hundred yards down the road. Then there was the affair of the cow.

I had gone down to Nansio township to see how the drainage ditches were holding up, and also to have a look at the concrete bridge which Eddie had built to take the westbound road over a stream on the outskirts of the town. The approaches were said to have been washed out by the rain and the abutments in danger of being undermined by the stream, now running fast and well above its usual level. The rain had slackened off as I splashed and slipped along the road down to the bridge. The little *dukas* along the way were not exactly doing a roaring trade, and Mr. Patel sat in his shop doorway looking even more misanthropic than usual. He was one of the leading local Indian traders, and uncharacteristic with his bellicose and quarrelsome manner.

At the stream, the approaches to the bridge had been damaged, and although immediately passable only to a Landrover, there was nothing that could not be repaired with an hour or two's labour and half a lorry-load of broken stone. However there was evidence of some excitement, and a small group of men were chattering and directing their collective attention downstream. About fifty yards below the bridge a cow was struggling fitfully, its eyes rolling with fear; its rope halter was tangled in the exposed roots of a tree on the river bank, and the pressure of the water pulled the rope tight round the animal's neck and every few seconds dragged its head under water. The owner seemed not to be present, and the spectators appeared not to have any intention of doing anything. It was *'shauri ya Mungu'*, the will of God.

I strolled over the bridge and down the opposite bank, and lying on my rain cape, tried to reach the rope below. Not a chance. The current was flowing strongly, and though the water was brown and turgid with the topsoil of farmsteads upstream, I knew it couldn't be more than about four feet deep. So I hopped in as casually as possible, to free the rope, but I miscalculated the depth and force of the water, and my feet did not find the bottom. I was instantly swept past the cow but managed to get a handhold on one of the tree roots. So with a bit of a struggle, my body trailing horizontally like a skein of waterweed, I was able to work my way up past the cow – ducking it again in the process – and wrestled with the rope. It took some little while to untangle it, for I had to do the job with one hand; the other was locked firmly on to one of the roots. At length the halter came free and I grasped the loose end as the cow was propelled downstream. Alas my arms were not equal to the strain; I let go, and concentrated on hauling myself out of the water with what aplomb I could muster, this time assisted by one of the bystanders. Meanwhile, the cow, mooing mournfully, was being swept down into Lake Victoria, only about two hundred yards distant. Here the flood slackened, and the cow soon found itself swimming in calm waters. A fisherman and his son who were paddling by in one of the graceful lake canoes grabbed the halter and headed for the shore. Judging that the cow would recover, I departed and squelched off in the direction of my car, an object of some curiosity to the few people who were out on that dismal Saturday morning. As I passed his shop, little Mr. Amin reacted briskly and produced a towel, and I was able to dry off my head, arms and legs.

My arrival home was the occasion for some merriment, and I explained my condition as I climbed shivering out of my sodden clothes. There was no hot bath, for we did not light the 'Tanganyika boiler' until early evening; however, a fire indoors was a matter of minutes.

Word must have got about. The next day I was visited by the headmaster of the Indian Primary School, whom I had first met when paying him a courtesy call; he was a small, quiet man with an interest in English literature, and I had often seen him in Nansio walking alone and apparently reciting to himself, or perhaps rehearsing a lesson.

He handed me a foolscap manila envelope, and with the briefest of courtesies mounted his bicycle and rode off. Inside the envelope was a page and a half of manuscript, couched in the extravagantly purple prose which is – or was – characteristically Indian. In this he likened my almost accidental rescue of the cow to some of the more notable epics of British imperial history in which our Victorian heroes covered themselves in glory. He was right about the facts as they had no doubt been related to him, but completely mistaken as to the motives – which had been casual in the extreme. And of course, he was unaware of my miscalculation as to the depth and the momentum of the water. Again, being a good Hindu, he was perhaps unduly influenced by my apparent concern for the cow – just a cow to me, but holy to him. At all events it was nice that someone had cared, for I saw neither hide nor hair of the animal's owner.

Diplomat-in-waiting

A few weeks before leaving Ukerewe I was reluctantly drawn into a district boundary dispute, just as I had been weeks after arrival in Manyoni eight years earlier. This time a chief in Musoma district claimed a small slice of Ukerewe, between the heads of the Speke and Baumann gulfs. When John Stephenson, DC Musoma, (invariably known as 'Steve') wrote suggesting a meeting near the boundary, I could not well refuse. After brief discussion with Chief Lukumbuzya, a date was agreed.

On this occasion I accepted the offer of a lift in Lukumbuzya's capacious Chevrolet station-waggon. Late one afternoon he dropped me off close to 'Steve's' camp, and then went back a few miles to spend the night with a sub-chief in Kasuguti. I was to join 'Steve' for an evening meal, and pitched my lightweight tent at a little distance from his own – a felicitous decision as it turned out. We sat in our camp chairs enjoying a beer, chatting desultorily as we watched the moving pattern of wildebeest, zebra, and Tommies grazing across the middle distance. If I seemed a little preoccupied, it was because of my impending departure on leave; I wanted to savour the moment, and this would be the last time I saw the sun dip behind the Ragata hills.

'Steve' was an entertaining companion, a tough stocky Kenyan who, like Tony Golding, had served with Somali levies in the Horn of Africa during the Second World War. He was lucky to have survived a mutiny by his platoon of half-disciplined troops whilst on a forced march in pursuit of bandits. With a combination of personality and sheer bravura he had disarmed his men, with the exception of a sergeant who remained loyal, and got them back to base without further mishap. We talked on into the night about anything other than the matter in hand.

Next morning we were joined by Chief Lukumbuzya and his opposite number from over the border. A short drive took us to the top of a low rise, from where we looked out over the area in dispute; open grassland, dried to the colour of sand, there was no habitation for miles, and no landmarks on which to base a sensible discussion. Lukumbuzya knew as well as I did that the whole thing was a charade, and he was content to go through the motions of ceding a square mile or so of empty country to Musoma. The visiting chief would be applauded by his elders when he returned, but on the ground nothing would change; there would be no demarcation, and the district maps would remain the same. A few years hence, unless our successors were more robust about these 'boundary *shauris*' than we were, someone would resurrect the dispute.

Adjourning for lunch, 'Steve' was dismayed to find his tent a smouldering ruin. His hapless cook had allowed his fire to get out of hand when a brisk breeze blew up, and the tent had gone up in flames along with its contents. My own tent, fifty yards away, and upwind, was unscathed. I commiserated with 'Steve' and offered a not-very-consoling drink. Lunchless, we went our separate ways.

On the return journey we were delayed for some time at the Rugezi ferry. Here, sitting in his Chevrolet, Lukumbuzya began to unburden himself as to his future prospects in an independent Tanganyika. It was not at the time evident that the traditional Native Authorities would *not* be incorporated in whatever definitive form of local government emerged, but there was certainly a possibility that they would be perceived by TANU as an alternative focus of personal and tribal loyalties at a time when national unity would be a major concern. Lukumbuzya had spent some hours with Julius Nyerere on his last visit to the district, and perhaps knew more about this than I did. He had a pleasing personality, and I found him to be a capable and forward-looking chief, and an effective administrator, whilst his contributions to decision-making in the District Council had typically been constructive, and focused on results. Although an admitted nationalist, he had never been overtly disloyal to Government or to me, nor had he fallen into the arms of TANU – if he had done we would not have been having this conversation. I felt confident in assuring him that any future government would need people of his calibre and experience, and that any anxieties he might have were groundless; it was I whose career was nearing its end. My prediction was correct, and Michael Lukumbuzya was recruited into Tanganyika's new diplomatic service. He died prematurely three decades later whilst serving as High Commissioner in Canada.

The Indian community

If there is only passing reference in this narrative to the Indian community, it is simply because it featured very little in our working lives; our primary preoccupation was with African development and the moulding of African institutions. Our Indian residents (and a handful of Arabs) we judged to be more than capable of looking after their own interests at local level without any intervention by officialdom. There were numbers of Indians and Goans in the civil service, many of whom had been recruited in the sub-continent; in general they occupied positions of responsibility for which there were, as yet, not enough trained Africans. Hence there were Indian doctors, commissioned police officers, and most typically senior accounts clerks. But far and away the greatest numbers were in commerce, with a sizeable contingent in the law. On the coast Indians featured largely in the import-export trade, and they dominated wholesale business. They also owned transport and construction companies, and in general were consummate entrepreneurs, albeit often on a very modest scale.

So it was in up-country districts, where the retail trade was very largely in Indian – mostly Gujarati – hands. This near-monopoly generated a good deal of resentment amongst Africans; this was compounded of envy and the awareness of dependence on the Asian traders for most of their retail purchases. It was also the case that Africans found it difficult or impossible to compete because they rarely had access to loans or credit with which to set up and sustain a business. Most African *dukas* were to be found in the remoter areas or where local needs could be met by a single small shop; being the only Indian family for miles around was not an appealing social option.

In Nansio township I made the acquaintance of all the Indian traders early on, and thereafter passed the time of day with most of them whenever I was down in the little lake port. In most cases we had little in common, but there were exceptions; Mr. Amin, who supplied European-type food; Ladha Meghji who owned the oil mill by the lake shore, and who was a man of some education; Mr.Kumar, who invited Sylvia and me to join him at the small local cinema to see 'Mother India' so that he could explain the plot as the epic unfolded; and of course the head teacher of the Indian school. Dr. Tiagi, the District Medical Officer for most of our tour, was a next-door neighbour, a convivial host and congenial guest. By way of contrast there was Mr. Patel, a disagreeable man whose voice could usually be heard raised in anger or irritation a hundred yards from his shop in both directions. Social relations between expatriate officials and the Indian community were friendly and relaxed, but I thought it expedient not to get too close, lest this be misinterpreted by an African public increasingly sensitised to the politics of race. I think most of my colleagues felt the same. By a similar token I avoided making close friendships with Africans; I did not want them being thought of as 'Uncle Toms' by their more nationalistic fellow-countrymen.

Official contacts with Indians were limited; they were law-abiding citizens who rarely appeared in court or needed advice or information. During my first year or so in Ukerewe there were two Indians on the District Advisory Council (along with an Arab and a non-official European), and they could usually be relied upon to make useful contributions to debate. Otherwise contact in an official capacity tended to be by mischance. Thus, a few months after our arrival in Ukerewe, there was an African boycott of three Indian traders in Nansio, allegedly organised by TANU. One of the trio was the delightful Mr. Walji, whose shop occupied a prime site on a corner adjacent to the pier. He was a public-spirited man who at any given time was financing an African youngster through Makerere University College, although he did not advertise the fact. It seemed particularly shabby that he should be victimised in this way. The three shops in question were quite close together, and I had a police constable sent to patrol the area and arrest anyone seen to be interfering with would-be customers. On the third or fourth day an arrest was made and the culprit charged and convicted. Knowing that he had been acting on instructions I fined him a few shillings, but warned that anyone else convicted in similar circumstances could expect a prison sentence. The boycott ceased, and the incident provided me with an excuse to call at the local TANU office and meet the district chairman and secretary on their own ground and have a tête a tête. I said that I accepted TANU's basic political objective, since it was also ours; the differences between us were over timing and means. We were for our various reasons concerned with the pace of constitutional change, but my primary responsibility was for the good government and development of Ukerewe district; this included the maintenance of law and order, and the less I was occupied with this the more time I could devote to local needs. Being a big fish in a small pond I thought I had probably established some credibility as a relatively progressive DC, as distinct from one who for the best of reasons wanted only to preserve the status quo; but I also wanted to make it clear I could not tolerate politically-motivated crime. We did not part bosom friends, but we established a modus vivendi which held up pretty well during the rest of my tour; and even during the few tense months in 1959 it was possible to join the two TANU representatives for a drink in a local bar if I chanced upon them in the course of an evening stroll.

There was in fact another boycott the following year, but this was a national affair initiated by Julius Nyerere – a boycott of South African goods in protest against apartheid. I suspect that in practice this hurt Tanganyika more than it did South Africa, but in Ukerewe the effect was negligible. I forget whether the boycott was intended to apply solely to the purchase of goods or whether it invited a general boycott of any trader dealing in imports from the Union. Whichever it was, the Ukerewe traders assumed the worst and played safe. Packing cases were destroyed, and labels indicating South African origin surreptitiously scraped off the offending items. In the case of canned foodstuffs this also had the effect of conferring anonymity on the contents. So poor Mr. Amin, grocer-in-chief to the expatriate community, having soaked the labels off his tins, felt obliged to offer them at half-price. We participated in the lucky dip and made our purchases, never knowing whether a tin contained soup, fish, vegetables, meat, or fruit until we opened it.

My only other engagement with the Nansio traders was to arbitrate in a labour dispute between them and their domestic staff. By our standards their household servants seemed to work excessively long hours, often from dawn until the employing family went to bed. Unusually, but not unreasonably, the domestics went on strike, and one of the shopkeepers asked me what I was going to do about it. I said I had no authority to do anything, but that if the shopkeepers and the strike committee were agreeable, I would try to come up with a solution which was acceptable to both parties. In the event discussions went ahead, initially with the two parties separately, and later jointly; eventually my judgment was accepted, with some grumbling on both sides – which I took to be a good sign. I have no recollection of the details, nor how long the agreement stuck; weeks later I was on my way to England and leave.

A reluctant farewell

Late in February 1961 I was in the throes of packing preparatory to departure. There were no professional packers, and the chore of filling twenty-odd trunks and wooden boxes was spread sweatily over a period of three or four weeks. Sylvia and the children had left in November, when we made a last joint voyage in the *Mukama,* wallowing across Speke Gulf to Mwanza. There we spent the night with Pat and Douglas and their two daughters in their bungalow on the hill. I saw Sylvia and the children off on the evening train to Dar, and next morning returned to Ukerewe after a brief call on Peter Bell.

The anxieties engendered by the threat of civil unrest eighteen months earlier had receded, and had been followed by a period of quiet if qualified optimism. It was increasingly possible to look to the local TANU representatives for support or at least acquiescence in our work, particularly in as far as it affected the welfare of the district. Modest Africanisation of the senior civil service was demonstrated by the posting to Ukerewe of an African Assistant District Officer (ADO), Joseph Macha. We needed an extra pair of hands, and here too was the opportunity of transmitting skills to one of our successors. But, desirable though this process was, it was too little too late. And recently there had been a growing sense of unease and uncertainty between 'us' up-country and 'them' in Dar-es-Salaam. It seemed to 'us' that local government was being allowed to drift, that with dwindling authority we were left to do our best in advising and encouraging District Councils, but with precious little guidance as to what end product was now intended. There were signs that the new model of local government would be very different from our own, but if the elected Government had a blueprint it was not vouchsafed to us up-country, and we were left to carry on as best we could – perhaps to create an illusion of continuity in the country at large whilst the reins of power were handed over at the centre. Thus in East Lake Province[44] for example, each DC had, usually solo, negotiated some form of revised local 'constitution' with local political interests – NA's, district branches of TANU, and representatives with more traditional views. All were agreed, with or

---

[44] In 1960 Lake Province had been split into two, East and West Lake.

without modification, existing forms being adjusted by reference to local opinion in one way or another. Immediately after its election, one new District Council tried to vote itself into office in perpetuity; our own – more modest or less ambitious – sought only to double the sitting fee of members, and pay a substantial honorarium to the elected chairman.

In Ukerewe I had set up a panel consisting of members from the old-style District Advisory Council, representatives of TANU, and Chief Lukumbuzya. After some months of deliberation and consultation we had produced a new 'constitution' setting out the composition and responsibilities of the District Council, election rules, and so on. By the turn of the year the election had been held and every single new member, about half the total, was a novice. Much of the collective wisdom and experience of their predecessors was in practice lost, for the older members were anxious not to incur the displeasure of the new ones, all TANU nominees to a man. This dilution of experience coincided with the allocation of executive power to the council; it was no longer advisory. To be fair, the newly-constituted council was characterised by good intentions and enthusiasm, and local issues were discussed earnestly in committee and full council. The staff committee was commendably conscientious, yet when filling vacancies, tended to appoint obvious no-hopers. And for a minor disciplinary offence which merited no more than a reprimand, it dismissed the excellent Secretary, their Clerk to the Council (these days grandly styled Chief Executive in the UK), since I had now taken a back seat. There was also a certain naïveté which equated deciding with doing, and a tendency to overlook or ignore the practicalities and problems of implementation. It was no advantage as far as I was concerned that amongst the new members was one of the trio of murderers who featured earlier in this narrative.

Our accelerated and ad hoc democratisation of local government at this time was the consequence of legitimate pressure for greater public involvement combined with a brief and almost absent-minded loss of interest and initiative at the centre; and this was in an area of activity, local government, which had been central to our rôle. And of course my own ability to bring experience and advice effectively to bear was limited by a certain disinclination of an over-confident new council to accept either, although this was by no means absolute. This pattern was of course repeated up and down the country sooner or later.

Added to all this was a niggling suspicion, perhaps unfounded, that some of our seniors in the capital were too busy securing their future career interests to devote the requisite time to district matters. 'Fanny' Walden had once remarked following a brief visit to Dar-es-Salaam shortly before his retirement, 'All you could hear down there was the clanking of climbing irons and the grinding of axes'; an exaggeration no doubt, but probably not wholly without foundation, and up-country we felt rather neglected.

The few months preceding my departure from Ukerewe, then, were muddled and frustrating in the context of local administration. After a succession of good years the cotton crop had been poor, and revenues were down; intended developments would have to be curtailed or abandoned if the council was to remain solvent. On top of this I had failed to convince the new members to abandon their plan to abolish the already modest school fees[45] if they were not also prepared to increase the local rate, then not much more than 50p a year per adult male. I was not surprised to hear, two or three years later, that the council had been dismantled and a Government Administrator appointed precisely because they had bankrupted the local treasury as predicted. The new Minister for Local Government, Rashidi Kawawa (later Prime Minister and Vice-President), had been largely if unintentionally responsible for this. Following the council's decision I had referred the matter to the ministry, and the Permanent Secretary had agreed with my view that the council should be overruled; the Chairman then appealed to the Minister who, on a forthcoming visit to the Province, made a detour to Ukerewe to review the matter. I sat in with him on the Finance Committee, the new members of which took the familiar line that 'we Africans must stick together and show the colonialists who is now in control'. It worked, prudence flew out of the window, and Rashidi Kawawa gave the Ukerewe District Council the green light to bankrupt itself. A few more pence on the local rate would have avoided this.

Anxious to complete unfinished tasks before going on leave, there was neither time nor inclination to brood over this disappointment. The house which had been home for two and a half years took on an increasingly forlorn aspect as familiar bits and pieces, none of them of any great value,

---

[45] Primary fees 25p a year, middle school boarding fees about £8 a year.

disappeared into trunks and boxes where they would remain for the next six months. I sold the car so that I could pay our last remaining bills; sadly, for it had during the previous six years taken us over 60,000 miles of unsurfaced road and track with only one breakdown and never a broken spring.

My successor arrived and I handed over to him with a certain egotistical resentment, and after the last signature was dry I was anxious to get away; I was sorry to be leaving the district, colleagues, and friends, but Ukerewe held no further allure with someone else in *my* seat. The departure date was determined by the first leg of an ambitious homeward itinerary which was to take me to Kenya, Ethiopia, Egypt, Lebanon, Israel, and France. The morning in question was dull, and I had to leave early to catch the plane at Mwanza. Our friends and neighbours were at the pier to see me off, joined by some of the district councillors, Chief Lukumbuzya, a small TANU contingent and a number of traders and townspeople. I boarded the *Mukama* for the last time, accompanied by our Swedish doctor and his wife who were visiting Mwanza for a few days, and Victor pushed us away from the pier with his boathook. It was chilly on the lake, and I pulled on a sweater and watched Ukerewe recede; the same view had evoked excitement as it appeared over the horizon from the deck of the mv *Alestes* all those months earlier, and now there was a great sense of loss. Ten miles or so south we passed the huddle of rocks which served to guide the lake traveller. There was the usual cormorant or two and the nonsense verse ran through my head as it invariably did at this point:

The common cormorant or shag
Lays eggs inside a paper bag.
The reason you will see no doubt,
It is to keep the lightning out;
But what those unobservant birds
Had never noticed is that herds
Of wandering bears may come with buns
And steal the bags to hold the crumbs.[46]

Would there be cormorants, I wondered, where next we came to rest? It

---

[46] Copyright © Estate of Christopher Isherwood.

seemed unlikely. My next posting was still uncertain; if either of two contradictory rumours was true, it would be either a stint in the Secretariat in Dar-es-Salaam, or Ngara district bordering the shambles of the newly-independent Congo Republic, where refugees were still imposing severe strains on the local community and administration.

Mwanza was still two hours away, and out there on the lake I was aware that something was missing. The accustomed stress and tension of responsibility had fallen away, and I was conscious of being tired; but it was too early to unwind, and the prospect of over four months leave induced restlessness rather than relaxation. These were the usual end-of-tour withdrawal symptoms when suddenly deprived of work and immediate purpose.

It had been a good tour, personally satisfying, sometimes exhilarating, frequently frustrating, occasionally – but only very occasionally – bloody. It was pleasing to know that for several years there had been a modest annual incremental improvement in the district's prosperity, evidenced in the increases of the numbers of bicycle and radio licenses issued, in Post Office savings accounts, in the sales of cement and permanent roofing materials and little consumer luxuries, and so on. As for my own stewardship, changes in local government have already been alluded to, and though intentions had been unexceptionable, the consequences had not been an unqualified success. We had started an ambulance service and begun a regular screening of schoolchildren for hookworm and bilharzia. In agriculture we had introduced improved seeds and persuaded a sceptical peasantry of the advantages of cattle dips and manure. A forest reserve to produce timber supplies in the future had been established, and we had distributed some thousands of free coffee seedlings. The building of a dam had opened up a few square miles of country for settlement, even though it now looked as if this would be entirely uncontrolled. The judicial and administrative function of Sub-Chiefs had been separated and a local magistracy established.

Caspair Lake Air Services had been persuaded to fly a de Havilland Rapide in from Mwanza twice a week, using the airstrip just along the road from my house; it was a delight to fly in. An ante-and post-natal service had been set up on the island, and this was to be matched by a similar service in Mwibara, where the White Fathers Mission had begun to build a new hospital on condition of an annual subvention from the District Council. A variety of public works had been undertaken, including the construction of two new primary schools, six new classrooms, three markets, and housing for nine African staff. Importantly, we had a new African DC in the making; however, his title and duties might change radically in the months ahead[47] – if the office survived at all.

Over a period of thirty months, these were the visible results of the interaction between members of the District Team as it was fortuitously assembled, Government, and public opinion expressed through traditional leaders, councillors, and latterly,TANU. With a different mix the results would not have been more or less significant, only different. Now it was someone else's turn. But with independence only eight or nine months away my successor's tenure was short, and he was Ukerewe's last expatriate DC.

I recollected also tasks intended and never carried out, and felt a twinge of guilt. Unreasonably so, for a ten to twelve hour day had been normal, often six days a week. Our longest break in two and a half years had been a Bank Holiday weekend en famille at Seronera in the Serengeti; here, after eight years in the country, we saw our first lion and buffalo. Nevertheless, perhaps I *could* have pushed ahead with planting Russian comfrey as a fodder crop in Ukara, and had a go at easing out old Chief Mataba. I really *ought* to have done more about the selection and training of a new Social Development Assistant; and that intended fishing co-operative over in Mwibara had perhaps deserved more encouragement. There was regret too that I had not socialised more with my African colleagues, despite the very good reason for not doing so already adduced. We had thrown occasional inter-racial parties, and having the District Council round for tea or drinks had become almost routine. It was certainly the case that I had devoted less time to training Joseph Macha the new ADO, than he needed and deserved; with pressure of work it was often easier to 'do it myself' and explain afterwards and too perfunctorily, instead of talking him slowly through whatever the problem or process was. I should also have given more time to Chris and Tom. Perhaps *next* tour I'd do better.

At Mwanza I was met by Geoff Thirtle, now in the Provincial Office after leaving Masasi. An hour later I was on board an East African Airways DC3

---

[47] They did, but the designation has now been reinstated.

bound for Nairobi. We lifted off the earth runway, dropped a few feet as we passed the ridge beyond, and droned onwards, gaining height very slowly. Our flight path took us northwards, close enough to Ukerewe to see the whole of the district spread out below, and hidden intermittently by a scattering of thin cloud. There was Irugwa island too, off the coast of Majita; conscience pricked again – I had never got round to visiting it and now I never would.

Saturated with the immediate past, the prospect of Addis Ababa, Asmara, Cairo, and Beirut was not as stirring as it should have been. But Israel was different, and offered a purpose. This had been sparked off some months earlier following an official visit to Tanganyika by two senior Israeli civil servants, an event which was reported in one of the Chief Secretary's monthly newsletters. On the strength of this I wrote to them at their ministries in Tel Aviv, expressing a wish to see something of Israeli rural and co-operative development; I thought there might be useful lessons for Tanganyika to learn. The result was an invitation from the departments concerned, and a week's programme which included visits to agricultural settlements, co-operative projects, and colleges where I met a number of students from Tanganyika. I would report on this after returning from leave later in the year. But we did not return; despite the very persuasive letter sent to most of us by Julius Nyerere urging us to stay on[48], family considerations prevailed over personal inclinations, and after much agonising I took the 'severance package'. The report on my visit to Israel occupied me rather desultorily later in the year, and was despatched to the office of Julius Nyerere a week or two after independence in December 1961. By then I had begun a new, and brief, career in ICI. A year later I was on my way back to Africa, this time to Nigeria with the British Council.

---

[48] See Appendix A

EPILOGUE

Ten years on

ICI was a good employer, and more generous than my previous one; but the work failed to excite, and hierarchical formalities contrasted unfavourably with the easy relationships of the Colonial Service. Sight of an advertisement for a post with the British Council in Nigeria coincided with the creeping onset of itchy feet; I applied for it and was accepted.

In mid-1971, whilst serving in London, I received from the Government of Tanzania an invitation to attend the tenth anniversary of independence celebrations. This had been forwarded from my previous post in Kuala Lumpur, from where a return air ticket would have been provided had I still been there. As it was I found myself, in early December, amongst a plane-load of similar invitees, half of them former DOs, bound for Dar-es-Salaam, and thrilled at the prospect of this fortnight's foray down memory lane.

It would be absurd to pretend that in colonial times all had been sweetness and light, particularly at the national political level. However there were no overt signs of rancour; rather a good deal of mutual back-slapping, laughter, reminiscing, and serious talk about issues which had concerned us ten or twenty years earlier and now exercised our successors. The programme in Dar-es-Salaam included attendance at a mammoth parade in the national stadium, a Government sundowner,[49] and a State banquet.

Guests at these two social events included representatives from all foreign embassies, and token contingents from countries too small or impecunious to have their own diplomatic representations. At the sundowner it was noticeable that the Tanzanian guests were mainly engaged in conversation with we 'ex-colonialists', whilst groups of East Europeans, Russians, Chinese, Americans and some British stood around looking slightly bemused at the easy and friendly relations between people who, in the context of their own dogma, were supposed to be enemies. Again, at the banquet, the police band played the same selection

---

[49] The familiar evening drinks party.

of tunes which they would have played twenty or thirty years earlier, and which any military band performs on any bandstand in Britain; and they willingly met requests from former 'colonials' who sporadically stepped forward and whispered in the bandmaster's ear.

At dinner I found myself sitting between the representative of the Albanian government and the Deputy Minister of Labour from Kenya. I did my duty by the Albanian, who trotted out a list of unimpressive statistics relating to progress in education, adult literacy, and the economy; battered and numbed by this barrage, I spent the rest of the evening in conversation with the Kenyan.

The formal part of the proceedings concluded with a speech by President Nyerere in which he paid a gracious tribute to his former expatriate civil servants – again, I suspect, to the puzzlement of communist-bloc guests. He also reminded us that at the time of independence he had announced that Tanganyika would develop more in the next ten years than it had done under forty years of British rule; he good-naturedly admitted that he'd been over-optimistic – and the subsequent developmental record had been patchy, attributable as elsewhere in Africa, to a combination of internal and external factors. But he was proud of what *had* been achieved, and wanted us to share it.

The next major event offered a choice between visiting a game reserve, and Zanzibar and Pemba. Zanzibar had united with Tanganyika in 1964 following a brief but bloody revolution, but retained its own Marxist government, and was heavily reliant on East German and Chinese support. Curiosity demanded the Zanzibar option. We flew over in a Defence Force 'Caribou' transport aircraft, and were entertained to lunch by the Chief Minister, Karume, and subsequently ferried to a number of showpiece projects in both islands; these were dispiriting rather than encouraging, and as a propaganda exercise the visits were entirely counter-productive. A bizarre feature of the tour was the allocation of members of the youth wing of the ruling party to our group – one of them to every three or four of us. Their function was clearly to stop any of us wandering off on our own, and to thwart conversation between ourselves and the local people. They were very conscientious and largely successful. Heavily indoctrinated as they obviously were, we managed to crack the shell of our little 'green guard' by engaging him in conversation and banter in his own language, and perhaps demonstrated that we weren't as black as we'd been painted.

A major project of the Zanzibar government at the time was to accommodate the entire population in permanent housing, and they were well on their way with the building programme. It was a wholly admirable intention, but flawed in practice; the largely rural population was being put into three and four-storey blocks of flats, appropriate to East Berlin perhaps, but entirely out of keeping in Zanzibar, and not best-adapted to the keeping of chickens and goats or the use of wood fires for cooking. We saw this mis-match of African life and European architecture at first hand, since we were accommodated overnight in a newly completed and partly occupied block.

Back in Dar-es-Salaam the main anniversary celebrations were over, but for us the best was yet to come. Our hosts had generously arranged for us all to visit the last – or indeed any – district in which we had served, and get us to the place of our choice by combination of land, air, and water. Unsurprisingly, I chose Ukerewe. One party of us set off in a 'Caribou' bound for Mwanza; the captain of the aircraft was a confident young Tanzanian officer who handled his machine as competently as could have been wished. I recollected that the Sardauna of Sokoto, a traditional ruler in northern Nigeria, had a few years earlier refused to allow himself to be flown by African pilots.

We trundled westwards noisily and uncomfortably, dropping a small contingent off at Dodoma, and then carrying on over and beyond Manyoni to Tabora , where a few more of the group were to leave. However, we landed during the opening salvoes of a crashing thunderstorm, and the pilot wisely decided to stop there overnight. We all stayed in the Government catering rest-house and were amused to see that the menu was substantially the same as it had been ten years earlier. Amongst the local residents who came to greet us was Eddie Murat, the Mauritian who had been my District Foreman in Ukerewe, now a Tanzanian citizen and accompanied by his Kerewe wife.

The delay in Tabora meant that I missed the early morning ferry from Mwanza to Ukerewe the next day. A local civil servant had been nominated to keep me company whilst his seniors decided whether to send me round to the island by road or whether I would have to wait until the morrow. Whilst he was away making a phone call I seized the opportunity to speak to a young woman air-taxi pilot who, it turned out, was killing time before flying her fare back to Nairobi. Yes, she had time to take me to Ukerewe, and would do so for a modest fee. My African companion returned, was consulted, and after further discussion the onward flight was agreed. We sped off to the airport, and twenty minutes

237

later we landed on the grass airstrip a quarter of a mile from my old home.

It was in many respects a homecoming, and I was made very welcome by the Area Secretary and local officials. A tour of the island took in the Rubya forest reserve; it was pleasing to see quantities of logs and poles lying on the quay awaiting shipment across the lake – saplings when I had last seen them. At the other end of the island I saw where the causeway had once been and the motor ferry which of necessity replaced it. The cotton ginnery at Murutunguru had disappeared, but I was able to renew my acquaintance with the White Fathers at their mission near by; sadly the ebullient Father Vachon was in hospital in Mwanza, but I managed to make a quick call on my return journey.

Nansio was much as it had been, with one notable exception. In 1961 it had been designated a Minor Settlement; it was now a Township, one step up the local government ladder. In recognition of this promotion, the local powers-that-be had decreed the felling of the avenue of trees which had flanked the dusty main street – mangoes, flamboyants, and a few jacarandas. Traders, hawkers, shoppers and idlers now sweltered in the sun. In passing, I noticed that the shelves in the *dukas,* formerly stacked with goods, were now three-quarters empty. Apart from this, walking through the town was a delight, exchanging greetings and news with old acquaintances. Several, including an elderly beer-brewer, clearly thought I had returned to take over the district again, and I hastened to disabuse them lest they incurred official displeasure – though the relaxed atmosphere suggested that this was unlikely. Conversation with the Area Secretary (approximating to a DC, but with more limited responsibilities) induced a distinct sense of déjà vu; the same issues and problems exercised him as they had me; in some instances old policies and practices continued, others had been abandoned, whilst with others our wheels had been reinvented. And there were innovations of course. One of these was a unified local government service with a view to spreading ability more evenly across the country; in our day the quality of local government staff had been dependent on the pool of talent available in the district, and in backward areas this could be very small indeed. In practice it appeared that results didn't always match intention, and the more able and ambitious tended to find their way to developed districts and larger towns, whilst remote and poorer areas whose need was greater still had to make do with the also-rans. But it was worth a try, and standards were probably less uneven than they had been a decade earlier.

Back in Mwanza after an overnight stay, I met the Regional Commissioner,[50] another old acquaintance; he had been the local Schools Supervisor at Kondoa during my first tour, and a very good one. He later went on to become a Minister, but subsequently fell from grace for reasons unknown to me. He took me under his wing for half a day, and was particularly pleased to conduct me round a cotton spinning and weaving factory stuffed full of the latest hi-tech textile machinery from Japan. It was impressive but arguably inappropriate, requiring a minimum of labour, and disposing of the Lake Region's cotton crop in a fraction of the working year. But this is an aside; as in Dar and Ukerewe, recollection of the past and celebration of the present were a pleasure.

After two weeks the ex-colonial party re-assembled in Dar-es-Salaam. Our visit had not been an investigative or inquisitorial one, and impressions were – well, impressionistic. I saw things which, without close questioning, seemed to merit criticism; and other things which were clearly commendable. Observable shortcomings were as far as one could judge attributable to the errors of judgement to which all governments and organisations are prone, and to circumstances over which they rarely have complete control; and there were misgivings as to whether the economy, even with added foreign aid, could sustain the otherwise commendable expansion of education, medical services, and so on. I returned to England in many ways reassured, and grateful for a memorable experience; but that was half a lifetime ago. Tanzania, like much of Africa, achieved its greatest post-colonial economic growth in the ten or twelve years after independence; for the next twenty years the economy declined, and reliance on foreign aid increased, a pattern which began to be reversed only in the 1990's. On the other hand the country has been remarkably stable, and in social and political terms seems very much at ease with itself.

Afterword

I have sometimes been asked, in the context of post-colonial African history, if I have regrets about my first career choice; the answer is an emphatic no. There is regret that post-war British Governments lacked the

---

[50] Formerly Provincial Commissioner.

resources and the will to fully meet their colonial responsibilities; that the colonial Government of Tanganyika failed to engage more constructively with the African political leadership and educated Africans in general; that TANU paid too little heed to the need for more trained and qualified Africans as a prerequisite for independence; that circumstances did not allow us to achieve more; and that more than forty years on Tanzania is still an extremely poor country. But as for the job itself and the work it entailed, it was richly rewarding in its own right, full of interest, variety, and opportunity to make a personal contribution – albeit often ephemeral – to the district in which one lived. It conferred greater satisfaction than any work I have done since; if the clock of history was put back, and with the foreknowledge of a severely curtailed career, I would make the same choice again. There has also been the bonus of lifelong friendships.

Appendix A

Office of the Prime Minister,
P.O.Box 9000,
Dar es Salaam.

1st May 1961.

Dear Barton,

I feel I should write to you personally at
this time when you and numbers of your colleagues may
feel that you must make decisions about your future.

Some Administrative Officers have, I know,
already decided to leave Tanganyika, and to them I would
say thank you for what you have done and good luck in
whatever you decide to do.

To those of you who are undecided, the first
thing I want to make clear is that my Government, and
therefore the great bulk of the people of Tanganyika whom
we represent, are really in need of your help; and we will
be for a long time to come. I have said so on many occasions,
both in Legislative Council and outside. So have several of
my colleagues, although their references to you do not always
get as well publicised as one or two speeches which are
contrary to Government's policy and which do harm to Tanganyika.
Anyway, let it be clearly understood that such wild remarks as
were recently reported as having been made by Mr.Mwanjisi in
Cairo do not reflect my views or my Government's or those of
the vast majority of the people of this country. You can
account for them by the heady atmosphere in which they were
delivered; and so I hope you will ignore them. At all events,
let me repeat here that it is not only technical officers we
wish to retain. We need our experienced administrators, our
corps d'elite as the Governor called you the other day, because
it is they who keep the whole machinery of Government working.

I did not feel I could write to you in this
personal fashion until we, as a Government, could see that
you were being properly treated materially. Now that the
Flemming award has been made and the compensation scheme is
in being, I feel entitled to ask you to stay and help us.
That is not to say that I think you will have no difficulties.
I know many of you will have serious worries about education,
although we have done what we can to help you there with the
allowances that make it easier for you to educate your children
in your own country. Some of you may feel, though I believe
you are wrong, that medical and other services may deteriorate;
or that there will be less companionship with people of your own
background on out-stations.

I do not brush these worries aside as though they
do not matter, but I want to appeal to the sense of mission which
our Administrative Officers have always felt. It is your sense
of mission which has seen you through the challenges of the past.
I can offer you challenges too and I don't think they are so very
different from the challenges that brought you out here. Together

we have still got to make something of Tanganyika that we can
all be proud of; and surely that is enough of a challenge for
anyone in a continent where so much ill-feeling and unhappiness
abound.

So I am not suggesting that from now on no irresponsible
statements are going to be made by junior politicians in this
country. Such a suggestion would be silly. What I am seriously
suggesting is that you should not be put off from your great task
by such statements and by such irresponsibility. I am not
suggesting that you will have no trials and difficulties and
frustrations in the future. I am suggesting that the difficulties
alone should not head you off from playing a part in this country
where the chances of constructing a genuine community of goodwill
are stronger than anywhere else in Africa.

It is my duty to appeal, as I have done above, to your
sense of duty towards Tanganyika. But perhaps you will feel that
it is not my business to appeal to your patriotism towards your
own country. Nevertheless, I want to do so, because I feel so
strongly that British interests and the interests of Tanganyika
are the same in this regard. All the leaders of British political
life and all the leaders of this young emergent country are
remarkably united in their desire to see Tanganyika off to a good
start and in their views as to how this can best be done. Would
not Britain's interests be damaged as well as Tanganyika's if you
and your colleagues left us in such numbers that the fabric of
government could not be properly maintained? Could you feel happy,
if you had left us for any but the most strong and compelling reasons
if we then proceeded to make a mess of our trust here because we had
not enough British administrators to help us?

And so I am asking you to stay with us if you possibly
can. Stay with us and help in a job which will, I am sure, be as
full and as varied and as challenging as anything you have done
hitherto. If you can stay indefinitely, that is what I would like
best - subject only to our Africanisation policies, and I have said
before that we are so desperately short of trained Africans that
these policies are unlikely to affect you adversely for a good time
to come. If you cannot stay indefinitely, then I would ask you
most seriously to consider whether you cannot stay for the next two
or three years with us, for it is those years, above all, which will
be our testing time.

I attach to this letter a note from my Permanent
Secretary, which, in the light of plans already announced, indicates
the kind of openings for which I need you. I hope you may consider
where you can best fit into the pattern and let your Provincial
Commissioner know.

Yours sincerely,

Julius K. Nyerere.
(Julius K.Nyerere)

OFFICE OF THE PRIME MINISTER,
P.O.BOX 9000,
DAR ES SALAAM.

CMC 17/65/049

1st May 1961

To: All Expatriate Administrative Officers

Openings in Tanganyika for Administrative Officers

        I append below details of the openings which will be available to expatriate Administrative Officers who elect to remain in the service of the Tanganyika Government under the provisions of the Compensation Agreement:-

1. **In the Field:**

    (a) **At Provincial Level**

        Plans for the reorganisation of the Provincial Administration provide for the establishment of strong Inspectorial Teams in each Province in order to allow inexperienced officers to take over as District Commissioners. The composition of these teams was discussed at the recent Provincial Commissioners' Conference and, as a result of the advice of Provincial Commissioners, it has been accepted that the teams will consist of the following officers:-

Province	P.C.	D.P.C.	Regional Appeals Magistrates (under Judiciary)	Lay Magistrates (under Judiciary)	Prov. M.L.G.H. Officers	Inspectorial Staff Officer
Central	1	1	-	1	1	1
Eastern	1	1	-	1	1	1
Lake	1	1	1	2	1	1
Northern	1	1	1	1 Mbulu	1	-
Southern	1	1	-	1 Masasi	1	-
Southern Highlands	1	1	1	1 Tukuyu	1	-
Tanga	1	1	-	1 Korogwe	1	1
Western	1	1	-	1	1	1
West Lake	1	1	1	-	1	-
Dsm.Extra-Provincial District	-	1	1	-	-	1
Totals:	9	10	5	9	9	6 - 48

(b) **At District Level**

(i) **District Commissioners and District**
Officers i/c Divisions:

Here again, the number of posts available to expatriate Administrative Officers will depend to a very large extent upon the speed with which suitably qualified African Administrative Officers can be recruited to the Service. However, it is clear that for some time to come there will be a need for expatriate District Commissioners and District Officers in charge of the following Districts and Divisions:-

Central Province	Lake Province	Northern Province
Kondoa	Maswa	Arusha
Singida	Musoma	Loliondo
	Mwanza (Urban)	Masai
	North Mara	Moshi
		Ngorongoro

Southern Highlands Province	Eastern Province	Southern Province
Iringa	Kilosa	Songea
	Mahenge (Ulanga)	
	Morogoro	

Tanga Province	Western Province	West Lake Province
Lushoto	Kigoma	Bukoba
Korogwe	Ufipa	Ngara
Tanga (Rural)		
Tanga (Urban)		

(ii) **Administrative Advisers:**

Plans for the reorganisation of the Administration also provide for the appointment of Administrative Advisers to District Commissioners and, while it is clear that every African District Commissioner will not require an Administrative Adviser, from reports received it is equally clear that some African District Commissioners will wish to have them.

(iii) **District Officers:**

For some time to come expatriate Administrative Officers will be needed in the majority of Districts in the usual District Officer roles.

(iv) **Magisterial Duties:**

Vide paragraph 1(a) above, plans for the establishment of Provincial Inspectorial Teams provide for the appointment of nine lay Magistrates under the Judiciary. These nine officers will be unable to undertake all the Magisterial work at present carried out by officers of the Provincial Administration and there will no doubt be other vacancies for lay Magistrates.

(v) Development Officers:

There will also be a need for expatriate Administrative Officers to take charge of various development projects in the field, particularly where such projects are financed by loans or grants from overseas.

2. In Ministries:

It is Government's policy that priority should be given to Africanisation in the field. Since the number of African Administrative Officers is unlikely to be sufficient to fill all the field posts, the staff in Ministries will be mainly expatriate for some time to come and, although some ministerial posts requiring specialised knowledge will be filled by technical rather than Administrative Officers, the majority will be filled by the latter.

There are now the following administrative posts in the various Ministries in Dar es Salaam:-

```
P.A.S.s              33
Asst.Secretaries     30
```

After the attainment of full independence, more Ministries may well be established and additional administrative posts would thus be created.

3. Training:

There is, and there will continue for some years to be, a need for expatriate Administrative Officers to act as instructors at both the Local Government and the Administrative Training Centre at Mzumbe.

4. Foreign Service:

Applications have recently been invited for vacancies in Tanganyika's Foreign Service. Owing to the limited financial resources of this territory, it is unlikely that a large number of embassies will be established immediately. However, there will be a need for some expatriate Administrative Officers to fill administrative posts in Tanganyika's overseas embassies.

5.   To sum up, the following openings will be available for expatriate Administrative Officers and W.A.A.s who decide to stay on in Tanganyika:-

   (i)   Posts in Provincial Inspectorial
         Teams - see paragraph 1(a) above: 48

   (ii) Posts of District Commissioner and
         District Officer in charge of
         Divisions - see paragraph 1(b)(i) above: 24

(iii)	Administrative Advisers – see paragraph 1(b)(ii) above:	say	10
(iv)	District Officers – see paragraph 1(b)(iii) above:	say	50
(v)	Additional lay Magistrates – see paragraph 1(b)(iv) above:	say	9
(vi)	Development Officers – see paragraph 1(b)(v) above:	say	3
(vii)	Ministerial posts – see paragraph 2 above:	say	45
(viii)	Instructors – see paragraph 3 above:	say	5
(ix)	Foreign Service posts – see paragraph 4 above:	say	6
		Total say	200

Although the figures shewn against (iii), (iv), (v), (vi), (vii), (viii) and (ix) above are notional only, the total number of posts (200) shews only too well the need for expatriate Administrative Officers to stay on when one considers that there are at present only 208 expatriate officers and W.A.A.s in the Provincial Administration.

In addition to the above, secondary education in Tanganyika is being extended rapidly and, if any expatriate Administrative Officer is keen on teaching and is prepared to attend a teacher-training course, there will undoubtedly be a vacancy for him in the Ministry of Education.

C.I.MEEK
Permanent Secretary

Appendix B

About Tanganyika[51]

General

Tanganyika occupies a land area approximately equal to that of France, Germany, and Switzerland put together. A narrow costal strip rises to an inland plateau averaging over 3,000ft (914m) high, with mountains in the north-east and south-west. There is normally a clearly defined dry and wet season, but rainfall can be erratic; the central region is markedly dry. The population was about 9 million in the mid-1950's, and is now over 30 million; most are engaged in agriculture, albeit a smaller proportion than 50 years ago. The predominant occupation is subsistence farming, and agriculture was, and remains, the chief economic activity. In the late Trusteeship period the main products were sisal, coffee, cotton, tea, tobacco, groundnuts (peanuts), cashew nuts, castor seed and sesame seed; maize, millet, sorghum and cassava were extensively grown for domestic consumption. A number of minerals were mined in relatively small quantities, but diamonds from Lake Province were by far the biggest source of revenue.

---

[51] Still the correct designation for the mainland part of the Republic of Tanzania, which includes Zanzibar and its lesser islands. For consistency and convenience I have referred to Tanganyika throughout, including the same geographical area before its present boundaries were defined.

History[52]

Until the middle of the twentieth century even reputable European historians took the arrogantly Eurocentric view that Africa had no history prior to the incursion of Arab and European outsiders. In fact the continent had a rich and diverse pre-colonial history, as a growing body of academic publications testify, although it has to be said that since Tanganyika was one of the last parts of Africa to be permanently settled, its history is correspondingly shorter and therefore less rich.

Up until the late 1800s, African colonists were still moving into a very sparsely populated Tanganyika from the west, south and north. By mid-century the older and newer populations had settled down into recognisable tribal polities, each with its own social and political organisation, language, and customs, but also having similarities based on mutual contact and observation, intermarriage and the mutually beneficial exchange of goods and services. These tribes number about a hundred and twenty, some of them very small indeed, numbering hundreds, whilst the larger ones ran into hundreds of thousands. At one extreme were sizeable, centralised mini-states with ruling and administrative hierarchies; at the other small entities in which, although a wider community of interest was recognised, all authority was simply exercised at village level. Some were autocracies, but most had elements of participatory democracy, with checks on arbitrary rule. Because there was no shortage of land, inter-tribal conflict was less common that is popularly assumed; negotiation was the rule, and hostilities tended to be ritual rather than bloody affairs. There were exceptions; for example the Ngoni, moving up from southern Africa, and having adopted Zulu weapons and tactics, ravaged the south-west until the 1890s, whilst the Masai were similarly in a state of intermittent war with their neighbours in the north-east.

The main threat to stability came from outside, with the revival of Arab trade into the interior on the initiative of Sultan Seyyid Said of Muscat early in the nineteenth century. Prior to the Portuguese ascendancy in the sixteenth

---

[52] Further reading: John Iliffe, 'A Modern History of Tanganyika', Cambridge University Press.

century there had been a flourishing trade through Arab ports[53] along the east coast, including traffic in slaves for domestic service in the Middle East. Inspired by the Portuguese use of slaves on plantations in Mozambique, and their export to both the West Indies and the French island colonies in the Indian Ocean, Sultan Seyyid followed suit, whilst also promoting the existing trade for ivory. However, it was in slaves that the greater profit lay, and in 1840 he moved his court to Zanzibar. In the third quarter of the 19th century, slaves were also employed on Arab plantations along the coast, and in Zanzibar.

Slave trading within Tanganyika was relatively small in scale, though sufficient to generate inter-tribal enmities. Most slaves were captured or bought in the Lake Nyasa region and in the eastern Congo; the latter were marched down to the coast via Tabora to Bagamoyo, whilst a lesser route ran down to Pangani. Far more disruptive of the indigenous societies still establishing themselves on the inland plateau of Tanganyika, and of relations between them, was the politics implicit in the control of these trade routes and the adjacent country. In the last resort they were largely, but not entirely, controlled by the Arab and coastal Swahili merchants; they sought protection and collaboration, and the tribes along and near the routes wanted payment in return, a situation which led to shifting agreements, alliances and tribal warfare as the different parties jockeyed for local advantage. After the 1850s the position became even worse as imported firearms became increasingly available. So it was that early European explorers and traders reported commonplace, though not universal, disorder in civil society. Meanwhile Zanzibar had separated from Muscat, and its Sultan claimed and exercised effective control over much of the coastal strip from northern Kenya to Mozambique. By the last quarter of the century European and American commercial interests were well-established in Zanzibar, not to trade in slaves but to seek commodities for export and to develop a new market. In this context cheap imported cotton cloth from India had an adverse effect on domestic textile production; the final blow came in the form of even cheaper unbleached cotton cloth from industrial America, an import marked in the Swahili vocabulary as *merekani*. By this time, too, numbers of Indians had

---

[53] Of which Kilwa Kisiwani was the main example in Tanganyika.

established themselves as traders in the coastal towns, and by the mid-20th century dominated retail business and much of the wholesale trade throughout East Africa.

Of the European nations involved in trade, the Germans began to take an interest in Tanganyika's hinterland, and even before the Berlin Conference of 1884-5 paved the way for the subsequent European carve-up of Africa, Carl Peters had already made a number of ambiguous treaties with African chiefs[54], and acquired dubious rights to over 100,000 square miles of territory. Thereafter, the German government, under Bismarck, took a hand in overcoming Arab resistance to their expanding trading activities, and the Sultan of Zanzibar was forced to abandon his claim to the coastal areas of what was soon to become German East Africa[55]. Penetration and occupation of the interior was patchy, and pacification was not complete until the final years of the century with the subjugation of the Hehe under their Chief Mkwawa. The peace was brief, and in 1907-8 the south and south-west erupted in the Maji Maji rebellion, which was put down with conspicuous ruthlessness. Germany's administration of Tanganyika always had a strong military flavour, and was dependent on a permanent presence of African troops officered by Germans.

Despite a reputation for thoroughness and efficiency, this German colonial enterprise was still in the red when war broke out in 1914; ironically a major and costly agent of development, the railway from Dar-es-Salaam to Kigoma on Lake Tanganyika, had only just been completed. Although she lost the larger war, Germany's East African campaign was notably effective; under General Von Lettow-Vorbeck, a force never larger than 3,000 Germans and 12,000 African troops played cat-and-mouse with a British, Dominion, and Colonial army numbering up to 74,000. At the armistice the German force was still intact and undefeated in Northern Rhodesia.

After the war, responsibility for the administration of German East Africa[56], was awarded to Britain under a League of Nations Mandate, a fact

---

[54] A practice also engaged in by the British in the Rhodesias and Kenya.

[55] The Sultan had also been preoccupied with fighting a rival Arab dynasty to the north

[56] Excluding Ruanda-Urundi which went to Belgium.

not unconnected with our having been on the winning side. Some fanciful suggestions were made for renaming the new acquisition, but fortunately the then Colonial Secretary insisted on an unambiguously native name; initially designated the Tanganyika Protectorate, this was soon changed to Tanganyika Territory. The terms of the mandate stated that 'until such time as the native peoples are able to stand by themselves under the strenuous conditions of the modern world …. The material and moral well-being and the social progress of the inhabitants forms a sacred trust of civilisation'; in other words a trust to be undertaken by the League and the administering authority. Nothing was said about how soon the inhabitants might expect to be able to stand on their own feet; the principle of eventual withdrawal had been established, but the timing was not yet on the agenda. The League doctrine, largely drafted by Britain, effectively became the basis of future British colonial policy, with the colonies seen as embryo self-governing Dominions within the British Commonwealth.

At the time of the Mandate the existence of colonies and protectorates was taken for granted, and their legitimacy was not an issue; in this context the League's expectations of British administration were modest. Economic expansion between the wars was fitful, attributable in part to the after-effects of the First World War and the Depression, but also to the current assumption that economic development was a function of private capital, not of governments. It was also British policy that dependencies should, as far as possible, be self-financing. This combination of circumstances meant that the promise of material and social progress referred to earlier was tempered by the limited revenues available to the Government of Tanganyika. These were simply inadequate for the job in hand, and development was slow.

More positively, a system of civil government was set up which had the potential for development on more modern and democratic lines; and at district level, local administration was based on the principal of indirect rule, in which, in varying degrees, authority was exercised by and through indigenous institutions and structures, with the guidance of colonial officials. As Sir Donald Cameron, an early governor, put it 'We cannot discharge our obligations (under the mandate) if we do not train the people in the art of administration, (and) to administer their own affairs … the wise and practical course is to build on the … tribal institutions which have been handed down

252

through the centuries. It is our duty to do everything in our power to develop the native politically on lines suitable to the state of society in which he lives … It is an essential factor (of indirect rule) that the government rules through these institutions which are regarded as an integral part of the machinery of government, with well defined powers and functions recognised by law, and not dependent on the caprice of an executive officer.' In practice, nominally native institutions were in a few areas creations of Arab and German rule, whilst in others they were simply too unsophisticated for modern government and were reinvented out of expediency.

The impact of the Second World War was inevitably disruptive of all forms of development, but from 1946 on there was a marked acceleration, reflecting the spirit of the Colonial Development and Welfare Act, passed by the British Government as an act of faith in the dark days of 1940. The Act acknowledged the future rôle of HMG in actively promoting development with an injection of funding from HM Treasury. There was a marked increase in the recruitment of administrative and specialist officers into the Tanganyika Government Service, and there was a significant expansion of education and other forms of social welfare, as well as the economy, in the post-war years. Even the notorious failure of the Groundnut Scheme, dreamed up in Westminster and implemented by the Overseas Food Corporation, had the advantage of putting money into the economy and local pockets.

Another major change, a direct outcome of the war, was the substitution of UN Trusteeship for the old League Mandate. This was welcomed by the small Tanganyikan political class as being favourable to their aspirations, as was the prospect of a three-yearly UN Visiting Mission to report on various aspects of Britain's Trusteeship. This pro-active stance of the UN coincided with the growth of an indigenous political movement, which in turn had been stimulated by Africans' participation in the democracies' war against the Axis dictatorships, by the anti-colonial attitudes of the U.S.A. and the Eastern bloc countries, and of course the achievement of independence by India and Pakistan in 1947. For many years there had been tribal associations which were primarily concerned with local progress, culture, welfare, and self-help, but which also had a political content which was susceptible to fertilisation and growth. At the centre, the old Tanganyika African Association gave way to the more overtly political and aggressive Tanganyika African National

Union (TANU) under the leadership of the young and charismatic Julius Nyerere in 1954.

In the same year a UN visiting mission advocated negotiation of a timetable leading to independence over 25 years. The British Government of the day opined that since the country could not possibly be ready for self-government until towards the end of the century, the recommendation was premature, and it was rejected. In the sense that a majority of the rural population – over ninety percent of the whole – were not overtly discontented and showed little obvious sign of sharing the minority wish for early independence, rejection of the UN proposal was not entirely unreasonable. But the outright refusal to even discuss the matter showed a lack of imagination and political acumen. It ensured international criticism, presented TANU with ammunition which it was not slow to use, and initiated several years of unnecessarily aggravated friction between TANU and the Government – and of course its officers in the field. An initiative by the Governor, Sir Edward Twining, for power to be shared equally by Africans, Asians and Europeans, had to be abandoned in the face of African hostility. Nyerere was not having multi-racial government; it had to be non-racial. In principle he was right, though it is conveniently overlooked that TANU itself was for some years open only to Africans, and that its propaganda – most notably in the provinces – had latterly become increasingly racist.

In 1958 a new Governor, Sir Richard Turnbull, quickly established a mutual rapport with Nyerere, whose essential moderation he recognised. He also saw, following the partial elections in the same year, that TANU had a virtual monopoly in its opposition to the colonial government; there were no local opponents to contend with. Negotiations in 1959 were accompanied by the threat of a general strike and civil disobedience, and led to the appointment of a fifth elected minister, and the promise of a general election in September 1960. This would be followed by internal self-government, with a majority of elected ministers. Little more than five years after HMG's rejection of the UN proposal, TANU was elected by an overwhelming majority, winning seventy of the seventy-one seats. To what extent the electorate was in part influenced by intimidation, and by the wish to be on the winning side, will never be known; but it registered a resounding collective vote for a legislature and government led by Julius Nyerere.

Meanwhile a separate and extended dialogue was taking place between the Governor, Colonial Office, and two successive Colonial Secretaries (Alan Lennox Boyd and Iain Macleod) regarding progress towards independence, with target dates ranging from 1962 to 1968[57]. Early withdrawal would ensure public goodwill and the co-operation of a moderate and respected leader. Conversely, a well-intended delay to allow ministers and senior African officials to gain experience might invite an insurrection led by more extreme politicians than Nyerere, and armed clandestinely by the Communist bloc. On the wider scene, a Conservative administration quite suddenly turned away from its colonial responsibilities and its associated costs and brickbats. With the Gold Coast and Somaliland gone, and most recently Nigeria, the easier and more prudent option was taken. After barely fifteen months of practice in office, Julius Nyerere found himself Prime Minister of an independent Tanganyika. By comparison, Ghana had seven years of internal self-rule before independence. At midnight on December 9th 1961, the Union flags came down and were replaced by the new national flag of black, green and gold.

After independence Tanganyika (following union with Zanzibar in 1964, Tanzania) experienced three decades of one-party rule and quasi-Marxist African socialism before turning towards a market economy and multi-party politics. It has been the recipient of massive aid, the population has more than tripled, and it is still one of the poorest countries in Africa. But it got rid of Idi Amin in Uganda unaided, and it is to its credit that a country of its size has held together, and peaceably changed governments from time to time without recourse to military coup or revolution.

---

[57] For details of these exchanges see:

Prof. John Iliffe, 'Tanzania Zamani',Vol III.No.2 1997 (ISSN.0856-6518)

Published for Dept. of History, University of Dar es Salaam and Historial Assoc. of Tanzania.

257

Singh, Sub-Inspector Gurmuk,
31, 47, 73, 75, 84, 135
Slave trade, 250
Sleeping sickness, 29, 67, 186
Soil erosion, 26, 37, 40, 203,
204
Spanton, Col. 6 KAR, 134
Speke Gulf, 158, 179, 181, 185,
228
Stanley, H.M., 65
Stephenson, J.G. (Steve), 223
Stubbings, B.J.J. (Basil), 157
Summerset, Ian, 159

Tanganyika African
Association, 253
Tanganyika African National
Union (TANU), 42, 164,
170, 173, 191-193, 211, 215,
215, 224-233, 240,
254
Tanganyika Standard, 130, 131
Taylor, Dr. Frances, 146
Tchoepe, Paul, 31
Thecla, Sister, OSB, 146
Thirtle, G (Geoff), 19, 23, 140,
144, 198, 233
Tiagi, Dr. R.D., 159, 206, 225
Tribal turnout, 41, 80
Troup, Donald, 108
Turnbull, Sir Richard, 162, 166,
254
Turner, Douglas, 26, 29, 45,
116, 186
Turner, P.A. (Pat,née Barton),
116, 167, 228
Twining, Sir Edward F., 14,
133, 254
Tymkow, J.M., 29

Ujiji, 65

Union Castle Line, 7, 8
United Nations Trusteeship,
253
United Nations Visiting
Mission, 253
Universities' Mission to
Central Africa (UMCA),
112, 116, 128, 144, 146, 157

Vachon, Father, 159, 238
Valentino, Father, 36
Vassiliou, Mr., 159
Veterinary Department, 126
Walden, S. A. (Fanny), 157,
165, 166, 173, 183, 190, 201,
230

War graves, 31, 112
Water
Dams, 112, 115, 173,
178-185, 232
Filters, 5
Supplies, 22, 32, 34, 38, 39,
67, 85, 112, 184
Water Development and
Irrigation Department, 39,
115, 134
Way, Bishop Mark, UMCA, 146
White Fathers, 159, 232, 238
Winnington-Ingram, Cecil, 29
World War I, 31, 252
World War II, 94, 253

Xhosa language, 33

Yao tribe, 113, 128
Young, John, 142

Zanzibar, 12, 13, 236, 248, 250,
251, 255

Printed in the United Kingdom
by Lightning Source UK Ltd.
104842UKS00001B/61-74